Civilities and Civil Rights

CIVILITIES AND CIVIL RIGHTS

Greensboro, North Carolina,
and the Black Struggle for Freedom

WILLIAM H. CHAFE

OXFORD UNIVERSITY PRESS
Oxford   New York   Toronto   Melbourne

Oxford University Press
Oxford London Glasgow
New York Toronto Melbourne Wellington
Nairobi Dar es Salaam Cape Town
Kuala Lumpur Singapore Jakarta Hong Kong Tokyo
Delhi Bombay Calcutta Madras Karachi

Library of Congress Cataloging in Publication Data
Chafe, William Henry.
Civilities and civil rights.
Includes index.
1. Afro-Americans—Civil rights—North Carolina—
Greensboro. 2. Greensboro, N.C.—Race relations.
I. Title.
F264.G8C47   323.42'3'0975662   79-12898
ISBN 0-19-502625-X
ISBN 0-19-502919-4 pbk.
Printing (last digit): 987654

Printed in the United States of America

To My Father
and
the Memory of My Mother

Preface

Twenty years ago four black students in Greensboro, North Carolina, sat down at a Woolworth's lunch counter and demanded the same service as that given white customers. Their action remade history, inaugurating the civil rights revolution of the 1960's and setting in motion the most turbulent decade of our nation's history. The students acted because they believed in American democracy. They had faith that white American citizens—when forced to confront the horror and indecency of racism—would move to guarantee equal opportunity for all people in jobs, education, and politics. Hopeful, idealistic, and more than a little bit frightened by their own daring, these young men took it upon themselves to dramatize the evils of racism, and thereby hasten the day when democracy could become a reality for themselves and all black Americans.

Much has happened since that February day two decades ago. At least some of the goals envisioned by the first sit-in demonstrators have been achieved. The civil rights laws enacted in 1964, 1965, and 1968 have ensured far wider legal protection of black citizens and have destroyed official sanction for most forms of racial discrimination. Yet the underlying goals of the sit-in demonstrators remain, in many ways, as far distant today as they were before the Woolworth's protests took place. Inequality and discrimination still suffuse our social and economic system, buttressed by informal modes of social control even more powerful than the law. Although the means of keeping blacks in their place may now be implicit rather than explicit, they too often are just as effective as in the past. Indeed, many of the hopes espoused by the

Greensboro demonstrators twenty years ago now seem almost naïve, the products of an innocence and idealism that we may never see again.

Civilities and Civil Rights traces how the sit-ins came to happen and how they grew. It tells of the heritage of strength and protest in the black community—a legacy that made it possible for the four sit-in demonstrators to consider acting in the first place. It also discusses the different ways in which white political and economic leaders sought to contain and diffuse the many stages of black insurgency. Above all, it tells about the ongoing and continuous nature of the struggle to achieve justice and equality in America.

Today, the aura surrounding the first sit-in demonstrations in Greensboro seems far away and unreal. Yet the core of that movement—its determined insistence on dignity, respect, and self-determination—remains, as then, the hope of our society. It is to that core faith and courage that this story is dedicated.

Chapel Hill, N.C.   W.H.C.
July 7, 1979

Acknowledgments

All books are collective products, but this venture, more than most, reflects the generosity and commitment of an entire community of friends, scholars, and historical "actors."

There is no way I can thank adequately the nearly one hundred people who took time from their busy lives to share with me their memories about events that, for most, represented central experiences of their own personal histories. They gave freely of their trust and recollections, and in the process made this book possible. Although some will disagree with my conclusions, this book could not have been written without their assistance, and I am grateful.

Many of these individuals also offered me access to private papers, organizational archives, and collections of photographs that illuminated still further the history of these years. At times the records involved just a single document or letter; at others, a volume of data. But in each case the material added invaluably to the body of evidence I was able to draw upon. Specifically I want to thank the following: Edward R. Zane, Otis Hairston, Kay Troxler, the board of the Greensboro YWCA, J. D. Tarpley, Joan Bluethenthal, Warren Ashby, David Schenck, Jr., Vance Chavis, Hal Sieber, John Foster, George and Anna Simkins, William Little, Lewis Brandon, Jack Betts, Jo Spivey, William Snider, Ed Yoder, and Alfred Hamilton.

The manuscript itself has been helped at every point by the criticism of friends willing to ask hard questions and push me to clarify and deepen my understanding of civil rights history. At an early point in the writing, William E. Leuchtenburg and James Patterson challenged me to sharpen my definition of the political configurations of Greensboro and North Carolina. It was also William Leuchtenburg who eight years ago first suggested this topic, and ever since has provided me relevant material from his own massive research into the history of post-1945 America. In response to a paper I wrote on the 1960 sit-ins, Raymond Gavins, Leon Fink, Harry Watson, Robert Brisbane, and Jacquelyn Jackson made helpful criticisms. Over the past two years especially, the comments of Vincent Harding have been crucial in my formulation and understanding of the issues discussed here.

As various articles became chapters and finally a book-length manuscript, my colleagues have been unfailingly generous in reviewing the results. Anne F. Scott—another person involved in the initial decision to undertake this project—pinpointed a number of areas needing clarification and offered her own valuable perspective on the years in question. Jacquelyn Dowd Hall, Donald Mathews, and Jane de Hart Mathews were decisive in helping me to rethink the conceptual framework of the book, as well as its organizational structure. Jack Cell, Richard Watson, and Jack TePaske each provided valuable comments on the political history of North Carolina during these years. I also benefited greatly from conversations about the manuscript with Clayborne Carson, whose own work on SNCC helped provide a framework for my understanding of Greensboro. As always, Harvard Sitkoff offered friendship and rigorous criticism, and together with Bob Hall, helped me to rethink some of the underlying interpretations I wished to present. David Budbill brought his sensibilities as a poet and novelist to the manuscript, suggesting many improvements in the narrative. Sheldon Meyer, executive vice president of Oxford University Press, has been wonderfully supportive since the beginning. Caroline Taylor, my editor at Oxford, has done a thousand things to make the manuscript a better book.

Throughout these years I have been constantly nourished in this endeavor by my colleagues in the Oral History Program at Duke University. Since 1972 the Duke Oral History Program has brought together more than twenty graduate students who have shared the belief that oral sources, used in conjunction with traditional historical evidence, can provide the basis for a better, more accurate understanding of our multiracial past. Since 1976 these students have participated in Duke's Center for the Study of Civil Rights and Race Relations which, with help from a grant from the National Endowment for the Humanities, has made it possible for us to focus our efforts specifically on the civil rights movement. Although the graduate students in oral history have not directly been involved in the research for this book, their own work on similar projects has proved indispensable to deepening my own understanding of where I must go and what I must do to answer their questions. In the best sense of the word ours has been a collegial relationship, with each of us teaching and learning from the others. Julius Scott, Teddy Segal, and Scott Ellsworth have been especially helpful.

As always there are two to three people whose contribution is so great that it dwarfs any effort to offer thanks. Larry Goodwyn, founder and co-director of the Duke Oral History Program, has been a part of this book since it began eight years ago. We have shared the process of discovery, the excitement of new insights, and the frustrations of trying to find words adequate to communicate what we have learned. His has been a collaboration so close and important that there is no way to express my appreciation. Sydney Nathans, a dear friend and brilliant critic, also has been involved from the beginning. But especially as the manuscript took final shape he played an indispensable role, repeatedly suggesting new hypotheses and driving me to confront problems. His friendship and wisdom have contributed enormously to this book. Finally there is Thelma Kithcart, a person whose spirit, good humor, and generosity have helped make all of this possible. She has typed all the transcripts of the interviews, done more drafts of the manuscript than she would like to remember, and perhaps more important than anything else, has made the oral history program at Duke University work. Her warmth, insight, and concern have helped to turn an academic program into a human community. For this and so much more, all of us say thanks.

From the beginning this research has been generously funded by outside sources. While still at the Rockefeller Foundation, Peter Wood made the Duke Oral History Program possible through his enthusiastic support of a five-year Rockefeller grant. The Greensboro study has been aided directly through research leaves funded by the National Endowment for the Humanities in 1974–75, and a Rockefeller Foundation Humanities Fellowship in 1977–78. The Duke University Research Council also provided travel funds in 1972.

Throughout this period of research and writing, Christopher, Jennifer, and Lorna have given me the love and support without which nothing else would be worthwhile.

Needless to say, the conclusions presented here are solely my own and do not necessarily reflect the views of those who have contributed so much to making this book possible.

W.H.C.

Contents

Civilities and Civil Rights

Those who profess to favor freedom
And yet deprecate agitation
Are men who want crops
Without plowing the ground
They want rain without thunder and lightning
They want the ocean without the awful roar of its waters

Power concedes nothing without a demand
It never did, and it never will

Frederick Douglass, August 4, 1857

Introduction

"The problem of the twentieth century," W. E. B. Du Bois wrote in 1903, "is the problem of the color line." This book began because I wanted to know more about how that color line operated, what kept it in place, and how the challenge to it evolved to the point of open rebellion during the years of the civil rights movement. In the largest sense, I hoped to probe the dialectic of social control and social change on the issue of race. What patterns of accommodation and paternalism had to be broken before change could occur? Which forces paved the way for protest? What triggered the immediate decision to sit-in or march? How did family, church, and school influence the people's response to civil rights? Who led the forces of resistance? Were "rednecks" the problem? And if not, who was?

Much of the existing literature on civil rights fails to answer these questions.[1] Journalists have described flash points of conflict such as Selma and Birmingham. Public opinion analysts have measured popular attitudes toward race. And scholars have traced the history of civil rights organizations, the impact of federal legislation, and the significance of leaders like Martin Luther King, Jr. Yet most of these studies have been written from a national perspective, distant from the day-to-day life of the local people most affected by the movement. Some historians have even suggested that presidential actions—hundreds of miles away from civil rights demonstrations—were responsible for initiating the challenge to American racism. While all these studies contribute to our understanding, very few have examined the story of social change from the point of view of people in local communities, where the struggle for civil rights was a continuing reality, year in and year out.

In an effort to incorporate this latter perspective, I decided to focus on what happened in a single city over a period of thirty years. The decision to choose one place grew out of a desire to become familiar with all aspects of the community—its churches, schools, clubs, and business organizations—that shaped the social context out of which the civil rights struggle emerged. The choice of a thirty-year period, in turn, reflected a concern with process. Although much can be gained by examining a dramatic event in a single moment, the dynamics of social change can be investigated only by following the stages through which a community arrives at a point of crisis. In this sense, a time span of three decades seemed the minimum necessary to gain historical perspective on the changing relationship between blacks and whites and the development of different levels of protest.

As a result of both these considerations, I decided to write about Greensboro, North Carolina. In his classic 1949 study of Southern politics, V. O. Key praised North Carolina for its "progressive outlook, . . . especially [in] industrial development, education, and race relations." The Tarheel State, Key wrote, was particularly noted for its distinctive pattern of race relations. Even though black citizens were disfranchised at the end of the nineteenth century, Governor Charles B. Aycock had embarked upon an ambitious program of educational reform to improve segregated black schools and to promote black self-advancement. Thereafter, according to Key, "the spirit of Aycock . . . persisted in a consistently sensitive appreciation of Negro rights." The state was run by sophisticated men—mostly lawyers—who served an "aggressive aristocracy of manufacturing and banking [interests]." These men recognized the value of maintaining an image of moderation and promoted the view that the state was "on the move" in the direction of racial tolerance. As a result, North Carolina has been portrayed by political scientists and lay observers alike as an "inspiring exception to southern racism."

The state's reputation was bolstered by the accomplishments of two men—Howard Odum and Frank Porter Graham. Both were associated with the University of North Carolina, long considered to be the South's best and most cosmopolitan state university. Odum came to UNC in 1920, having grown up in the Deep South and earned two doctorates, one in folklore, the other in sociology. Deeply committed to the idea that scientific investigation could lead to a solution of the South's race problem, Odum established the *Journal of Social Forces* and, later, the Institute for Research in the Social Sciences. Both would provide data on white and black folkways, which then would help erase

prejudice and misunderstanding. Although Odum himself harbored racial stereotypes, he was viewed by many as a leader in North Carolina's
enlightened approach toward blacks.

Frank Porter Graham, in turn, represented almost everyone's ideal of
the quintessential Southern white liberal. An inspiring teacher, Graham
had come to the University in 1915. As its president during the Depres-
sion years, and the 1940's, Graham defended dissent on campus, refused to fire a faculty member who dined in public with a black communist, and consistently supported labor organizers in the South. He was
"the most Christ-like man I've ever known," Senator Wayne Morse of
Oregon later said. Although neither Odum nor Graham was willing to
attack segregation openly, the two men gave credibility to the idea that
North Carolina was a different kind of state, closer to the national
norm, free of the bigotry and closed-mindedness associated with the
Deep South.

Yet throughout the twentieth century North Carolina's progressive
image existed side by side with social and economic facts that contra-
dicted profoundly the state's reputation. In the late 1940's, North Carolina had the lowest rate of unionization in the country. The state ranked
forty-fifth in per capita income, possessed one of the highest levels of
illiteracy in the South, and placed almost last among the states in
average manufacturing wage. Despite Frank Porter Graham, union organizing efforts were consistently broken by a combination of economic
intimidation and physical violence. Even though the University was
known throughout the country for its excellence, schoolchildren in the
state received less public support per pupil than in almost any other
state. Thus, North Carolina represented a paradox: it combined a reputation for enlightenment and a social reality that was reactionary.

Greensboro was a microcosm of the state at large. To a CIO labor
organizer entering the city in the late 1930's, Greensboro would have
appeared as a series of mill hills, each dominated by a large textile
complex. The industrial areas were loosely connected by a downtown
area of banks and shops where roads to and from the mills intersected.
The union organizer would quickly have concluded that a cadre of
bankers and industrialists ran the city, systematically repelling any effort
at labor organization and exploiting a working class that received low
wages, suffered from industrial diseases, and had little if any opportunity
for independence. Within the total community, blacks constituted a
dependent "under class," yoked to menial service jobs in factories and
homes.

By contrast, the image of Greensboro that dominated most perceptions was that of a bustling "New South" city, free of old prejudices and ideally prepared to lead the region toward new levels of prosperity and enlightenment—in short, a beacon of Southern progressivism. With a strong industrial base in textiles as well as some of the largest insurance companies in the region, the city boasted a balanced economy that promised continued growth. Its five colleges—three white and two black—provided a source of culture and intellectual stimulation, giving the city an aura of cosmopolitanism. Like the state, the city was governed by sophisticated lawyers associated with large corporations. Like the state also, Greensboro prided itself on a reputation for racial tolerance. White business and educational spokesmen pointed to Greensboro's race relations as a model of cooperation, taking special pride in the city's "better class" of colored citizens.

Appropriately, the story of civil rights in Greensboro from 1945 to 1975 embodies the paradox that lies at the heart of North Carolina's history. In 1954 Greensboro became the first city in the South to announce that it would comply with the Supreme Court's ruling, in *Brown v. Board of Education*, that segregation in schools must end. Six years later the city was the birthplace of the sit-in movement—an act of protest that would help to transform the nation. By 1963 the number of people demonstrating in Greensboro's streets exceeded that in any city except Birmingham, and a young Greensboro black named Jesse Jackson had begun his rapid rise to leadership in the civil rights ranks. Six years after that, armed confrontation between National Guard troops and black college students accompanied Greensboro's emergence as a center of the Black Power movement in the Southeast. Finally, in 1971—seventeen years after the *Brown* decision—Greensboro integrated its public schools, becoming one of the last cities in the South to comply with federal desegregation orders. It would be difficult to imagine a richer narrative framework within which to examine the struggle for civil rights or the paradox of the South's most progressive state.

Before proceeding, some clarification of terms is perhaps in order. I have used the phrase "white liberals" to describe white Southerners who perceived existing race relations as unjust and who were willing to participate in programs to fight segregation. "Rednecks" and "poor whites," in turn, refer not to specific social or economic groups, but to the labels widely used by upper-class whites to describe those at the other end of the political spectrum who seemed to them intolerant, bigoted, and otherwise unwilling to endorse an urbane approach to matters of race. Words such as "integration" or "desegregation" changed their meanings over time, but, as a general rule, the former describes the maximum degree of racial interaction thought possible in a given situation, the latter the minimum.

Most difficult to define is the culture of white progressivism that has for so long dominated North Carolina's political and economic life. The more I studied Greensboro, the more it became clear that progressivism did not operate as a political system with rigid regulations and procedures. Rather, it functioned as a mystique, a series of implicit assumptions, nuances, and modes of relating that have been all the more powerful precisely because they are so elusive.

In this sense, the "progressive mystique" is best understood through certain motifs that reflect—almost unconsciously—the underlying values of progressivism. Most North Carolina progressives, for example, believe that conflict is inherently bad, that disagreement means personal dislike, and that consensus offers the only way to preserve a genteel and civilized way of life. The underlying assumption is that conflict over any issue, whether it be labor unions, race relations, or political ideology, will permanently rend the fragile fabric of internal harmony. Hence, progress can occur only when everyone is able to agree—voluntarily—on an appropriate course of action. This concern with consensus appeared in Greensboro during the early 1950's, for example, when the ruling body of the First Presbyterian Church divided over whether to invite a Catholic priest to participate in an interfaith service. As a result of the conflict, a second meeting was convened. By a vote of thirty-seven to nothing, the church members decided not to issue the invitation. Only if all the people were prepared to move together, it seemed, would there be any movement at all.

On the other hand, progressives in North Carolina have also emphasized the importance of being hospitable to new ideas. Discussion of varying philosophies is viewed as part and parcel of a civilized life, even if action on some of those philosophies is *verboten*. In fact, the ease with which alternative political theories receive a hearing becomes a sign of how enlightened and tolerant a community is. Thus, many progressives in Greensboro during the 1950's took special pride in the existence of a political conversation group whose participants were free to say anything they wished about race, class, or other social issues. Members of the group, who ranged from newspaper editors to corporate lawyers and liberals, viewed the candor of their discussions as evidence of the community's openness. After all, even the delicate issue of racial change could be discussed, and discussion, in turn, could be seen as a step toward action.

Still another feature of the progressive mystique is what V. O. Key has called an attitude of "community responsibility toward the Negro." Rooted in a paternalism so unconscious that it would never be called such by whites, this "sense of responsibility" operated on the premise that those who are better off have a moral obligation to help those who are worse off. The result, historically, has been a patron-client relationship between white benefactors and black petitioners, the latter coming to friendly whites to seek specific objectives such as a new school or a recreational facility. After exchanging pleasantries, the white benefactor would render the aid he thought appropriate, more than ever convinced that the exchange testified to how good communications between the races were in North Carolina.

Surrounding all of these motifs has been a pervasive commitment to civility as the value that should govern all relationships between people. Civility is the cornerstone of the progressive mystique, signifying courtesy, concern about an associate's family, children, and health, a personal grace that smooths contact with strangers and obscures conflict with foes. Civility was what white progressivism was all about—a way of dealing with people and problems that made good manners more important than substantial action. Significantly, civility encompassed all of the other themes of the progressive mystique—abhorrence of personal conflict, courtesy toward new ideas, and a generosity toward those less fortunate than oneself.[2]

As creators as well as victims of Southern history, blacks know well the meaning of civility. As much as any group, they have given meaning to the ethic of hospitality. No people are more generous to victims of misfortune, none more open toward strangers. Yet blacks also understood the other side of civility—the deferential poses they had to strike in order to keep jobs, the chilling power of consensus to crush efforts to raise issues of racial justice. As victims of civility, blacks had long been forced to operate within an etiquette of race relationships that offered almost no room for collective self-assertion and independence. White people dictated the ground rules, and the benefits went only to those who played the game.

But if the etiquette of civility precluded honesty in direct contacts with whites, it could not suppress that honesty—that protest—within the black community itself. In churches, schools, pool halls, and corner

gatherings, another culture existed—one of assertion rather than deference. Sometimes blacks said they wanted a separate world where whites
could never enter. Other times they voiced a determination to share
fully the benefits of the white world. Always there was the mocking
humor of blacks making fun of whites who thought they knew their
"niggers" but never could understand what black people were all about.
The result of these gatherings was an agenda of demands: better job
opportunities, decent housing, good police protection provided by black
officers, quality textbooks and equipment for schools. Whether the protests appeared as a desire for integration or simply for better facilities for
blacks, they reflected an incipient rebellion no less powerful for not
being able to find open expression.

White progressives of Greensboro did not know this world. So deep
was the need of whites to believe in "good race relations" that they took
ritualistic deference as an authentic expression of black attitudes toward
them. Most white progressives would not have understood the middle-
aged black man who drove his car downtown each day because under
no circumstances would he ride on a Jim Crow bus. Nor had many of
Greensboro's white leaders ever walked through the campus of Bennett
College, a woman's school in the heart of the black ghetto. Its tall trees,
red brick buildings, and white framed faculty houses were sources of
pride to the entire black community. The Dean of Bennett, a gentle,
strong woman, walked down the tree-lined paths talking with students
about their heritage and the importance of standing up for their rights.
This world white Greensboro did not know—could not know—given
the prism of the progressive mystique. Yet it was this world that in the
1950's and 1960's gave rise to the black part of the dialectic that would
be the civil rights struggle in Greensboro.

This book, then, is about many things. It is about the progressive
mystique, how it operated, and the extent to which civility was or was not
compatible with the promise of racial justice. It is also about the history
of black protest and the stages through which that protest moved in
response to shifting circumstances. Finally, this book is about the interre-
lationship of black and white, best captured in questions about how the
two races communicated over a thirty-year period. How did the perception of blacks by whites, and of whites by blacks, affect the unfolding of
the civil rights drama? What steps were necessary to break through the
progressive mystique and achieve authentic communication? Above all,
what does the history of the civil rights struggle in Greensboro tell us
about the present and future nature of contacts across the color line?

This story could neither be told nor researched on the basis of written sources alone. Traditionally, historians have used newspapers, diaries, manuscript collections, and government documents as a basis for their investigations. But, until recently, almost all of these sources have represented a white perspective. Whites have run the newspapers, held the public offices, deposited the manuscript collections, and preserved the diaries. Whether consciously or unconsciously, the record has therefore transmitted a white point of view. Simply stated, that perspective cannot do justice to a past that has been multiracial throughout, with blacks as primary actors as well as objects of actions undertaken by others.

As a consequence, this book is based upon a combination of oral and written sources. Only through extensive use of oral interviewing, grounded in the written sources, has it been possible to gain even a glimpse of the rich multiracial fabric that is Greensboro's civil rights history. Oral sources are used here not as a substitute for other historical research techniques—rather as a supplement. But without a combination of the two there would be no possibility of discovering what happened in Greensboro.

The story that follows tells what occurred in one city in one state during the 1940's, 1950's and 1960's. It also speaks to larger issues at work in our society and culture. The progressive mystique is not unique to Greensboro, North Carolina. Instead, it reflects underlying themes very much present in our national politics and culture. V. O. Key called North Carolina a bridge between the Deep South and the nation as a whole. He was right. The state reveals much about both. Nor is the story of black protest distinctive to Greensboro. The stages of insurgency pursued by black activists there paralleled developments throughout the South. The themes enacted on Greensboro's stage, therefore, may provide insight into the drama unfolding elsewhere as well. Finally, the story of whether, and how, Greensboro's black and white people addressed the underlying issues of justice, self-determination, and autonomy may tell whether we as a nation will be able to come to grips with the central theme of our history. This, then, is the story of one city. But it is also the story of America.

PART I
Years of Protest

CHAPTER ONE
Inch by Inch—

The present generation . . . sometimes doesn't appreciate what
was done by those who came before them to make things possible.
Vance Chavis, black political leader in Greensboro
and former school principal

The gods bring threads to webs begun.
Susie B. Jones, former Dean of Admissions at Bennett College

The night after the Supreme Court handed down its landmark ruling in
Brown v. Board of Education in May 1954, members of the Greensboro
school board gathered for their regular monthly meeting. Immediately
they proceeded to a new item of business—a resolution brought by
Chairman D. Edward Hudgins committing Greensboro to implement
the Supreme Court's desegregation edict. The decision, Hudgins said,
was "one of the most momentous events" in the history of education,
and he urged his colleagues not to "fight or attempt to circumvent it."
School Superintendent Benjamin Smith sounded the same theme. "It is
unthinkable," he said, "that we will try to abrogate the laws of the
United States of America." Any effort to evade the decision, Smith
declared, would be a disaster to the country and signify the end of
democracy. Dr. David Jones, the only black member of the board,
strongly supported Hudgins and Smith. "Isn't there a possibility," he
asked, "that we of Greensboro may furnish leadership in the way we
approach this problem? Not only to the community, but to the state and
to the South?" After a brief debate the board voted six to one to endorse
Hudgins's resolution.[1]

Greensboro's decisive response seemed a good omen to those who
perceived the city as a leader of the modern South. Greensboro prided
itself on being cosmopolitan—a place where progressive attitudes were a
hallmark of political discourse and where the "good life" of affluence
and cultural sophistication was available to large numbers of people.
The city was the home of five colleges, including Guilford—a nationally known Quaker school—two state colleges, and two small liberal arts

campuses. Local leaders also pointed proudly to historically good relationships between Jews and Christians, including the election of a Jew
as president of the Chamber of Commerce and, later, as mayor of the
city. This record, together with the cultural and academic life of the
community, signified to many that in black-white relations as well,
Greensboro could serve as a beacon for others to follow. "I have lived in
Greensboro for sixty-seven years," Dr. David Jones told the local newspaper, "and I have never seen this community perturbed over the solution of a social problem. They will face up to it as they always have."

I

Greensboro's early history provided some justification for the belief that
the city was atypical in its racial attitudes and destined for a position of
leadership in a changing South. In the antebellum years Guilford
County had been a center of antislavery activity, a way station on the
Underground Railroad, and a gathering place for Quakers. After the
Civil War, Greensboro became the home of Albion Tourgée, a famous
leader of Northern "carpetbag" forces who commented on the area's
openness to political and social innovation. The county's social and
economic structures similarly reflected a degree of difference from the
traditional "plantation South." Although 4000 slaves lived in Guilford
County in 1860, there were also 600 free blacks, and the economy was
never as dependent upon staple crop production of tobacco and cotton
as the majority of the region was.

In the years between 1870 and 1900, Greensboro's economy continued to display flexibility. Although, numerically, blacks concentrated
overwhelmingly in semiskilled and unskilled positions, they also constituted nearly 50 per cent of all the skilled workers in Greensboro, serving
as brick-makers, stonemasons, carpenters, foundry workers, and skilled
railway employees. In the two spoke-and-handle factories in the city,
blacks and whites worked in comparable positions and received similar
wages. In residence patterns the city also showed some integration. In
1880, on seven of nineteen streets, black and white households existed
side by side. Although blacks represented, over-all, an economically
disadvantaged group, there were enough openings in crafts as well as in
industrial jobs to sustain some optimism about the city's economic and
social future in race relations.

Yet by 1900 Greensboro had rejected these potentially egalitarian
patterns and had moved sharply toward a system of rigid racial and
economic discrimination. As elsewhere in the South, the Populist in-

surgency—with its threat of class and biracial rebellion—led white members of the business and political elite to make scapegoats of blacks and to institutionalize white supremacy. Faced with the prospect of poor whites and blacks joining to topple the upper class from power, white leaders of the community set out to drive a wedge of racial prejudice between poor whites and blacks. "Employers, editors, and other influential town leaders," historian Samuel Kipp has noted, insisted upon exclusion of blacks from economic and political opportunities. As white farmers flocked into the city from agriculturally depressed surrounding counties, employers fired blacks from lumber, woodworking, and furniture factories and replaced them with white men and boys. At the same time, white women replaced black women in the tobacco factories. Blacks were proscribed from most skilled occupations, and the local Southern Railway office discharged all black conductors, engineers, and firemen, replacing them with whites.

The rise of overt racial oppression coincided almost exactly with the emergence of Greensboro as a "New South" city. Between 1880 and 1900 Greensboro's population increased fivefold, from 2000 to 10,000. The three decades after the turn of the century witnessed an even more spectacular population boom, with the city growing to 53,000 residents by 1930, almost a third of them black. Even as the local newspaper replaced farm news with the call for industrialization, new textile mills—using white unskilled labor—moved into the city. In 1895 Moses and Ceasar Cone arrived from Baltimore to begin construction of giant factories on the outskirts of the city. By 1905 their White Oak Denim mill employed 2500 operatives, the Proximity Mill more than 1000, and the Revolution Mill 750. During the 1920's the Cone hegemony was challenged when Burlington Industries—later to become the largest textile firm in the world—started its meteoric rise in Greensboro. By that time also, two of the largest insurance companies in the country, Jefferson Standard and Pilot Life, had established headquarters in the city. Greensboro was already well on its way to earning the description later given it by Princeton sociologists as one of "the most prosperous and industrialized political units in the state."

For both black and white citizens of Greensboro, the city's "New South" ascendancy produced stark economic divisions. Blacks, of course, suffered most. Whereas in 1870 nearly 30 per cent of Negro workers had been employed in skilled occupations, by 1910 the figure had dropped to 8 per cent, with four out of five blacks working either in semiskilled service jobs or as unskilled laborers. In 1884 16 per cent of the black labor force had held jobs comparable to those of whites in city factories. By 1910 not a single black was listed as a factory worker. Although a small and significant black middle class lived in Greensboro—a class primarily associated with the city's black colleges, its public schools, and its health care facilities—the vast majority of Greensboro's Negro population struggled to survive through serving whites. As late as 1950 nearly 40 per cent of all black workers held jobs in personal services.

White Greensboro also exhibited sharp class divisions. The city's textile mills required the continued presence of a large industrial work force, with almost 20 percent of the city's workers in 1930 employed as mill hands for Cone, Burlington, and other textile manufacturers. Yet pay and working conditions remained poor, largely due to the effectiveness with which textile owners combated efforts at unionization. The city's insurance companies, universities, banks, and retail stores, meanwhile, supported a developing white-collar population that helped give the city an aura of middle-class respectability. Overseeing both groups was a thin layer of corporate managers who routinely wielded political as well as economic power. Public and private interests became synonymous when city fathers paved Summit Avenue from the central business district to Cone Mills on the outskirts of town, and provided public transportation to and from the workplace. Conversely, private subsidy of mill village health facilities and recreation centers helped to reinforce the city's image as a progressive place.

Serving as a foundation for the entire social structure was a pattern of pervasive discrimination based on race. "In place of involuntary servitude," Samuel Kipp has observed, "Southern white society was erecting a caste system designed to preserve white control and ensure the continued subordination of blacks." It was the caste system that led to the enactment in 1914 of a city ordinance that barred blacks from purchasing homes on any street where a majority of residences belonged to whites. That same law forbade the building of any place of public assembly—a theater, for example—on a block dominated by members of the other race. Although subsequently invalidated, the legislation provided an accurate measure of early-twentieth-century race relations in Greensboro. By 1920 blacks no longer could work alongside whites in factories or offices, or live in the same neighborhoods as whites did. Politically, in turn, a new system of paternalism had emerged, with members of the white elite ready to assist those blacks willing to accommodate to white interests. Perhaps the most outstanding aspect of the caste system was its ability, in Kipp's words, to maintain "the rigidity of interracial barriers while at the same time permitting differentiation and diversity in the social structure of each race." Kept apart by the insurmountable obstacle of color, whites and blacks would then divert their energies into conflicts within their own groups over status and prestige. The end result was perpetuation of both a class and a race system "predicated upon black inferiority and subordination."

II

Within this over-all structure, the citizens of black Greensboro struggled to keep intact their own community institutions and to advance, wherever possible, the political and educational opportunities of the next generation. As always, the quest occurred within a context defined by white power and hence fraught with ambiguity and tension. To achieve a better life economically, politically, or educationally, blacks had to deal with "the Man," and use whatever wiles were necessary to pry loose the money or actions required to help their race. Black institutions were a centerpiece in this struggle. Only with a home base created by and for black people could the energy be found to engage white society on its terms. Thus the tortured dialectic of self-determination and dependency unfolded, each swing of the pendulum measuring the degree to which blacks had moved toward being able to define their own destinies.

By the mid-twentieth-century, Negroes in Greensboro could claim, with some justification, to live in both the best of times and the worst of times. Despite important class differences, race provided a common bond of oppression shared by the poor migrants who sought refuge in temporary shacks and by teachers living in sturdy brick homes. As late as 1950 the median income for the most populous section of black Greensboro was only 40 per cent of the citywide figure, and in 1960 only 23 per cent of all black families earned more than $5000 a year. On the other hand, Greensboro's black community was clearly better off than that in most of the state. Throughout the 1930's, 1940's and 1950's, Greensboro blacks boasted a higher median education level than blacks did in cities such as Durham, and a higher median income as well. Although nearly 40 per cent of the black labor force in 1950 worked in personal services, another 15 per cent were employed in professional and related occupations. Furthermore, many black working-class families had succeeded in saving enough to purchase their own homes.

The relatively better economic opportunities of black Greensboro served as a double-edged sword, attracting ambitious black recruits to the town but also generating anger at the persistence of white oppression. Vance Chavis, a young black schoolteacher, moved to Greensboro from Charlotte in the 1920's because "Greensboro had a little better atmosphere and it was more permissive. A black man could get along better." Yet that atmosphere could not eradicate or diminish the pervasive presence of Jim Crow, the systematic segregation of people by race, that drove Chavis to forswear public transportation, even in emergencies. Nell Coley, another teacher who came back from eastern North Carolina in the 1930's, pinpointed the paradox created by being black in a better educated and more self-aware community. "Blacks were out of it and didn't even think about it in the east," she said. "They were out of it and they knew they were out of it in Greensboro. There's a difference." Ironically, the presence of some opportunities simply accentuated discontent at the absence of any substantive equality. As one black noted acidly, "Greensboro [was] a nice-nasty town."

In the effort to overcome continuing oppression, Greensboro's black public schools provided a primary source of strength, even as they illustrated the larger problem of dependency upon whites. Blacks took pride in the accomplishments of their schools. In 1932, when the city first appointed a supervisor of black education, there were seventy-five Negro teachers in the community, 68 per cent of them without a college degree. Twenty years later, the total number of black teachers had grown to 200; all held B.A. degrees, and 65 per cent of them had received the Master's degree. Dudley High School, constructed during the 1930's, quickly gained a reputation comparable to that of Dunbar High School, in Washington, D.C., as a model of educational excellence. Of the ten Negro elementary schools accredited in North Carolina in 1950, six were in Greensboro. The statistics suggest how unusual was black Greensboro's educational record, and how potentially powerful a source for change.

The achievements of Greensboro's black schools reflected in large part the genius of John Tarpley. A native of Texas, Tarpley came to Greensboro in 1926 as a teacher at Bennett College. Shortly thereafter he was named principal of the city's black high school, working up from that position to become supervisor of all the Negro schools. With consummate skill, Tarpley moved back and forth between the white and black communities, establishing those relationships with white leaders that were necessary to improve the schools even as he built a reputation

among his own people as a defender of black rights. Despite some
progress, Greensboro's "separate but equal" black schools suffered from
poor equipment and textbooks that frequently were rejects from the
white schools. When Tarpley approached the Superintendent to seek
improvements, he always brought two plans—one for full equalization
that he knew would be turned down, and a second that would meet
many of his needs even as it appeared to be a compromise in the eyes of
his white superiors. Although some blacks viewed Tarpley as an "Uncle
Tom," his strongest teachers defended him as a "stalwart," a man who
"never had any fear." As one colleague commented: "John Tarpley was
there where the myth of separate but equal operated, and he always let
them know in no uncertain terms that he knew it was a myth. . . . He
didn't buckle and run at all."*

Tarpley's skills also proved instrumental in the creation of other community institutions, most notably the Hayes-Taylor YMCA. In the late
1930's several black leaders met to consider how to raise funds for an ur-
gently needed recreational center for the city's black youth. Without
capital of their own, the group deputized Tarpley to approach Ceasar
Cone for a gift of $50,000. Cone agreed, on the condition that blacks
themselves raise the money to purchase the land on which the Y would
be built. After much sacrifice the black community fulfilled its part of the
agreement, so Cone donated the building, naming it after Sally Hayes
and Andrew Taylor, two black servants who had been employed by his
family for more than forty years. Within a few years the YMCA had become a focal point for the black community, serving as the site for community-wide meetings as well as a training ground for young athletes and
civic leaders. Under the directorship of David Morehead, the Y increased
its membership from 400 in the early 1940's to 2300 by the early 1960's,
with an operating budget that grew tenfold during the same period.

The black churches of Greensboro, of course, were the institutions
that entered most forcefully into the lives of Negro citizens. Ranging
from pentecostal storefronts to the huge AME Zion and Baptist congregations, the churches provided a week-in and week-out affirmation that
in struggle there was meaning. Not all black ministers sanctioned pro-

*Tarpley displayed his political skill during World War II, when he was head of the
Negro teacher's association in the state. After creating a committee on the morale of
classroom teachers during the war period, Tarpley went to the Governor and persuaded
him that using his wartime emergency powers to equalize the salaries of white and black
teachers would be an effective means of boosting the morale of Negro teachers. Through
such behind-the-scenes manipulation, Tarpley accomplished a major victory without
resort to litigation.

test; indeed, many represented the quintessence of caution. Yet the clergy supplied steady leadership, and the churches—whatever their politics—offered the reassurance that continued striving would eventually bring victory. From a more practical standpoint, the churches also provided a training ground for political leaders and a meeting place where the aspirations of the black community could find collective expression.

It was the black colleges in Greensboro, however, that most exemplified the pride and hope of the community. North Carolina Agricultural and Technical College (A&T), established in 1893, had only a class "C" rating in the state in 1925; thirty years later it had risen to a class "A" rating, with a $12 million physical plant and 3000 students. Bennett College, a private black women's school, underwent a similar transformation. When David Jones took over as president of the Methodist school in 1926, it had lost its accreditation, was down to ten students, and had an endowment of only $100. Thirty years later, Bennett boasted an endowment of $1.5 million and was known throughout black America for its excellence. The two colleges provided not only a source of pride for the community, but a rallying point as well. "A college had to mean more to the black community," Nell Coley remarked, "because [blacks were] denied entry into the mainstream." As ongoing centers of intellectual debate, cultural activities, and political discussion, the colleges served as a constant reminder of the better life not yet available to most black Americans.

Bennett, in particular, stood forth as a model of racial strength. A private school, it was not forced to kowtow to public prejudices in order to secure legislative appropriations. Just as important, its leaders maintained a standard of independence that suffused the campus. Dr. David Jones was "one of the last great Negro college presidents," one faculty member recalled, "a man [of] vision and determination . . . with an aura of majesty. . . . [He] did not tolerate shilly-shally." Formerly on the staff of the Committee on Interracial Cooperation (a pioneering venture in Southern interracial activity founded during the 1920's), Jones instructed his students not to spend money where they were mistreated and always to devote part of their week to helping the community. When local business interests complained that Bennett was hiring all black labor for the construction of new buildings, Jones responded that he would rather give back the construction funds than change his hiring practices. In the 1930's, Bennett students helped lead a student boycott of downtown movie theaters in protest against Hollywood's use of blacks in only stereotyped roles. Continuing to challenge local customs, Jones asked Eleanor Roosevelt to speak at Bennett during World War II. After she accepted, he invited all Greensboro's schoolchildren—white and black—to come together at Bennett to hear the First Lady, scandalizing many whites, who were incredulous at the audacity of a black man asking white and black children to "mix together" on a black campus. (The children came in large numbers.) Although some viewed Bennett as an elitist institution, Jones had succeeded in making the school a visible symbol of self-determination and dignity.

In fact, two different styles of leadership existed side by side in black Greensboro. One was willing to challenge directly the oppressiveness of white power; the other sought to work within the structures of white power for black advancement. Randolph Blackwell perhaps best embodied the first style. Born in Greensboro during the 1920's, he grew up in a family that instilled racial pride. Although Blackwell's parents were not well off, they would not permit him to hold any job that placed him in a position subservient to whites, such as shoe-shine boy or newspaper carrier. Blackwell's father worked on the railroad, and during the period of 1927–34 he devoted much of his spare time to Marcus Garvey's United Negro Improvement Association. Blackwell recalls attending meetings in Greensboro where as many as fifty of Garvey's followers would be present. While a boy, he was taken by his father to Atlanta to visit the prison where Garvey was held, and to see a black insurance company with all black workers. In high school, Blackwell was inspired by two teachers who were active members of the National Association for the Advancement of Colored People, and in 1943, after hearing an address by Ella Baker, a field secretary for the NAACP, he helped to start a youth chapter in Greensboro. Five years later, as a student at A&T, Blackwell ran for the state assembly, basing his campaign upon a challenge to the dominance of white political and economic leaders. Eventually, in the 1960's, Blackwell became a leader of the Southern Christian Leadership Conference. "From almost the point at which I could walk and talk," he later recalled, "I was involved in something related to social change."

The second style of leadership was best personified by Dr. F. D. Bluford, president of A&T College. A&T's continued existence depended upon white legislative support; therefore, Bluford continually found himself having to accommodate to white expectations. As a consequence, he discouraged protest on campus and performed in public those acts of deference to white leaders that past history had shown were necessary to improve funding chances for A&T. Faculty members quickly got the message that, as one put it, "You could make it here if you didn't go too fast" or protest too much. Participation in the NAACP was discouraged, and any form of overt resistance was forbidden. There was a price for Bluford's accommodation: he was denounced as "the last of the handkerchief heads," and the president's house was referred to frequently as "Uncle Tom's Cabin." In fact, Bluford was caught between two worlds. As one of his successors remarked, it was almost impossible to "play that game and still live and come out [whole]. . . . What do you do? You can fight to get freedom and you can protest. . . . But how do you get the things that you need?" For the Blufords of Greensboro, the ultimate question was not what felt best, but what could be done to help the community. "If he had to go down to Raleigh and suffer indignities, he would," one faculty member remarked.

Despite the apparent polarization of styles, the two men represented alternate sides of the same effort to achieve racial dignity and progress. The juxtaposition was vividly illustrated in a private conversation between Blackwell and Bluford. In the midst of his 1948 campaign for the state legislature, Blackwell—then a student—lambasted local textile magnates. His campaign literature was highly visible on the A&T campus. He knew his actions embarrassed the administration, and he expected reprisals. One day, during a discussion with students, Bluford walked by and said, "Blackwell, I'd like to see you in my office." "Here it comes," thought Blackwell, "Now I've had it." Instead, when he arrived in Bluford's office, the president told him that he was free to use one of the college auditoriums if he wished. The only condition was that Blackwell must never ask for permission, because if Bluford were called on the carpet, he needed to be able to say that he had not sanctioned Blackwell's actions. Blackwell concluded that, despite Bluford's dissembling before the white community, he was a man with "a sense of dignity . . . a man [who, although] thoroughly discredited and constantly abused, also had some of the same yearnings as those of us that were out there raising hell."

Throughout the 1930's and 1940's, the two traditions of caution and activism—both responses to the realities of white power—played off against each other, each more or less prevalent depending upon the circumstances or the frame of reference of the observer. There were countless examples of accommodation and subservience. In order to survive, it was necessary for black people—nearly half of whom worked in service positions—to pay obeisance to the cultural expectations of those who paid their wages. Many children were taught early to "bow and scrape before white folk," lest they endanger themselves and, later, their families. Even active supporters of protest sometimes obscured their activities. Belonging to the NAACP during the 1930's, one activist later recalled, was like being a Black Panther in the 1960's. As a consequence, many NAACP members feared losing their jobs if their support of the organization became known to whites. Public school teachers, for example, often preferred paying their membership dues in cash so that there would be no canceled check available to be used as a basis for retribution. Given the hard lessons of day-to-day survival, there frequently was no way of reconciling overt independence with the need to put supper on the table. As one black leader commented, "a lot of black people [developed] a way of answering you the way they thought you wanted to hear."

Yet there were others who provided a daily reminder of full insistence on equality and dignity. None exerted a greater influence on generations of Greensboro black young people than Nell Coley and Vance Chavis, two teachers at Dudley. Both openly announced their participation in the NAACP and encouraged others to emulate their protest activities. Both also urged students to take home to their parents the message of registering to vote, Chavis even having students in his class address envelopes to prospective voters. By their own examples, each held forth a standard of pride and assertiveness that students found hard to forget. Chavis taught physics, but, as one student recalled, he also taught the importance of "not selling one's soul." Continually, he implored students "not to go in the back way at the movie theater and climb all those steps in order to pay for segregation." Chavis helped organize students to support the theater boycott during the 1930's, reminding them that he himself refused to ride the buses and railroad because of his unwillingness to accept any form of Jim Crow.

Nell Coley delivered the same message to her English classes. "We were always talking about the issues," Coley recalled. "We might read [a poem or a novel] as a kind of pivot," but the words of John Donne or Thomas Hardy were always related to the inalienable rights of all human beings to respect, freedom, and self-definition. "I had to tell youngsters," Coley said, "that the way you find things need not happen. . . . You must not accept; I don't care if they push and shove you, you must not accept that [treatment]. . . . You are who you are." Through her own example and the discussions she conducted, Coley drove home the theme that nothing was beyond the reach of those who dared. Recalling her years at Dudley High School with Vance Chavis, she commented: "We were leading the children to be the best persons that they could be. . . . We were being ourselves in the context of the times in which we were living. And if the spin-off leads to kids who are going to be leaders in [protests], so be it. . . . But I don't think we were deciding it that way. We were just trying to inspire young folks, trying to make them realize their potential."

In less visible ways, many of the same themes were reinforced in the home by parents. Traditional modes of racial behavior did not always prevail in daily life. David Morehead, long-time executive secretary of the Hayes-Taylor YMCA, remembers vividly a day when he was pelted by a shower of rotten eggs supplied to ten or eleven young white children by a white storeowner. When he told his mother what had happened, she marched directly to the scene of the incident, confronted the storeowner, demanded an apology, and made clear she would hold the storekeeper accountable were the episode repeated. Randolph Blackwell's father demonstrated a similar resoluteness, challenging a white foreman who sought to intimidate him, and doing so in front of his children. Such episodes, of course, were by no means the rule. Yet in a world where direct-action protest was usually impossible, seeing a parent defend his or her family against white authority, hearing discussions about voting, or sitting in a classroom taught by Nell Coley or Vance Chavis was of critical importance to a young black in sustaining a vision of what true equality might mean.

In this larger framework of caution and protest, the world of politics offered a barometer of black assertiveness and black status. Although North Carolina had joined other Southern states in disfranchising Negroes at the end of the nineteenth century, a growing number of blacks were able to register to vote in the 1920's and 1930's. One of the differences about Greensboro, Vance Chavis observed, was that whites did not overtly attempt to discourage blacks from voting. Moreover, starting in 1933, blacks ran for city-wide office on a regular basis. Robert C. Sharp, secretary of the Colored Ministerial Alliance, entered the race for city council in 1933 and was supported by approximately 12 per cent of those voting.* Sharp ran again in the next two elections,

---

*Greensboro elected its council in a city-wide election, not on a ward-by-ward basis. The top seven vote-getters won election, but, depending upon the number of candidates, it theoretically was possible for all winners to poll over 50 per cent of the vote, or for some to poll substantially less than 50 per cent. Voters could mark seven selections on the ballot, but they could also vote for less than seven if they so chose.

never receiving more than 15 per cent of the ballots cast, and being outpolled even in black areas by white candidates. Still, news reports noted the increasing registration of blacks after 1935, and a new responsiveness by the city council to black needs as evidenced by construction of a recreation park and swimming pool in the black community.

As elsewhere, World War II brought an acceleration of black political and protest activity. Sharp ran for city council again in 1943, this time receiving 31 per cent of the votes cast and coming in ninth out of twelve in the general election. Six out of seventeen city council candidates addressed an open-air rally in the black section of town, with at least two offering support of black issues. In addition, Sharp for the first time outpolled white candidates in precinct number five in the heart of black Greensboro. The same general picture prevailed in the 1947 elections when a new candidate, F. A. Mayfield, a construction engineer and former professor at A&T, received 25 per cent of the total votes cast.

The most significant change, however, began with the 1949 election, when for the first time two black candidates survived the primary and entered the general election. Mayfield was joined in the race by Brody McCauley. The two competed closely in the primary, each receiving 20 per cent of the vote, but in the general election, Mayfield outpolled McCauley two to one and ended up with 25 per cent of the total vote. More important than the returns, however, were the behind-the-scenes developments reflected in the two candidacies. In fact, McCauley and Mayfeld represented distinct segments of the black community. Although McCauley' was listed in the white newspapers as a restaurant owner, his "restaurant" consisted of a pool hall, a barber shop, and a café. McCauley was a "street" candidate, his natural constituency differing significantly from those "established" blacks who traditionally had been involved in politics and who supported Mayfield.

The decision to run McCauley, in turn, grew out of an effort by young blacks—led by Randolph Blackwell—to challenge the traditional political system in Greensboro and build the foundation for a mass-based political culture. Ordinarily, white politicians hired black "bosses" to dispense money on election day, and set up rallies where white candidates would speak. The first step in Blackwell's assault on such practices was to attend the rallies, ask candidates critical questions they did not expect, and then—with his friends—consume the food, beer, and cigarettes being handed out. The second step was to use Brody McCauley's candidacy to mobilize blacks who previously had been left out of the political system. "We saw in the running of Brody,"

Blackwell recalled, "an opportunity to involve people that had not been traditionally thought of as voting citizens. So that by running him we were able to pull the guys out of the poolroom and bars and get them registered." Although McCauley himself never really "campaigned" in the traditional sense, the voter registration effort associated with his candidacy produced lines two or three blocks long.[2]

In the end, the 1949 election proved to be a decisive intermediate step toward greater black political strength. The registration campaign produced 333 new voters in the fifth precinct, far outpacing the new registrations in any other area of the city. Just as important, the candidacy of McCauley altered prevailing political patterns dominated by whites and set the stage for further political initiatives by blacks. Although the white press commented sarcastically on the inability of blacks to unite behind a single candidate, the division between McCauley and Mayfield widened the black political constituency and changed the ground rules governing political activism. Even those identified with the "establishment" candidate applauded the new level of mass involvement. "You really turned them out," Dean Warmoth Gibbs of A&T told Blackwell, "you really turned them out." Such comments reinforced Blackwell's sense that his efforts would have an impact. "He didn't go into any discourse about . . . how glad he was," Blackwell remarked about Gibbs, "but I knew that I enjoyed his approval by that one statement. And you know, that's a very careful way of keeping alive something that you thought was important without running the risk of jeopardizing the school by openly identifying with it."

The seeds planted in 1949 came to fruition in 1951, when the first black was elected to the Greensboro city council. The victory was a product of many forces. In 1949 the Greensboro Citizens Association (GCA)—an alliance of older, well-respected black leaders—had formed to eliminate "those political parasites . . . who were selling the vote." By focusing community attention on issues such as streetlighting and recreation, the GCA sought to accomplish many of the same reforms as Blackwell's student-based coalition did. The GCA came into its own in 1951, when, in conjunction with Bennett College, it mobilized the largest and most effective voter registration campaign ever held in Greensboro. Each year the Bennett Homemaking Institute sponsored a community project that emphasized issues of general concern such as child care or better schools. The 1951 project was entitled "Operation Doorknock," and its goal was to register every black citizen who could be reached. Led by Professor Hobart Jarrett, a GCA leader, the project sent students into every black neighborhood to seek applicants for voter registration. For a week regular academic classes were suspended as students canvassed, provided child care, and coordinated transportation to the registration centers. "It was as strong a community project as I had seen," Jarrett said. "The city school people, the laboring people, everybody fell right into it." In precinct five, 560 new voters were registered, nearly 100 more than the total vote cast in that district in 1949. In precinct nine, the new voters totaled 446—almost double the ballots cast two years earlier. Whites could not help being impressed. "The surge of new registrations," the Greensboro *Daily News* commented, "has promoted immediate speculation that the Negro contender will have to be reckoned with."

That contender was Dr. William Hampton, president of the GCA, universally respected, and by all odds the kind of consensus candidate who had the best chance of gaining white support as well as solid backing from the black community. A quiet, unassuming man, Hampton was known throughout the black community for his work as a physician and staff secretary at the all-black Richardson Hospital. To the white community, in turn, Hampton appeared to be an ideal, responsible spokesman for black interests. His desire, Hampton told the voters, was to serve the entire community and acquaint other councilmen with "conditions in my part of the city with which they may not be familiar." Hampton was "such a personable person," Vance Chavis commented, that hardly anyone could dislike him. As a "nonpolitical" civic leader who rarely had taken positions on controversial questions, Hampton seemed ideally equipped to capitalize on the gains of the previous few years.

On election day Hampton scored a stunning victory, receiving support from 54 per cent of those casting ballots. Indeed, Hampton would have won even *without* the black vote, polling 41 per cent of the vote in white areas. In the past no black candidate had ever tallied more than 31 per cent of the total vote. Now, Hampton had far exceeded that, winning substantial support in every white precinct, regardless of its social and economic makeup. Even more impressive, however, were Hampton's figures in the black precincts. Previously, white candidates had done as well or better than blacks in the Negro precincts. But in 1951, for the first time, black citizens engaged in "bullet" voting, marking their ballots for only one person instead of the seven they were entitled to choose. As one black politician noted: "You don't help a black by putting his name on the ticket and then voting for six white candidates because [then] you are scattering your vote." In 1951 blacks acted on that injunction. Out of 1592 ballots cast in precinct five, Hampton received 1559. His nearest competitor polled 545. In precinct nine Hampton received 598 out of 703 votes, with his closest challenger getting only 189. If the victory testified to Hampton's skill in securing white support, it demonstrated even more dramatically the newfound political solidarity of black Greensboro.

With the triumph of 1951, many black leaders in Greensboro had good reason to look ahead with optimism. Much had been accomplished, despite the legacy of the social and economic caste system. Greensboro had the best black public schools in the state, two of the most respected black colleges in the South, a network of thriving churches and voluntary associations, and a deep-rooted sense of community pride. Greensboro's black citizens had succeeded both in building their own institutions and in advancing the possibilities of breaking into the still-closed larger society. The question that remained was whether Hampton's victory represented the first step in a fundamental transformation of the racial status quo, or simply a tactical adjustment in the continuing hegemony of white paternalism.

III

The answer depended in significant measure on white Greensboro's readiness to criticize, or even become conscious of, its previous treatment of Negro citizens as passive objects. In preceding years blacks had been viewed as dependent extensions of the white community, not recognized as independent people with an agenda of their own. Did Greensboro's progressivism provide room for self-doubt and a skeptical re-examination of that past? And if so, were those in positions of power ready to help chart a new course in full cooperation with blacks?

The response of Greensboro's white newspapers to the city council elections did not suggest an immediate readiness to criticize Greensboro's racial heritage. Instead, said the *Daily News*, Hampton's victory was just one more example of "the understanding, mutual respect and cooperation" that had always characterized race relations in the city. Repeatedly, Greensboro's white leaders praised the "excellent" race relations in the community, citing how well blacks and whites understood each other. Yet such attitudes testified more to the depth of the continuing problem than to progress in solving it. The idea of "excellent race relations" revealed much about the psychological needs of white people and little about the authentic state of interracial communication in

Greensboro. Most contact between whites and blacks occurred in situations shaped by a gross power imbalance that made impossible any forthright exchange of views. If interracial activities were defined as those where communication took place on grounds of "understanding, mutual respect and cooperation," past achievements were meager.

Not surprisingly, most cooperative interaction between blacks and whites took place on the city's college campuses. During the 1930's and 1940's the Greensboro Intercollegiate Fellowship held occasional meetings that brought together faculty members and students from A&T, Bennett, Guilford, Greensboro College, and Women's College. In the same years the Guilford County Interracial Commission, a voluntary group consisting mainly of academics and professional people, sponsored conversations on how to overcome the barriers of racial discrimination. Their efforts were exploratory, focusing mostly on theoretical topics of mutual interest, but gradually the group moved toward practical action as well. During the late 1940's and early 1950's biracial teams quietly visited county offices, large department stores, and other downtown public facilities to urge that Jim Crow signs be removed from water fountains and bathrooms. Over a period of months, and without any formal action, most of the signs were painted over. Despite such real and symbolic successes, the Interracial Commission at no time felt sufficiently confident of outside support to go "public" with the issue.

Ironically, the only truly integrated situation in the community was a by-product of tragedy. During 1947 and 1948, a massive polio epidemic struck Greensboro. In the midst of the crisis, people forgot the power of custom and drew upon every resource available. Nurses were recruited from throughout the state, and a polio hospital was created with black and white patients side by side, treated by an integrated staff. Since the National Polio Foundation paid for most expenses and refused to permit differential treatment, there was little resistance or furor. As one doctor recalled, "the value of it was that it started off at the very beginning that way, and there was no trouble." Significantly, school classes held at the polio hospital were also integrated—long before the *Brown* decision. But once the epidemic had passed, some people began to object to white and black nurses eating together, and hospital administrators established separate facilities. When one white nurse questioned the new segregation, she was dismissed.*

*For one brief moment, the Chamber of Commerce was also integrated. After receiving a recruitment letter in 1948, C. E. McAden, the black owner of a dry-cleaning establishment, sent his membership dues to the chamber and was sent by return mail his member-

The only other example of integration occurred on the playing field. White and black basketball teams from the "downtown" Y and the Windsor Recreation Center held exhibition games to raise funds for the polio hospital. Consistent with the purpose of the contests, seating was nonsegregated. In addition, white softball teams from various companies regularly played black teams, the teams alternating fields and usually appearing before integrated crowds. When a black semipro baseball team lost two players to injuries, white players from the downtown Y took their places. Placards advertising the games depicted the team as interracial, and seating at the contests was integrated. Still, such desegregation was mostly accidental, and occurred primarily in the black community, with whites coming into an integrated setting rather than vice versa.

In this over-all environment, there were just two predominantly white institutions—the YWCA and the American Friends Service Committee (AFSC)—publicly indentified with an effort to change racial attitudes. Each drew upon a religious impulse that questioned the principle of segregation; both were affiliated with national organizations committed to racial equality; and both drew heavily on political liberals, primarily women, who were willing to challenge tradition. Yet even in their departure from the status quo, the two organizations reflected the ambiguities of race in Greensboro and the power of conventional white mores.

The downtown YWCA was dominated by middle-and upper-class white women, many of whom were also members of United Church Women, a group that held yearly interracial meetings throughout the late 1940's. With a strong religious commitment to brotherhood, many of these women were troubled by the racial double standard of their region. Betsy Taylor, for example, grew up in a devout household. She had always questioned local racial customs, and when she and her husband returned to Greensboro in the late 1940's, they built two Holiday Inns that were open to blacks as well as whites. The Taylors made a concerted effort to become acquainted with Negroes, and both

---

ship card and a medallion to hang in the window. When the Norfolk *Journal Guide* published word of the breakthrough, the chamber was mortified, rescinding its action. Chamber membership qualifications stated that "all persons of good character who sympathize with the objectives of the Greensboro Chamber of Commerce" were eligible. Mr. McAden refused to give up his membership voluntarily. Not until almost 20 years later would the next black be admitted to the chamber.

believed that only through open communication could barriers of racial injustice be overcome. Although Betsy Taylor's commitment to desegregation was more explicit than that of most Y members, she reflected a concern about race that was widespread in the organization.

Still, the issue of desegregation at the YWCA was introduced initially by black women, who in 1946 formed their own separate chapter of the Y. With its one thousand members, the Susie B. Dudley YWCA presented the downtown Y with a challenge it could not avoid. First, the new organization threatened to outpace the downtown chapter in membership and support. Second, it forced the white Y either to affirm its commitment to the national Y credo of racial justice or to sanction separate institutions for blacks openly. If it chose the latter course, it would follow in the footsteps of the national YMCA, which had long approved separate white and black organizations. Significantly, there was no issue more capable of angering the YWCA than placing it in the same category as the YMCA.

In its handling of this dilemma, the Y illustrated how tortured were white attempts to make even slight alterations in the racial status quo. Although the YWCA had held interracial meetings during the early 1940's, it was always under circumstances that ensured compliance with traditional racial etiquette. Thus, for example, the Y's of Bennett and A&T were invited to a city-wide meeting downtown, but not at a time when a meal would be served. Similarly, after the formation of the Dudley Y, its representatives were invited to join the city-wide board of directors. But again, it was understood that the black board members should not attend the monthly dinners that preceded the board meetings. Thus, each month the two black representatives on the board would arrive after dinner had been cleared. Even that compromise was sufficient to drive some prominent whites to resign from the board in protest against the Y's breach of tradition.

In fact, the issue of interracial dining proved an accurate index of the YWCA's over-all attitude toward integration. By 1950, the board had decided to hold dinner meetings for all members and to include blacks on its city-wide nominating committee. More important, the Y had decided to press the city's Council of Social Agencies to include blacks. When that organization responded that it could not do so because its meetings were held over lunch, the YWCA offered its own dining facilities. During the early 1950's more and more YWCA activities took place at both branches, with one working women's club alternating meeting places and taking steps to assure interracial contacts by assigning each woman a number at the door, and then establishing small discussion groups by a random selection of numbers.

Yet the most important spur to the YWCA's affirmation of interracialism came not from within, but in response to an outside attempt to merge the black YMCA and the black YWCA into a single segregated facility. The controversy began in the spring of 1948, when the YWCA asked Ceasar Cone for $50,000 in order to renovate and rehabilitate the Dudley YWCA. In response, Cone angrily declared that he had meant his original gift to the Hayes-Taylor YMCA to be spent on a facility for both sexes. The crisis came to a head when Cone wrote, in December 1948, that he would contribute his money only for the enlargement of the Hayes-Taylor physical plant, and on condition that any future grant by the Community Chest to the YWCA be for the purpose of a joint facility within the black community.

Over the ensuing months, both black and white YWCA members sought a path of compromise that would maintain their independence from YMCA domination. Black women took pride in belonging to a "women's" organization that gave them the opportunity for self-expression, the head of the Dudley YWCA declared; they had not found the same opportunity at the women's auxiliary of the Hayes-Taylor YMCA. Sounding the same theme, the executive director of the white YWCA argued that a women's organization "develops potential leadership in women, beginning with our youngest members . . . This concept of the YWCA is one that is hard for men to apprehend and appreciate . . . This may [sound like] the battle of the sexes if you like, but the YWCA . . . is an example of how the women's movement has helped women along the way to more useful citizenship." Thus, early arguments against merger emphasized a feminist view that women needed to be independent of male control if they were to realize their potential.

Cone's response suggested how accurate the perceptions of YWCA leaders were. First, Cone criticized black women for not having a male advisory committee, since women "always had to call on men for financial help." His gift to Hayes-Taylor, he said, had been based on the premise that men had the ability to get things done. Second, Cone expressed concern about the relationship of economy to charity. Both could be served, he argued, only if there were a joint black facility. As if to confirm the worst fears of the women, Cone suggested that the new joint buildings have only one executive director and one program, with the women looking to men for leadership. Not surprisingly, the Dudley branch rejected the proposed merger.

Over the next five years, interracialism gradually replaced feminism as the primary argument against union with the YMCA. In fact, fear of control by the YMCA seemed to reinforce the move toward greater desegregation in the YW. The more the Y could claim to involve women from both races in all its activities, the less justification there would be for creating a single segregated facility for both men and women. Throughout the early 1950's, the YWCA emphasized its oneness. It would be foolish for the Community Chest to fund a joint facility, the YWCA argued, when its own two branches served women of both races. Furthermore, such a step would remove the only institution in the community where interracial activity could occur.

In the end, the YWCA settled for half a loaf. Although it eventually secured money for a new building of its own in the black community, Ceasar Cone succeeded in having the Community Chest adopt a $300,000 budget to enlarge the Hayes-Taylor YMCA and include facilities for women. In the fall of 1954, Cone and Burlington Industries' founder, Spencer Love, the two most powerful economic giants of Greensboro, gave $100,000 each to construct an indoor swimming pool for blacks at the Hayes-Taylor Y, making their gift contingent on the pool being utilized by both black boys and black girls.

On the other side, the YWCA encountered mounting opposition to its own interracial activities. When the Y acted on its commitment to desegregation by hiring a black receptionist, the action was met by a storm of protest. Prominent members of the YWCA board resigned, the head of the United Fund warned that the Y was endangering contributions by alienating the community, and pressure was applied to halt any further hiring of blacks. As Betsy Taylor recalled, "the roof was nearly blown off." Six months after going to work for the YWCA, the black secretary was hired away at twice the salary by President Bluford at A&T. In the minds of many, her transfer of employment was no accident.

On balance, then, the efforts of the YWCA toward some degree of interracial progress provided little basis for optimism. Some of the most powerful people in the city, as well as leaders of the Community Chest, appeared committed to maintaining segregated recreational facilities for blacks and whites. There seemed little support for accelerating the YWCA's endeavors toward interracial contact. Indeed, when word leaked out that an integrated group of cerebral palsied youngsters swam together in the YWCA's downtown pool, a new campaign was launched to force the Community Chest to cut off support for the Y.

Just as important, the white members of the YWCA faced internal conflicts over racial equality. Even if they went a significant distance given the racial climate of the late 1940's, many still accepted the values of a culture permeated by assumptions of white superiority. At least some black members of the YWCA wondered whether all the words about human relations were not simply "a lot of talk." The YWCA had journeyed further than most, but there was good reason to believe that its own fear of control by the YMCA was at least as important in the events of the early 1950's as its commitment to racial justice was.

The American Friends Service Committee experienced the same kind of resistance and tension in its advocacy of racial progress. In the early 1950's, the AFSC located its Southeast regional headquarters in Greensboro and embarked on an ambitious program of seeking "merit employment." Recognizing that racial injustice took its greatest toll in the economic marketplace, the AFSC set out to break down job barriers by persuading employers to hire blacks for nontraditional positions, thereby both increasing economic opportunities for blacks and promoting a lessening of prejudices through more frequent contact between whites and blacks. AFSC staff members attempted to impress employers with the quality of job applicants, thus appealing to their self-interest. With a special focus on Greensboro, the AFSC staff contacted nearly every major employer in the area between 1952 and 1956.

The most glaring disclosure of the AFSC study was the severe limitation on economic opportunity for Greensboro's black citizens, even those with a college education. In one case the wife of the social studies chairman at A&T, herself formerly a college instructor, went to a prominent department store in search of a sales position. The only position available, she was told, was that of maid or waitress. When the same woman applied to the telephone company for a job as a long-distance operator, she was informed that the company did not hire Negroes. A local doctor indicated that he would be happy to hire the woman as a receptionist if he were somewhere else, but—after all—he needed to make his living in Greensboro. A second woman, an A&T graduate and the person finally hired at the YWCA as a receptionist, had been forced to work as a part-time maid at two places prior to her employment at the Y. And when the local Sears store hired five A&T men, it assigned them to work as porters. Later the company let the men go because, in the words of a Sears spokesman, "they did not accept the bounds of propriety as a Southerner sees them." Writing about the South three decades earlier, Richard Wright had described his experience of being hired as a janitor in an optical factory with the promise that later he would be taught how to grind lenses. The apprenticeship never materialized, of course, and when Wright raised the issue, he was ostracized as a "bad nigger." More than one Greensboro black had the same experience. An A&T student who worked in the printing office at Cone Mills was told that if he stayed on after graduation he would be taught how to handle the presses and machines. The next year he was still waiting for his first lesson.

Significantly, the desegregation that did occur on the job took place where one would least expect it. In a local printing company white and black pressmen worked side by side, and the company hired a black woman linotype operator as well. A refrigeration service company employed a black mechanic. A Chevrolet dealer agreed to train a black salesman. (The same dealer held yearly interracial profitsharing dinners for his workers.) But most of this "merit employment" took place in small businesses. The owner of a local coal and oil company hired a black truck driver, and the manager of a filling station employed mechanics of both races. "Integration was all around," one AFSC staff member reported, but not in places that were most visible to outside observers.

The typical example of employee desegregation occurred in a tiny factory operated by Robert Ford. A Northerner, a Catholic, and the husband of a pediatrician, Ford had come to Greensboro to manage a surgical tool company. "I was the farthest removed from any kind of social activist as you could be," he said. "I didn't know anything about this. But suddenly I got hit with a problem in my conscience. Here's a guy who wants a job and he has qualifications, and I can't hire him." Ford discovered that a few blocks away at A&T there was a ready supply of machinists; faced with a shortage of workers, he set out to hire some of the black graduates. When one of his old employees threatened to leave, Ford went to his priest, who told him that the issue was a matter of conscience. Ford hired the black worker and thereafter ran his shop as an integrated working place. "There was no dedication to liberate the Negro," he said. "I had nothing to do with that. I was just a businessman trying to run a business."

Generally, however, AFSC efforts met delay and resistance, particularly in the largest companies and in those businesses where clerical and sales positions were sought. Of the large corporations, only Western Electric agreed to cooperate, hiring two black secretaries and promising to open fifteen departments to black employees. After two years of seeking an appointment, AFSC staff members finally interviewed

Spencer Love of Burlington Industries. Love declared that at the time he anticipated no integration. His own experience, he said, demonstrated that in textiles, the Japanese were more skilled than whites, and blacks less so. When the AFSC suggested that Love hire a black secretary as an example to the rest of his work force, the textile executive responded with disbelief. What would he do about toilet facilities? he asked. The same general reaction came from Cone Mills, the largest employer in the area. Although Cone operated one diaper plant with an all-black work force, there were few if any blacks in nontraditional positions in other Cone factories. Cone defended his policy by saying that white workers would not permit desegregation. The AFSC responded that state and local AF of L members had offered precisely the opposite assessment—they were willing to integrate, but employers would not let them.

Sometimes, management greeted the idea of merit hiring with outright hostility. An executive of R. J. Reynolds raised the specter of communism coming to Greensboro under the guise of the AFSC, since communists, after all, sought the same goals. An executive of Carolina Steel and Iron Company, in turn, openly endorsed total separation of the races, all the while talking about what he had done for "his blacks." Another executive in the same company declared that industry should not be pushed too fast. Integration, he said, should happen first in the churches. The man attended one of the most conservative churches in the city. Even academics were resistant. "If you were to ask me to employ Negro professors," the president of Women's College said, "I'd have to tell you that we're not ready for that."

One of the more interesting AFSC ventures involved the newly built Cone Hospital, established under the term of its bequest to serve members of both races who could not afford to pay. Dr. Joseph Lichty, administrator of the hospital, initially told the AFSC that he wished to build a completely integrated hospital, with black and white doctors and nurses working together to serve an integrated patient poulation. Within a short time, however, it became clear that his hope would not be realized. Black doctors who applied to the staff were turned down and the nursing staff was segregated. Although the hospital hired one black technician, other efforts to integrate the professional staff were unavailing. An initial effort to have black and white patients stay on the same hall generated immediate protest. The board of directors, Lichty reported, had been besieged by "the elite" of Greensboro society, who insisted that the desegregation be stopped.

The negative aspect of the AFSC experiment was perhaps epitomized by the experience of one young black woman who was an AFSC "pioneer" at a prestigious local retail store. Hired as a stock person, she had been told that when business was heavy she could also wait on customers, with the prospect that someday she might move up to be a saleswoman. After that, the young woman, on one occasion, sold some goods to customers. Her employer then forced her to resign, claiming she had not distributed evenly the sales she made to other sales clerks. The employer criticized the woman for calling other clerks by their first names, even though she had been introduced to them that way. In the employer's view, the black woman should have used proper titles with all clerks, even though they would continue to use her first name. All in all, he commented, she had been too aggressive. Although her sales personality was good, she was simply not "fitting in." When asked by an AFSC staff member to name another black he would prefer instead, the employer cited a maid in the store, who always called everybody Mr. and Mrs., and did not mind asking her superiors for a church donation, which they always gave because they liked her so much.

IV

As Greensboro prepared to face the prospect of school desegregation in 1954, then, the situation remained ambiguous, containing grounds for pessimism as well as hope. The black community seemed eager and ready for a new era of race relations. Despite a social structure based on caste and an economic system that used race to polarize the work force, the black community had struggled effectively to develop its own institutions and to build a base from which to enter the larger community. There were problems, to be sure—conflicts over whether to pursue the politics of protest or deference, anger at the timidity of some church leaders, divisions between the working class and the black bourgeoisie. But the black experience at Bennett and A&T, in the public schools, and in the world of electoral politics reflected a community that was vibrant, on the move, and committed to securing equality of treatment.

Given the realities of power, however, the larger issue was how white Greensboro would greet the prospect of a new era of race relations. On that question, several areas of concern existed. The first was the role of those who held most of the economic, social, and political power in Greensboro. Historically, it has been customary to think of upper-class whites as more tolerant in their attitudes toward race than "poor whites." According to this view, the only barrier that has prevented "well-born" leaders from pushing for faster progress toward race equality has been fear of provoking "redneck" resistance. By implication, intelligent whites of good social breeding would long since have supported a racially just society had they been able to act upon their own beliefs.

Yet the history of Greensboro prior to 1954 raises profound questions about the validity of such a view. Some affluent whites did promote racial justice, helping to guarantee that Greensboro's atmosphere would at least be "civil." There were no lynchings in Greensboro, and on an individual basis blacks enjoyed a greater chance to secure just treatment. But the primary resistance to significant racial breakthroughs also came from white leaders of the upper class. On the issue of job desegregation, it was in small shops, printing companies, and gas stations that progress occurred. Those who controlled the largest number of employees, on the other hand—Spencer Love of Burlington Industries, the Cone family, Carolina Steel and Iron Company, Jefferson Standard Insurance Company—took either a hard-line position against "merit employment" or responded with nothing more than the rhetoric of good intentions. To be sure, the downtown YWCA—a leading supporter of desegregation—represented part of the white elite in Greensboro; but these were women—itself an important difference—and some of the most powerful members of the Y left when the organization became involved in interracial activity. The Community Chest, led by William Preyer, a member of one of Greensboro's most prominent families, actively opposed the hiring of a black receptionist at the YWCA and implicity threatened curtailment of support for the Y if such practices continued. When Cone Hospital took some tentative steps toward desegregating its patient population, it was "the elite of Greensboro" that protested most vigorously to the hospital director and board of trustees. It was also the retail stores frequented by the upper class that reacted most negatively when asked to hire blacks as sales clerks. In short, those whom one might have expected to be most progressive in the white community seemed to have resisted rather than promoted racial change. That resistance was partly rooted in the desire to avoid conflict with one's peers, partly in the inability to recognize a black point of view, and partly in the understanding that caste was an effective way of preventing class issues from being raised. But whatever the reasons, support from these white leaders would be crucial if the community were to provide the kind of leadership envisioned by David Jones and Benjamin Smith and Edward Hudgins on the school board.

A second area of concern was the paternalism characteristic of

Greensboro's white elite. No benefactors did more for the black community than J. Spencer Love and Ceasar Cone. The latter provided the building for the Hayes-Taylor Y, and the two together made possible the construction of an indoor swimming pool at Hayes-Taylor in the mid-1950's. Yet the benevolence of both appears to have been premised on maintaining the racial status quo. Indeed, some felt that the construction of the swimming pool in 1955 was a means of guaranteeing that blacks would swim together in their own pool and not attempt to use the "white" pool downtown. Support by such men of black institutions may have been indispensable, given the context of the 1940's and l950's; but that support carried with it the implicit price of "not rocking the boat" on racial issues.

Just as significant was the nature of the interpersonal relationships through which Love and Cone maintained contact with the black community. John Tarpley, principal of Dudley High School and supervisor of all black schools, was the black leader who kept in touch with Cone on issues of mutual interest. Tarpley effectively represented his constituency; yet, given his dependence upon Cone, he necessarily was forced to work within Cone's expectations. David Morehead, executive secretary of the Hayes-Taylor Y, served a similar function with J. Spencer Love. The first contact with Morehead occurred when Love's secretary asked Morehead to find two chauffeurs to drive the Love family to Florida. Although Morehead did not run an employment service, he provided the help, feeling that if Love had wanted the employment office, he would have called it. Subsequently, Morehead helped secure two other household workers for the Love family. After that, the two men met, and Love asked what he might do in return for the favors that Morehead had done for him. Anticipating such a question, Morehead requested support for the indoor pool at the YMCA, and Love joined with Ceaser Cone in funding it. Every year thereafter, Morehead noted, Love would give him an hour or so in the springtime, and the two men would ride in the country and talk about the needs of the black community. Tarpley and Morehead referred to the two textile magnates as among their dearest friends, and used these relationships to promote the best interests of the black community. Moreover in the convoluted world of racial politics in America, both had a genuine devotion and fondness for their white benefactors. Yet they too were used, and, in the reciprocal nature of benevolent paternalism, they served well the interests of Cone and Love in maintaining contact with, as well as control over, the black community.

Nor was such paternalism found only among defenders of the racial status quo. When one AFSC staff member visited a local clothing store he observed a black clerk behind the counter waiting on a customer. The man's report on the incident was condescending and incredulous. The black clerk, the memo stated, had not only completed the sale "properly" but had also answered the phone and provided the customer with a receipt, all without any difficulty. Indeed, the report concluded, the entire store had been "entrusted" to the black clerk for the whole lunch hour. At least some white YWCA members shared the same attitudes. One woman recalled "what a wonderful opportunity" it had been to meet with "colored men and women who were intelligent, educated, refined and cultured [as opposed to]ditch-diggers, bus boys, and things like that." Although such sentiments may not have characterized most white YWCA leaders, some members of the black community wondered about the "good image makers of the YWCA" and how deep their convictions on racial justice went.

The greatest power of paternalism, of course, was its ability to define for the black community what its proper "place" should be. Even as William Hampton was elected to the city council, the Greensboro *Daily News* gave notice that it would watch carefully over his tenure. "We are confident," the paper editorialized, "that we do not have to remind him of the responsibility and opportunity which are his." Hampton got the message. When, two years later, he finished first in the primary—a rank which if duplicated in the general election usually meant being chosen mayor—Hampton renounced the possibility. "I wouldn't do anything," he said, "to lessen the progress that has come in these years, and I am fully cognizant of support that white people have given me." Such obeisance to white standards enraged some blacks. Julius Douglas, pastor of St. James Presbyterian Church, attacked the existing leadership as "the sorriest possible bunch."

Thus, in the spring of 1954 Greensboro faced the prospect of desegregation with a mixed history. On the one hand, whites viewed the city as one of the most forward-looking urban areas of the South. In the same relative sense Greensboro was a better place for blacks to live than elsewhere. As Vance Chavis recalled, "No one ever called me nigger here," a truth that both illustrated and defined the progress made by the city's black community. Yet an underlying pattern of racism and paternalism remained, condemning most blacks to economic poverty, and preventing all but dependent relationships between whites and blacks.

As the time for decision on school desegregation neared, the Greensboro *Daily News* described its version of the dilemma facing the community. The editorial was entitled, "Time for the Golden Mean." "During fifty years," it said, "the Negro race has moved rapidly to take its rightful place in the mainstream of the nation. But these extremists on both sides—the Talmadges and the NAACP—should remember the moderate views held by most Southerners. They cannot be pushed too fast. . . . These times call for courage combined with the golden mean." The question left unanswered was, what did it mean to be a moderate in Greensboro, North Carolina?

CHAPTER TWO

The Politics of Moderation

There has been a kind of liberal strand running through the air—
but make no mistake about it, Greensboro is not all that liberal.
Nell Coley, a black schoolteacher

We're just like Georgia and Alabama except we do it in a tuxedo
and they wear suspenders.
A prominent white attorney in Greensboro

The law is the landing force [of change]. It makes the beachhead. But the breakthrough, if it is to be significant, is broadened
by forces from behind which take advantage of the opening to go
the rest of the way. Where these forces are present, significant
alterations of social practices result. Where they do not exist, the
law has been unable to hold its beachhead and the legal action
becomes a kind of military monument on which is only re-
corded, we were here.
John B. Frank, legal scholar

To those who believed that Greensboro might lead the rest of the South
toward racial justice, the early response to the school board's desegregation resolution provided hope and reassurance. On May 19, 1954, the
morning newspaper applauded the school board's willingness to face
facts. "How one felt or what one did about segregation before Monday . . . has become relatively academic now," the *Daily News* editorialized. "Segregation has been ruled out and the responsibility now is to
readjust to that reality with a minimum of friction, disruption, and set-
back to the public school system." A few days later, the Greensboro
Jaycees—the largest chapter in the state—endorsed the school board's
resolution by a margin of four to one. The same day, the Greensboro
Ministerial Alliance added its support.

Acceptance of the *Brown* decision appeared to extend into the general
community as well. A newspaper survey reported that most "ordinary
citizens" had accepted the Supreme Court's decision as inevitable. "I
really haven't had a chance to think it out," one white mother said, "but I
feel the best thing to do is to go ahead and accept the decision and make

the best of it." Even those most upset by the Court's action spoke of compliance. Guilford County School Superintendent E. D. Idol observed that the Court's ruling would at least alleviate the need to bus black children past white schools. White liberals interpreted such responses as a sign that Greensboro was ready to come into its own as a leader of the "New South."* As one minister recalled, "I was tremendously proud of the school board and grateful that we had the kind of leadership to take that step. I thought it was indicative of a progressive attitude."

To a great extent, black leaders shared in the general optimism. Most appeared to agree with NAACP attorney Thurgood Marshall that "once and for all, it's decided, and completely decided." The school board's action represented the latest in a series of forward steps, especially the election of Dr. William Hampton to the city council in 1951 and then—through Hampton's aid—the appointment of Dr. David Jones to the school board in 1953. Moreover, black leaders felt that they could trust at least some white leaders. One NAACP member remarked that "Superintendent Benjamin Smith was no wishy-washy fellow. He was for real." Another called Smith "a man of integrity and conviction and guts." With such a man at the helm, there seemed a good chance that the school board "meant what it said—a definite commitment to go ahead with desegregation." Ezell Blair, a black teacher, understood the enormity of the forces against change, but believed that the black community and at least part of the white community were ready. "The climate was right," he said. "Greensboro had the greatest opportunity of any school system in the South if the local people were willing to go along."

Within three years, this ebullient optimism had been shattered. Although token desegregation occurred in Greensboro beginning in 1957, in the eyes of most blacks it represented more a defeat than a victory. Supporters of far-reaching desegregation were unable to prevail, notwithstanding what appeared to be support on the school board for such a policy. To unravel the threads of this decline of hope is to reveal many of the underlying reasons for the turbulence of the 1960's and the radical protests that decade produced.[1]

---

*As noted in the Introduction, white "liberals" are defined here as those who recognized the injustice of the existing racial system and were willing to work openly to bring about improvements. They are not to be confused with white "progressives" or white "moderates," who welcomed an atmosphere of tolerance but did not initiate or endorse change in the racial status quo.

I

The failure to achieve greater progress in school desegregation in Greensboro had many causes, but the best place to start is with the school board's own confusion over what Hudgins's resolution meant. Although six of the seven members had committed themselves to compliance with the *Brown* decision, individuals on the board diverged sharply in their private interpretation of what compliance signified. In retrospect, it appears that only Superintendent of Schools Benjamin Smith and black school board member William Hampton—named to succeed Dr. David Jones in 1955— believed in speedy desegregation.

There seems little doubt that Smith accepted both the rightness and necessity of desegregation. A native Southerner, Smith had served the school system in Shelby, North Carolina, before coming to Greensboro. Smith was widely recognized as one of the leading educators of the state. Prior to the *Brown* decision, he had upgraded a black employee to the position of storekeeper for the entire school system. Later he had requested help from the AFSC in hiring a black electrician—at the time a "nontraditional" job for Negroes. As soon as the *Brown* decision was handed down, Smith eliminated all references to a dual school system, listing schools alphabetically rather than by race, holding joint meetings of principals and supervisors, and deleting mention of racially separate organizations from the faculty handbook. "Integration is as inevitable as the sunrise," Superintendent Smith told friends and reporters. "We must not repel! We must not defy. Circumvention and resistance can but meet with coercion and cause confusion, conflict and turmoil." A devout Methodist, Smith was unable to reconcile racism with his religion. "There is nothing wrong with Christianity," he once wrote. "It has simply never been tried." Black teachers had watched Smith grow during his nearly two decades with the Greensboro school system and had come to believe in his devotion to the idea of an interracial America. Significantly, both whites and blacks shared the same perception of Smith's character. One white colleague described him as "an old army man" who, when he saw a straight line to follow, never deviated from it. A black associate, in turn, compared Smith to "a bulldog [who] won't let go until he gets his ideas over." To both observers, Smith's posture on compliance with the *Brown* decision exemplified this tenacity.

The other white school board members, however, were of a different mold. Although Chairman Ed Hudgins had drafted the compliance resolution, he believed that desegregation would be "traumatic for the average white Southerner." Hudgins was concerned primarily with forestalling emotional defiance in the community. An attorney and a former Rhodes scholar, Hudgins had confidence that "the broad-gauged" enlightened citizens of the community could deny rednecks or hard-core conservatives any room for maneuver by issuing a statement of principles. But denying conservatives a base for resistance was not the same as pushing forward, and Hudgins himself did not contemplate any immediate action toward desegregation. Rather, he endorsed Judge Parker's interpretation of the *Brown* decision in the 1955 *Old Fort* case—that it "does not require integration, it merely forbids discrimination"—and thus believed that compliance would involve primarily the elimination of *legal* sanction for segregation, with the chance that at some time in the future a few Negroes might be admitted to white schools.

Other white board members either accepted Hudgins's view or adopted an even more conservative stance. John Foster, who succeeded Hudgins as school board chairman in 1955, believed strongly in the necessity of "facing reality," but he recalled that the board's action on the Hudgins resolution was "not a real solid, firm vote." "It was more or less an easing of conscience," he said, a recognition of the board's responsibility to abide by the law. Such an interpretation helps to explain why the seventh board member, described by some as "very conservative," downplayed the significance of his negative vote, saying only that he felt the Hudgins resolution was untimely. If the school board hoped primarily to neutralize the issue, there would be less reason to express opposition to the principle of desegregation. Foster himself believed that separate schools for blacks and whites should prevail for the foreseeable future. Thus it appears that most board members wished primarily to control the situation—to keep the lid on—and prevent the kind of disruption that might hurt the city's image and create instability. As had been true so often in the past, the promise of change obscured an agenda for continued control.

In arriving at their positions, white school board members misread profoundly the sentiments of the black community. Foster was convinced that "the average Negro did not want desegregation"—a judgment he based upon personal contact with the maid in his home, the man who drove his truck, and the janitor at his place of business. Although he acknowledged that a new assertiveness had "crept" into the manner of blacks who repeatedly visited school board meetings, Foster viewed such delegations as atypical and unrepresentative. The NAACP, Foster believed, was like a labor union that claimed support but whose members "never pay any dues." On that basis, he concluded that most blacks were dubious, "just as dubious as whites, just as dubious as they could be" about desegregation.

Significantly, white school board members sought corroboration for their point of view from their black colleagues who, given the power relationships surrounding racial contacts in the South, could achieve positions of eminence only by at least seeming to accommodate to prevailing white assumptions. Thus, while the black community perceived Dr. William Hampton, the black school board member, and Dr. John Tarpley, the supervisor of black schools, as strong supporters of change in the racial status quo, many white board members saw them as allies working for the common goal of maintaining order. Hampton was praised by white leaders as "level minded" and a realist who could be depended upon to help chart a moderate course between extremes. Foster noted that when a black activist became particularly "obnoxious" Dr. Hampton could be counted upon to "handle him well." White leaders relied upon both men to look after the black community; indeed, their presence provided the school board with a ready-made excuse for discounting more militant black activists. After all, Hampton "represented" the black community. Both men, of course, played other roles than those of accommodationists, and frequently stood strongly in support of black delegations to the school board. Nevertheless, white officials selected for attention those cues that most clearly conformed to their own preconceptions and needs.

Just as important as school board ambivalence about desegregation was the refusal of Greensboro's most powerful business leaders to speak out. In the opinion of most people, Spencer Love, the head of Burlington Industries, could have exerted the most influence. A friend of Love recalled that when employees discovered that the Burlington executive favored John F. Kennedy for President in 1960, all the Nixon bumper stickers in the parking lot at Burlington Industries suddenly disappeared. A tough, sometimes ruthless executive who cultivated both tension and profound personal loyalty in his staff, Love was reported to have total control of his empire. As one AFSC staff member wrote, "If and when Bur-Mills moves, the most impressive and influential textile company in America will have moved." Yet Love refused to take an active role on the desegregation issue. Some evidence indicates that he had personal doubts concerning integration. Others have speculated that he wished to use the race issue with white workers, exchanging his silence on segregation for worker refusal to join labor organizations. Whatever the case, Love told interviewers that he felt it inappropriate for a man in his position to speak publicly on the issue. Although he fit perfectly Hudgins's category of a "broad-gauged" enlightened citizen, Love preferred to await the "crystallization" of community sentiments rather than take the lead.

Other business executives acted similarly. Ceasar and Herman Cone both refrained from public statements, deciding to follow whatever trends developed in the community at large. Howard Holderness, the president of Jefferson Standard Life Insurance Company, was the one school board member who opposed the Hudgins resolution. Lesser business leaders were even more reluctant to "get out front" and hoped that the whole question would go away.

Nor did leaders of the white religious community exert influence. Although Harold Hipps, associate minister of West Market Street Methodist Church, declared that it was anarchy to oppose a Supreme Court decision, most ministers were less bold. In the spring of 1955 the First Baptist Church allowed an interracial meeting of the Baptist Student Union to use its facilities, but the board of deacons would not permit conference delegates to attend Sunday service lest integrated worship become a precedent. The lack of support for desegregation was most notable at First Presbyterian Church, Greensboro's most prestigious congregation. Attended by the heads of most major corporations as well as their executive officers, First Presbyterian could have provided a crucial lever for change, had church leaders lined up in support of desegregation. Instead, an associate recalled, the minister of the church "encouraged foot-dragging" and revealed his own distaste for desegregation by announcing that it was "his duty" to inform the congregation of the national church's stance on these issues. Looking back fifteen years later, one Greensboro minister observed: "a lot could have been done to get the business power structure behind what was taking place . . . but no one person really emerged as a leader. The potential for leadership was fantastic, but they all hung back. The greatest reason was just the desire to avoid conflict."

Thus, sixteen months after the school board's apparently decisive action, it became clear that white Greensboro had moved into a holding pattern on the issue of desegregaton. Speaking to a Sedalia audience, Roy Wilkins noted that Greensboro had "grabbed the national spotlight in 1954, but not a peep has been heard from that day to this." The failure of leadership shattered the confidence of those who earlier had believed with the Greensboro *Daily News* that Greensboro might provide a model for integration. "If we are honest with ourselves," one white liberal wrote, "we will have to admit that so far North Carolinians have not measured up. . . . No ways and means have been described for complying with the decision. . . . What has happened to us? First, . . . we seem to have forgotten that the principle of the court decision is valid. . . . Second, our leaders and those of us who are white apparently do not understand what Negroes want. And how could we when we do not listen to them and when none of their representatives are appointed to the [state] advisory committee on education?" The letter-writer was prophetic. There was little likelihood that integration would occur as long as black people had no voice of their own and were viewed primarily through the lenses of white paternalism.

II

Appropriately, Greensboro's response to *Brown* fit the pattern established by North Carolina as a whole. State leaders had initially greeted the *Brown* edict with grudging acceptance, and in some cases warm approval. The situation in some ways resembled that of the South immediately after the Civil War, when Northern victory was accepted as a *fait accompli* and the Confederacy waited with resigned acceptance for whatever programs the victors would impose to exact punishment and displace the old regime. Governor William B. Umstead expressed disappointment with the Court's decision, but acknowledged that "the Supreme Court . . . has spoken." Over the next few weeks, Umstead directed his actions primarily toward working out means of compliance. A conference of state educational leaders met one week after the *Brown* decision to discuss the problems of school attendance, transportation, and teacher assignment that would have to be faced under the new ruling.

The response from other political leaders proved encouraging—at least initially—to supporters of desegregation. In a keynote speech to the state Democratic Convention in Raleigh just four days after the *Brown* decision, Irving Carlyle of Winston-Salem, a widely respected state political leader, declared that "as good citizens we have no other course except to obey the law laid down by the United States Supreme Court." Carlyle's remarks were applauded heartily by the 3000 delegates, who also enacted a resolution affirming belief "in the supremacy of the law for all citizens" and condemning, "without reservation, every effort of man, singly or in organized groups, to set themselves above the law." A few weeks later, Kerr Scott triumphed in a primary election for a United States Senate nomination, even though his two opponents portrayed him as a supporter of desegregation and a friend of the Negro. Church leaders also reacted with support for *Brown*. North Carolina's Catholic Bishop ordered an end to segregation in all the state's parochial schools, and the North Carolina Council of Churches urged its member congregations to support the decision of the Supreme Court "in the spirit of Christ." The evidence seemed to support the contention of the Raleigh *News and Observer* that "the South will not rebel at this decision; educating its children is too crucial a task."[2]

Yet within a few months the mood in the state had changed, swinging first toward postponement of any consideration of compliance, then toward forceful opposition to desegregation. Just as during Reconstruction the absence of decisive action from President Andrew Johnson in the immediate aftermath of victory encouraged a resurgence of Confederate resistance, so in the second Reconstruction the equivocation of the White House and delay in the federal courts created room for Southern politicians to raise the possibility of successfully circumventing the Supreme Court's decision. Repeatedly, President Dwight Eisenhower refused to say whether he approved of the Supreme Court's decision. When he indicated by his actions as well a distaste for rapid enforcement of the decision, Southern politicians, in effect, were freed to act in opposition to the Court. Thus, in North Carolina economic and political leaders retreated from the early move toward compliance, and instead began to confer legitimacy on resistance. By the spring of 1955, North Carolina's General Assembly had resolved that "the mixing of the races in the public schools . . . cannot be accomplished and should not be attempted."

The movement away from compliance occurred under the shrewd leadership of Luther Hodges, a former textile executive who succeeded to the governorship when Umstead died in the fall of 1954. Although Hodges had had no prior experience in elective office before his race for the lieutenant governorship in 1952, he proved to be a brilliant politician, defining issues in ways that provided his opponents little room for maneuver. Throughout his governorship, Hodges appeared as a principled guardian of North Carolina's progressive tradition, fighting off extremism on the racial issue and devising a middle way for North Carolina's schoolchildren.

Hodges's leadership of the anti-desegregation forces began in the winter of 1954 with his endorsement of the special "Advisory Committee on Education" report declaring that desegregation should not be attempted. Named by Umstead, the nineteen-member committee was chaired by State Senator Thomas Pearsall. It contained three blacks, all of whom were employees of the state; two of them—Dr. F. D. Bluford of North Carolina A&T and Dr. J. W. Seabrook of Fayetteville State Teacher's College—depended totally on the state for support of their colleges. The advisory committee recommended passage of a Pupil Assignment Act removing control over education from the state and returning it to local school boards. The purpose of the change, Hodges wrote a constituent in 1955, was "to be sure that the state is not involved in any state-wide [desegregation]suit" by the NAACP or others. More importantly, the pupil assignment bill established multiple criteria such as residence, previous schools attended, and other "local conditions" that could serve as the basis for perpetuating segregation without mentioning race.

The plan was a clear effort to circumvent the *Brown* decision. As the Pearsall Committee stated, "a factual local condition, even if color is one of the causes, is a different thing [than racial separation by statute]." Although ultimately all criteria of the law were related to race, there were enough reasons for school assignment that were not explicitly racial to guarantee that no black would ever go to a white school. Under the terms of the Act, one supporter pointed out, even the most highly qualified black could still be excluded on non-racial grounds. The 1955 Pupil Assignment Act appeared to be an airtight bulwark against desegregation. Parents of black children who wished to challenge segregation would have to go through endless administrative procedures to transfer their children, and each case would have to be argued on an individual basis.

Initially, at least, Hodges appeared satisfied that such measures were sufficient to forestall any attempt at integration. During the April 1955 legislative session in which the Pupil Assignment Act was passed, Hodges argued against a constitutional amendment that would have appropriated public funds for private schools. Such a bill, he said, was "extreme and untimely. It is an unnecessary bill . . . . If that weapon is ever used in North Carolina its results will be appalling in ignorance, poverty and bitterness." Most segregationist lawyers agreed that the Pupil Assignment Act provided the most effective barrier to integration then available.

Yet by the summer of 1955 Hodges had moved well beyond his

earlier position. Already he had appointed a new seven-man Pearsall Committee to continue studying the school situation, this time excluding all blacks and naming only individuals known for pro-segregation points of view. During July, I. Beverly Lake, a conservative Assistant Attorney General and a possible foe of Hodges in the 1956 gubernatorial primary, urged that the state should prepare to fund private schools with tuition grants for individual students. Although privately angry, Hodges refrained from criticizing the suggestion, and instead praised Lake as one of the state's most effective lawyers. When the state NAACP then demanded that Lake be dismissed for proposing such ideas, Hodges lashed out at the organization, accusing it of trying to divide North Carolinians into racial camps. The next day the Governor himself raised the issue of closing schools for the first time.[3]

The full ramifications of Hodges's new posture became apparent only when he addressed the state by radio and television on August 8, 1955. In that address he declared that the state confronted two stark options. "If we are not able to succeed in a program of voluntary separate school attendance," he told the TV audience, "the state . . . will be face-to-face with deciding whether it will have some form of integrated public schools or shall abandon its public schools." As Hodges presented the issue, voluntary segregation offered the only possibility of avoiding the equally untenable extremes of integration or closing the public schools. Black education in North Carolina had been a great success, Hodges claimed, but only because of the "devoted friendship and assistance of white citizens." Integration would cause those same white citizens to withdraw their support, leading to the abolition of the public schools and lasting injury to the cause of black education. Hence, the circular argument ended, segregation provided the only "middle ground" for both whites and blacks, particularly given the fact that whites alone could be trusted to provide for black schools.

In that August speech Hodges displayed the full force of his political skill. Lambasting the NAACP, he blamed black protest for the crisis. Hodges chose language seemingly designed to inflame racial hostility, even as it drew upon the deepest presumptions of white supremacy. The NAACP, he declared, was seeking to destroy "our interracial friendship" and was the "enemy of the principle that the Negro race can take care of its own children." Rather than teaching blacks to be proud, Hodges claimed, the NAACP taught them to be ashamed of their color and to seek the destruction of their race by "burying it in the development of the white race." Unabashedly, Hodges invoked the imagery of miscegenation. The NAACP, he said, would have the black race "*lose* itself in another race," encouraging Negroes to sacrifice "their identity in *complete merger* with [whites]." (Italics mine.) Through such reasoning, Hodges concluded that blacks who were proud of their history had no alternative but to accept and affirm the separation of the races. The law, he declared, had established the principle of equal citizenship under the law. That was sufficient. "Only the person who feels he is inferior must resort to demonstrations to prove that he is not. A person convinced of his own equality . . . of his own race respect, needs no demonstrations to bolster his convictions." Thus, proud blacks should repudiate protest organizations and work to develop their own schools and teachers.

Such arguments led Hodges to one final postulate: blacks who continued to protest on behalf of their legal rights must bear complete responsibility for closing down the public school system. "The white citizens of this state," he insisted, "will resist integration strenuously, resourcefully, and probably with growing bitterness." Hence, anyone who pushed for such integration carried the burden of the counterresponse. The lesson of history, he declared, was that when the law ran contrary to the popular will, it was the law that had to be changed. Hodges acknowledged that in raising the possibility of closing public schools he might frighten some people. But his purpose was to underline the necessity of maintaining voluntary segregation and to educate the people on where responsibility rested for the present crisis. By the time he had finished the speech, Hodges had succeeded in pre-empting all attacks from conservatives and in creating a situation where anything he proposed—short of an outright endorsement of the Ku Klux Klan—could be portrayed as "moderate."

With the political landscape cleared, the basic remaining issue was how to implement the new policy. Specifically, Hodges had to decide whether to call a special legislative session in the spring or summer of 1956 to take further action. The argument against such a session, Hodges's staff wrote in September, was that "the people of this state are still, in the main, apathetic in regard to this problem . . . it may be assumed that this feeling is shared by many of the members of the General Assembly. There is also a feeling among many that there is no way to head off integration in schools and that we should attempt to work out plans for gradual integration." In addition, the staff noted, a special session might provide a "fertile field for demagoguery" and stir up opposition of political candidates "not now existing." On the positive side, a special session would take place in the spring, at a time when blacks were filing applications for transfer to previously all-white schools. By calling a special session in such circumstances, Hodges could focus attention on the issue himself, reap maximum political benefit, and at the same time prevent his political enemies from stepping into the situation.

In fact, Hodges appears to have already made up his mind in September to proceed with a special session. He requested from the Chief Justice of the North Carolina Supreme Court an opinion on the legality of using public funds for private schools. Moreover, his close personal aide, Paul Johnson, had already outlined the key features of what subsequently came to be known as the Pearsall Plan—a local-option clause permitting a school district, or any portion thereof, to close its schools by public referendum if desegregation occurred, and a constitutional amendment granting state tuition aid for white students in those districts to attend private schools.

As the time neared for Hodges to announce his bid for re-election, the Governor's commitment to a special legislative session became even more explicit. By February, Hodges had endorsed a legislative resolution protesting the "unjustified usurpation" of power by the Supreme Court. Two days later, in announcing his candidacy, he boasted that North Carolina was further advanced than Virginia in its segregation policies, and pledged legislation providing tuition grants for private schools "if necessary." In July the legislature met in special session and enacted the Pearsall Plan, drawn up by the Governor's Special Advisory Committee and providing the constitutional framework outlined by Hodges's aide ten months earlier.

With shrewdness and skill, advocates of the Pearsall Plan presented their amendments to the voters as "safety valves" against integration. On the one hand, supporters of the Plan argued that the white citizens of North Carolina, and especially poor whites from eastern North Carolina, would never permit desegregation to occur.* On the other hand, they recognized that outright defiance of the Supreme Court would be foolhardy. In that context, the provisions of the Plan became a "middle way," permitting individual districts to close down their schools if they wished, but avoiding state-wide resistance of the federal courts. The

---

*Eastern North Carolina, a rural area with large numbers of blacks, had traditionally been viewed as the most racist area of the state. It was there that the Wilmington Race Riot of 1898 had occurred, overthrowing a biracial coalition government there and leading to statewide disfranchisement of blacks in 1900. The area has been seen as being more like the Deep South than the rest of the state.

Pearsall Committee had not said that there should be absolutely *no* mixed schools in North Carolina. Nor did it oppose some desegregation where local voters were willing to tolerate it. But for those not willing, the Plan offered a perfect escape.

Ingeniously, the Pearsall Plan thus became a progressive alternative to extremism. Significantly, the extremes to be avoided were, on the one hand, the violence of die-hard white racists and, on the other, the demands of black integrationists for equality under the law. Through such manipulation of public opinion, the Pearsall Committee managed to equate the NAACP and the KKK. Indeed, the Plan was interpreted as the quintessence of moderation—a blend, the Charlotte *Observer* noted, of "conscience and common sense, . . . an effort to preserve the public schools and at the same time North Carolina's identity with constitutional government."

In fact, the Plan represented a subtle and insidious form of racism. Nothing illustrated this better than the attitude of the Pearsall Committee and its staff toward blacks. In most cases the committee ignored Negroes entirely, acting as if they did not exist. But where blacks were recognized, the results were even more revealing. Early in the fall of 1955, the executive secretary of the committee requested members of county boards to get in touch with blacks who had signed petitions urging integration. The purpose was to "ascertain their reasons" and find out "if they are in earnest." Some might be persuaded to change their minds!* The same memorandum argued against creating any biracial committees. "The association between the races," W. W. Taylor wrote, "is so close, especially in rural areas, that someone can usually be found who has some influence with each member of the Negro race." Hodges and Pearsall assiduously searched for blacks who would support their Plan, especially in the school systems, and were surprised when the response was negative. Hodges even went so far as to take his proposal for voluntary segregation directly to the statewide black teacher's association. They rejected it unanimously, instead praising the *Brown* decision as "just, courageous, and timely."

Most revealing of all, perhaps, was the incredulity with which Pearsall and Hodges viewed blacks who asserted an independent view. Both

*On the surface this request suggests two contradictory explanations: either the committee consciously was seeking to coerce blacks, in a hypocritical attempt to display black support for segregation; or it genuinely believed that no black would seriously want desegregation. In all likelihood, both explanations are correct, the contradiction being resolved by the larger truth that whites could not conceive of any blacks questioning a white view of reality.

men, together with their supporters throughout the state, were convinced that unrepresentative black citizens had created the crisis by seeking equal rights. "We are concerned," Pearsall wrote to Hodges, "about the *intemperance* of the statements of some of the Negroes who have spoken out. It may well be that the members of the white race are more interested in the education of all children, including Negro children, than are those Negroes who have spoken so intemperately." (Italics mine.) Others shared the same cultural worldview. "We were shocked," wrote two Pearsall Committee staff members who attended a court hearing, "at the . . . *rudeness* and *complete self-confidence* of the Negro attorneys." (Italics mine.) Black witnesses in a Montgomery County school case had actually gone into detail on how their race had been discriminated against by school authorities. The Pearsall staff left "with a very depressing feeling . . . that any appeal to reason will be. wasted on the Negroes of North Carolina. . . . We have a definite feeling that the NAACP and the attorneys representing it feel they are engaged in a crusade." Not surprisingly, the same staff members spoke glowingly of their visit with one of the South's most outspoken segregationists, Judge Leander Perez of Louisiana.

Such attitudes inevitably generated opposition from nearly all black Carolinians as well as an appreciable number of whites. As the Southern Pines *Pilot* pointed out, underlying all the provisions of the Pearsall Plan was the assumption that the Negro occupied the role of "attacker—a creator of intolerable situations—and the white man the role of rescuer." It was shocking, Negro minister Otis Hairston said, "to hear the current governor of North Carolina talk like the governor of Mississippi." A number of white liberals found it ludicrous that Hodges should ask blacks to sacrifice a fundamental constitutional right. As one observer commented acidly: "paraphrasing Mr. Churchill, never before in human history has one man asked so many to give up so much."

Still others regretted that North Carolina's leaders had turned away from the higher path of leadership toward racial justice in favor of legal subterfuge. "It is all so sad," one liberal wrote, "to see our beginning leadership among the Southern states crushed back. Such selfishness and blind political trading: Luther Hodges had a chance for greatness . . . ." The noted playwright Paul Green interceded with Hodges, urging his support for compliance with the *Brown* decision, only to find that the Governor had embraced instead "the old familiar message of an ancient and reactionary South." Some of the leading constitutional lawyers in the state testified that the Pearsall Program was a plan of nullification whose purpose was "the coercion and intimidation of Negroes." But their words had no impact. When a constitutional lawyer from Duke University testified against the Plan, a Pearsall Committee staff member planted the rumor that he was a communist sympathizer. For those who had hoped for a different kind of leadership, Hodges's plan was "a retrogressive glorification of the status quo," placing "a seal of whole-hearted approval on a process of evasion."

Still, what remained most impressive was the extent to which political and editorial leaders across the state accepted Hodges's definition of the situation and endorsed the Plan as the only "moderate" solution for North Carolina's school crisis. State Senator Terry Sanford, one of the most progressive voices in the state, endorsed the Pearsall Amendments as a force for "moderation, unity, understanding, and goodwill," and urged the state to use the time gained by the Pearsall Plan to create "an Age of Reason." The Fayetteville *Observer* argued that the Supreme Court had set fire to every schoolhouse in the state, and "the Pearsall Plan is a fire extinguisher." More liberal newspapers, in particular, seized on the notion that the Plan would permit some desegregation if local opinion would tolerate it. Thus, the Greensboro *Daily News* endorsed the Plan's "flexibility" and the possibility of "gradualism" in desegregation, even as it applauded the Plan's safety-valve features if "Negro citizens persisted in creating . . . crisis." Although the Richmond, Virginia, *News-Leader* called the terms of the Pearsall Plan "hard and bitterly resentful," newspapers inside North Carolina insisted upon describing it as "the middle way." In words that might have been written by Governor Hodges himself, the Greensboro *Daily News* editorialized: "North Carolina wants no violence and North Carolina wants no abandonment of its public school system. The path is tortuous and narrow. But with moderation, goodwill, understanding, and wise, sound and far-seeing statesmanship, we can and shall tread it safely."

The central argument advanced by proponents of the Pearsall Plan was that unless it were approved, poor whites would rise in rebellion and force the General Assembly to enact a far more devastating program of massive resistance. As evidence of poor-white political attitudes, Hodges's allies pointed to the famous 1950 primary election in which Frank Porter Graham—a liberal and a recent appointee to the United States Senate—was defeated in his bid for election because of the race issue. Although Graham had won the first primary go-around handily, he lost the run-off four weeks later by 18,000 votes. Nearly every politi-

cal observer attributed the turnabout to the virulent race literature circulated by Willis Smith, Graham's opponent. In screaming headlines,
handbills called upon white people to "Wake Up Before It's Too Late!"
Graham, the leaflets said, wanted blacks to work side by side with white
women, to eat with whites in public places, and to send their children
to schools with whites. "Frank Graham favors mingling of the races,"
Smith's posters declared. The mob mood at the end of the campaign,
political scientist Samuel Lubell wrote, could only be compared to that
preceding a lynching. If North Carolina's moderates wished to avoid a
repeat of such political hysteria, Hodges's supporters suggested, they
should unite forthwith behind the Pearsall Plan.

Despite its powerful appeal, however, such an argument was flawed.
First, Graham's defeat had resulted from other causes in addition to
race. As a former president of the University of North Carolina, Graham attracted not only the support of the University's friends, but also
the enmity of thousands across the state who resented Chapel Hill's air
of self-importance and elitism. Graham's fondness for internationalism
and liberal causes also left him vulnerable to charges of being "soft on
communism"—a powerful weapon in its own right during the age of
McCarthyism. Nor did Graham's association with President Harry Tru-
man help. Second, and more important, the election statistics failed to
corroborate Hodges's argument. Although North Carolina's eastern
"redneck" counties had voted against Graham, Samuel Lubell noted,
"the big break against him came in the economically conservative
middle class." Graham's opponent was a former president of the American Bar Association and chairman of the Board of Trustees at Duke
University. He appealed more to affluent and middle-class North Carolinians than to poor whites in the east. "It was not only the bigots who
turned against Dr. Frank," Lubell concluded, "but many progressive
North Carolinians [as well]."

In this context, Hodges and his allies misrepresented the threat of a
"redneck" rebellion. Without question, most poor white farmers and
workers harbored anti-black attitudes. But there were no redneck hordes
in power, nor was there any likelihood of their coming to power. Instead, a diffuse political constituency existed that could be manipulated
by those who did hold power. By no means was it clear that only racists
could appeal to this constituency. Despite his liberal racial views, for
example, Kerr Scott won strong backing from poor white workers and
farmers during his successful gubernatorial race in 1948. The same
groups supported him again after the *Brown* decision in 1954, when he

won a primary contest for the United States Senate nomination over opponents who tried to tag him an integrationist.

Even the Ku Klux Klan posed less of a threat than state leaders implied. No gatherings of the Klan occurred without police surveillance, and official documents suggest that state intelligence agents as well as the FBI had thoroughly infiltrated even the highest ranks of the Klan in the state. For the most part local "Klaverns" engaged in endless discussions of plans that never materialized. Although it is important not to underestimate the implicit danger that was present whenever the Klan met, it is equally important to realize the degree to which these activities were under the constant control of state authorities. Thus at the end of the argument about the "redneck" threat one returns to the beginning: the crucial role of those who held power in the first place. They, not the poor whites, were in charge.[4]

The notion of an angry white crowd about to rebel appears to have been as much a political creation of Governor Hodges as a fearsome social reality. Hodges's own staff members commented upon the mood of apathy and resignation in the state toward school integration. In addition, legislators from eastern North Carolina—the most segregationist area—had withdrawn bills to close the public schools and provide tuition support for private schools. When one assemblyman proposed to deny state aid to any county desegregating its schools, his bill never even received a committee hearing. Moreover, all these measures were either killed or withdrawn prior to Hodges's voluntary segregation speech in the summer of 1955. Thus, far from responding to a widespread demand for a new legislative package, Hodges was creating the issue as his own and dictating the terms of the debate.

The absence of significant opposition seems to confirm that the political climate was far less volatile than the Governor suggested. If the specter of a right-wing revolt had been real, one might have anticipated strong conservative opposition to Hodges's "progressive" approach. Yet the North Carolina Patriots—the state's White Citizens Council—endorsed the Pearsall Plan. Furthermore, a constitutional amendment to eliminate the state requirement for public schools—proposed by I. Beverly Lake—received no support at all. Throughout, observers commented on the consensus behind the Plan. As one legislative aid boasted, "we have the votes that can pass the Pearsall Plan anytime." Only two legislators cast their ballots against the Pearsall Plan in the General Assembly, one representing a primarily black constituency, the other from the mountains.

But were there other alternatives? Did North Carolina's leaders have viable political options? A substantial body of evidence suggests that Hodges could have found as much support for compliance as for resistance. After traveling across the state for two years, Reid Sarrat, the respected editor of the Winston-Salem *Journal Sentinel*, concluded in 1956 that "a large number of intelligent, influential North Carolinians believe that the best way . . . is to comply. I believe that the state would support a program of compliance." Others commented on the number of city and county school boards that were ready to implement desegregation plans prior to Hodges's initiatives against integration. At least seven of the state's largest cities were in that category in 1956.

Public-opinion research offers additional evidence, highlighting people's openness to strong leadership. An extensive sociological study of the white population of Guilford County (which contains the city of Greensboro) revealed that 18 per cent of the population was ready to resist desegregation at all costs; another 18 per cent wished to push ahead much faster with integration. The vast majority, however, were in the middle. Preoccupied with jobs, families, and other concerns, they were ready to respond to strong and sensible direction from above. Significantly, the survey disclosed that resistance to desegregation diminished as the questions moved from attitudes toward behavior. Thus a respondent might oppose the *idea* of having children attend schools with blacks, but when asked how he or she would react to the actual situation, the same respondent moved toward acceptance. Indeed, the lag between cultural attitudes and specific behavior provided one of the stronger arguments used by opponents of the Pearsall Plan. As Irving Carlyle pointed out, "opposition to integration and approval of destruction of the public school system are by no means one and the same thing, and one does not necessarily follow from the other." Yet Governor Hodges repeatedly acted as though the two issues were identical, refusing to provide the leadership that would have moved the mass of undecided people toward desegregation.

On balance, then, the evidence suggests that Hodges chose the Pearsall Plan because of political expediency and his own racial views rather than because of a mass demand for more extreme action. At a time when strong leadership for compliance stood a good chance for success, Hodges chose to legitimize opposition to desegregation. In the process he defined the issue so that no one either to the left or the right had any room for maneuver. By raising the threat of more extreme resistance from poor whites, Hodges frightened most liberal forces in the state into supporting the Pearsall Plan as a means of buying time and preserving civility. By lambasting the NAACP and evoking fears of racial "mixing," he united white conservatives behind his Plan to defeat the common black enemy. The only people left out were those 25 per cent of the state's citizens who happened to be black.

In the end the Pearsall Plan accomplished all the objectives its sponsors had envisioned. It postponed meaningful desegregation in North Carolina for more than a decade—longer than in some states where massive resistance was practiced. For Hodges, it proved a brilliant political success. In the country at large as well as in North Carolina, he was viewed as a moderate and enlightened governor who had found a peaceful way to handle school desegregation. Most important, the Pearsall Plan enabled North Carolina's business and political leaders to continue boosting the state as a progressive oasis in the South, a hospitable climate for Northern investment, a civilized place in which to live. Ultimately, therefore, the Pearsall Plan met all the requirements of the state's white leadership. In the words of the Shelby *Star*, it would "maintain separate school systems," but with a "tone of moderation."

III

The black leaders of Greensboro, meanwhile, pursued their own agenda, regardless of the response of white politicians and businessmen in the state and city. If anything, Hodges's commitment to segregation reinforced black protest activities. The Negro citizens of Greensboro, Julius Douglas wrote the local newspaper, could only resent the logic that asked them to be part of a system of programs "designed to make a mockery of constitutional government." A white liberal woman found that blacks who had once been "cordial and cooperative" had now become "reserved and questioning," exhibiting "deep frustration verging on race resentment." In Greensboro, as in other communities, Hodges's actions served most effectively as a recruitment tactic for the NAACP. Under the leadership of Edward Edmonds, a minister and sociologist who came to Bennett College in 1955, the NAACP sharply increased its average membership to 1200 people.

Building on the achievements of the late 1940's, the protest movement in Greensboro swelled during the 1950's. The *Brown* decision did not cause an upsurge of protest, Vance Chavis recalled, but it helped stir "people to come out and express how they felt more." When Meyer's Department Store advertised a cooking class at the store and appended the words, "Sorry, no accommodations for colored," blacks held indignation rallies, and some canceled their charge accounts at the store. Although the protest only resulted in an indirect apology from the store, it signified the kind of activism that was to become more frequent as the decade went on.

The most dramatic protest materialized at A&T and involved Governor Hodges himself. Hodges had been invited to attend the Founder's Day ceremony in the fall of 1955. The ceremony was held after Hodges's voluntary segregation speech in August and his subsequent appeal to the all-black North Carolina Teacher's Association to endorse separate schools, although the invitation had been extended prior to them. Both episodes, of course, were in the forefront of the students' minds. President Bluford had warned the undergraduates that they would be punished if they misbehaved, but campus observers knew that if Hodges insulted the audience he would receive an appropriate response. Arriving fifteen minutes after the ceremonies had begun, Hodges in effect gave two speeches. In the first he praised A&T's founders and scrupulously referred to blacks as "Negroes." Then he launched an attack upon the NAACP, specifically criticizing "some of your unwise leaders." In the process, he began to use the word "Nigra." Almost instantaneously, students started to scrape their feet on the floor and to cough. Ruffled, but blind to the reason for the disturbance, Hodges asked if he should continue. "As you wish," responded Bluford. Hodges finished his speech and stalked out. The next day, newspapers throughout the state reported that the black students had humiliated and embarrassed the Governor. Two days later, Dr. Bluford went to the hospital. Within the month he was dead. His last words, according to some, were: "They called me an Uncle Tom, they called me an Uncle Tom."

The demonstrations at A&T set the tone for the increasing assertiveness of black protests in Greensboro during the middle and late 1950's. A group of black professionals went to the local public golf course in 1955 demanding the right to play. The city had rented the course for $1.00 a year to the chairman of the recreation department to be operated as a private concession. As the blacks arrived, the golf pro cursed and asked why they were there. "For a cause—the cause of democracy," they answered. That night, the black protesters were arrested. When a federal court eventually ruled that all citizens had a right to play on the course, it was opened to blacks. But then the clubhouse mysteriously burned down, so the city ordered the course closed.

Not surprisingly, the greatest upsurge of activism occurred over the public schools. "The NAACP recognized very early," Edward Edmonds remarked, "that one of the ways to move black folks is to move them about their children. You can't be conditioned for years to achieve, to become somebody, and then have your kids denied. School was a very sensitive thing . . . a pressure point . . . so we had all kinds of support from people willing to go down and confront the school board." Beginning in December of 1955, a steady procession of delegations from the Dudley and the Lincoln PTA's (both black schools) attended monthly school board meetings demanding improvement in black school facilities. Between October 1956 and April 1958—a period of eighteen months—representatives of black organizations appeared at all but two meetings to protest or lobby about black school facilities and the need for greater desegregation.

Black parents were especially persistent in their demands for a new gymnasium at Dudley High School. The existing gym, they argued, was far too small, with inadequate space for spectators; worse, the brick walls of the gym were only eighteen inches beyond the end lines of the basketball court. The Dudley delegation demanded either immediate action on a proposed new gymnasium or the opening of the white high school gymnasium for black basketball games. The school board responded that it could not alter plans and that the white gym was being used on every occasion that Dudley had a basketball game. Instead, it suggested that the basketball court be reduced in size so as to permit the end lines to be moved inward by two feet. Not to be outwitted, the Dudley PTA proposed that Dudley rearrange its schedule to play on the nights when Senior High was free. When the board responded that all dates suggested by Dudley were already full, the PTA leaders requested a list of "open" dates at Senior High so that they could make their schedule fit. With no recourse left, the board instructed the Superintendent of Schools to make the white gym available when it was not in use. In fact, Dudley played only a few games there because shortly thereafter the board of education rearranged its building schedule and constructed a new gymnasium at the black school. An an NAACP leader put it, "the minute you use their facilities, they find the money."

The school campaign of black parents and the NAACP demonstrated the increased assertiveness of blacks. They would not permit the school board to deny their children what had been so long promised—a better education. Although an apparent contradiction existed between the demands for a new "black facility" and integration, the two prongs of the NAACP attack were in fact complementary. "We were carrying on two fights at the same time," Edmonds noted. Each reinforced the other, and both contributed to the prospect of better education for black children. Furthermore, each campaign bespoke a growing commitment to open protest within the black community. After the *Brown* decision, Chairman John Foster of the school board later recalled, visits from the NAACP and black parents were not only "more frequent . . . and more assertive, [but] less patient. They wanted it done, boom, boom. The group felt that if they did anything that might appear to be a concession, they might be doing a disservice to their people."

During those same years, a number of black parents applied to have their children reassigned to schools that previously had been all-white. Although many whites believed that the applications came from an unrepresentative group of agitators and elite educators, in actuality the parents reflected a cross section of black Greensboro. Among those seeking transfers for their children were a milkman, a printer, an express handler, a barber, a maid, a student at A&T, a minister, and a worker in the stockroom of a local mail-order house. "[White people] couldn't charge it up and say that [only] the smart-niggers applied," one parent later noted. Furthermore, these people—all in a dependent economic situation—were willing to undergo the threat of social ostracism and economic reprisal in order to seek a better life for their children.

It would be a mistake, of course, to overemphasize activism and underemphasize the continued intimidation of protest. Many churches in black Greensboro, one activist noted, were "pretty conservative . . . and frightened." In addition, there were important tactical divisions among black leaders. More forthright protest leaders such as Edmonds and Douglas found Dr. Hampton's mild demeanor a sourse of frustration. "We approached him . . . for speaking out on the board," Edmonds recalled, "and he very clearly told us that he represented all the people, white and black, and therefore he could not evidence any particular support for us." On the other side, many blacks found men like Douglas and Edmonds "too far ahead in their thinking for a whole lot of people." Edmonds "stirred up things" in a manner that offended the style of some blacks, as well as nearly all whites. His contract at Bennett was terminated at the end of the 1950's, and many blacks concluded that his departure was at least in part because he had created too much trouble as head of the NAACP, thereby provoking the hostility of powerful white interests and their black allies. But if the dialectic between assertiveness and caution was not resolved totally, there could be little question that blacks in Greensboro were not intimidated by either Governor Hodges or his pro-segregation platform. Even if white leaders wished to forestall change, the black community had an evolving agenda of its own.

IV

For the moment, however, control over race relations remained in the hands of white political and economic leaders in the city and state. The more progressive of these felt isolated by the actions of Governor Hodges. He had, in effect, taken away any room for maneuver by defining anything beyond the most token desegregation as extremist. In anger, some Greensboro political leaders would later accuse the Governor of letting the local school board "bleed and die." Some white liberals in particular perceived the Pearsall Plan as doing a great disservice to the city. "Greensboro was ready to move," one liberal declared, "and then it all collapsed." Yet most whites in Greensboro shared Hodges's assumptions. Superintendent of Schools Benjamin Smith was the only prominent leader to speak out against the Pearsall Plan. "I should rather fail in supporting a right cause than win in supporting a wrong one," he said. But though friends in influential places wrote Smith of their sympathy for his position, none spoke out publicly. By keeping silent, white leaders, in effect, recognized the right of the governor to speak for them. In Greensboro, as in the state at large, the white elite was simply not ready to move beyond paternalism into a new relationship of equality with blacks.[5]

An even deeper reason for the lack of white protest was the mutual dependency that existed between supporters of the Pearsall Plan in the state and local school board leaders. All along, an underlying premise of the Pearsall Committee was that in some local communities token desegregation would have to occur so that the state as a whole could escape federal-court action. During the debate over the Plan, supporters minimized the requirement that some desegregation would have to take place. But more sophisticated advocates had always argued that a minimal degree of black attendance in a few white public schools would be necessary.

No one made that argument more effectively than Colonel William Joyner, a conservative from eastern North Carolina, and one of the primary architects of the Pearsall Plan. "I cannot believe," he wrote in November 1956, "that a state can long conduct its public schools in a manner which is in defiance of what the Supreme Court of the United States has said is a constitutional right." The course of massive resistance, Joyner argued, would inevitably bring federal retribution. Thus, the only way in which North Carolina could succeed in its strategy would be to allow a tiny number of blacks to attend white schools, thereby ensuring that more than 99 per cent of the white population could continue to attend segregated institutions. One of his worst nightmares, Joyner said, was of being in a federal court trying to defend the state school board "when a showing is made that nowhere in all the state . . . has a single Negro been admitted to any of the more than 2000 schools attended by white students." Would it not strengthen the state's legal position, he asked, "if we could point to one or more instances . . . where a Negro has been admitted to a white school?" Such a course of action, he concluded, "is a small price to pay for the ability to keep [racial] mixing within the bounds of reasonable control."

It was in this context that token desegregation occurred in Greensboro in the late summer of 1957. School board members recognized that a do-nothing stance would bring a court suit that they would inevitably lose. A number of blacks had applied for transfer, arguing, cogently, that only white schools contained all of the equipment and facilities necessary to provide them the best education. The school board carefully laid the groundwork for processing these applications. Black students were required to fill out complicated forms and have them notarized; white parents, in turn, were told that they could secure automatic reassignment for their children if the parents objected to desegregated schools. To strengthen the over-all effort, Chairman John Foster of the Greensboro school board negotiated with Winston-Salem and Charlotte, arranging that all three school boards announce their desegregation plans on the same night. "If we act separately," he told them, "the segregationists get three shots at us. If we act together, they get one big shot and boom that's it."

On the night of July 23, 1957, the Greensboro school board met to consider the black applications for transfer. A large crowd milled around as C. L. Shuping, a representative of the North Carolina Patriots, declared that no man in public service "has been as damned, villified, and cursed as Ben Smith." With accuracy, the local chapter of the White Citizen's Council singled out for abuse the white school official most committed to obeying the Supreme Court's edict. After the school board had apologized for the attacks upon him, Smith spoke:

I greatly regret ending my professional career in turmoil; I could
have run away. I am past retirement age, but there comes a time

when a man must stand for what he believes to be right. No one likes to hear what I have heard tonight, but I hope all the unpleasantness will be directed against me and not my successors.

One month later, six black students entered previously all-white schools, one in the Senior High School, the others together in Gillespie Elementary School. There was little public outcry.

From a national point of view, Greensboro's action appeared to be a progressive breakthrough. *Newsweek* called the city a symbol of the "New South, astir with a new liberalism." A group of Princeton sociologists heaped praise on Greensboro's leadership and predicted that "desegregation will not only surely triumph but will do so quickly." *Time* applauded North Carolina's "strong governor and purposeful law enforcement," and although it recognized the extent to which Greensboro's decision was motivated by self-interest, it characterized the city's action as a "bold offensive."

From the perspective of many Greensboro blacks, however, such phrases described a city on another planet. Compared to the hopes that had existed in 1954, the decision to engage in token desegregation represented a bitter disappointment, not a cause for joy. The black community correctly perceived the 1957 action as carrying out the spirit of the Pearsall Plan—a spirit it identified unmistakably as racist. "The white power structure was trying to appease," black teacher Ezell Blair recalled. "They wanted a token thing . . . so that they could call Greensboro 'the Gateway city,' an all-American city—and they got it."

Not all school board members, of course, acted out of conservative instincts. Benjamin Smith and William Hampton hoped that this initial venture might lead to further modification of Greensboro's racial system, creating room for more far-reaching actions later on. There remained a faith that when Greensboro's moderate leaders saw how easily desegregation was implemented, they would be willing to support integration in additional schools, the job market, and cultural activities.

Yet these people, too, had been crippled by the Pearsall Plan. In making token desegregation the outer limits of permissible action, the Pearsall formula cut the ground from beneath those whites who wished to move further toward racial equality. Given the political climate created by Luther Hodges, it was no longer possible to build a white constituency for full-scale desegregation of schools or jobs; the Pearsall Plan had defined such alternatives as beyond the pale. When, on top of these political pressures, men like Smith had crosses burned on their lawns and windows broken in their houses for advocating even token desegregation, the message was clear; the dominant political culture had ruled out of order—for the moment, at least—any further challenge to the racial status quo from white people.

Thus, the Greensboro decision to have six blacks attend previously all-white schools must be seen as an integral part of a state-wide effort to sustain the Pearsall Plan and prevent meaningful integration. Through minimal concessions to the *Brown* decision, it was hoped that the federal courts could be kept at bay. John Foster, the school board chairman, later recalled how angry and frustrated he became when segregationists from eastern counties attacked him for his liberalism. "I tried to tell them," he said, "that dammit, we were holding a big umbrella over them. We're protecting them really. Because we are at least getting into a position where the state of North Carolina can't be forced into integrating." As Colonel William Joyner told Greensboro's Kenneth Whitsett, head of the North Carolina Patriots, "the sacrifice of some children to mixed schools must be made so that many other children will not similarly be subjected to the evils of mixed schools." If some eastern North Carolina segregationists failed to understand the political equation, the lesson was not lost on most blacks. Summarizing what had happened in Greensboro during the fall of 1957, Vance Chavis noted: "this [desegregation] was nothing but a one-way street. . . . It was a shrewd way of getting around the integration of the schools." Events would soon prove how right Chavis was.

V

The history of Greensboro and North Carolina during the three years after the *Brown* decision illustrated vividly the dynamics underlying North Carolina's politics of moderation. Both state and city leaders boasted of the "Tarheel middle way" as the course best designed to preserve civility and maintain progress. By renouncing the harsh language of massive resistance, white leaders believed, they could reinforce the progressive image of their city and state and, at the same time, alter only minimally the racial status quo. The virtue of such an approach was its style. As the Shelby *Star* noted, North Carolina "did not adopt the rigid attitude that some Southern states have committed themselves to." Yet the results were the same—the maintenance of "separate school systems." As the centerpiece of this approach, the Kingston *Free Press* noted, the Pearsall Plan offered "an open invitation to moderates of both races to continue voluntary segregation until further evidences of good faith and willingness to comply with the law can be achieved. . . ." Within such a framework, of course, moderate change was the same as no change at all. As sociologist Thomas Pettigrew observed in 1961, "good race relations, for the moderate, refer to the relaxed . . . paternalism where the white man's superior status [goes] unquestioned."

A central ingredient of the politics of moderation was the form of communication that existed between whites and blacks. White leaders, both in the state and in Greensboro, listened only to those blacks who conformed to their expectations. Inevitably, the maid in the house, the janitor in the office, or the president at the black state college would not contradict what the white "boss" wanted to hear. To do so would be to risk one's security and livelihood. Yet whites continued to solicit—and use—such deference to justify the racial status quo. Conversely, those blacks who supported protest were often reluctant to make their participation in groups like the NAACP a matter of public record lest they become victims of economic reprisal. Yet that reluctance also led whites to conclude that black protest was minimal. The result was a vicious cycle of distortion and misunderstanding, rooted in the system of white supremacy, and causing a man like John Foster to dismiss black discontent on two grounds: his employees told him that blacks were happy, and he could see no support for protest because blacks did not pay what he regarded to be "public" dues to the NAACP.

For William Hampton, such forms of communication created an inescapable trap. Forced to work closely with white officialdom if he were to have any influence at all, Hampton found his cooperation interpreted as a sign that blacks were satisfied, while his support of protest was discounted as a "sop" to black militants. Within such a contorted framework, both sides lost. Not only did whites miss the opportunity to build on the leadership that Hampton had to offer; Hampton himself suffered disdain and contempt from those blacks who saw how he was being used. As Edmonds commented: "Hamptom did not represent our point of view. Hampton was a white in black skin—he was an impediment to our work. Nothing is worse . . . than a person who is supposedly identified with you speaking in the opposite direction. The opposition could always say, 'look, that is not the black point of view' because Dr. Hampton was black." Thus, the politics of moderation not only destroyed any chance for authentic communication across racial lines; it even impeded communications within racial lines. The same politics would inevitably propel blacks to develop new forms of communication that would eliminate any room for misunderstanding.

A second ingredient of the politics of moderation was an insistence on defining the world in polar opposites, both of which made the middle seem automatically reasonable and just. Throughout the 1950's, North Carolina's white political leaders claimed to represent a moderate alternative between bigoted poor whites on the one hand and black extremists on the other. Such a definition produced two pernicious consequences. First, it cast as villains North Carolina's black citizens—the only participants in the situation who unquestionably had the law on their side. And, second, it permitted North Carolina's white leaders to use the specter of lower-class white rebellion as a rationale for their own posture. By making "rednecks" the primary reference group on the political spectrum, those in power were able to portray any position less extreme than that of the Klan as "moderate." At the same time they were able to divert attention from their own roles in perpetuating the caste system. Poor whites did not have the power to shape policy. Yet their anti-black sentiments were used to justify continued inaction by those who did have power. Whether or not a calculated strategy lay behind the use of the "redneck" argument, it served the ultimate purpose of protecting the interests of those in power.

Issues of class were also implicit in the politics of moderation. Both the movement for black civil rights and the drive to organize workers threatened inherited patterns of paternalism and challenged business and political leaders who wielded the greatest power. American Friends Service Committee staff members found textile executives least willing to support merit employment for blacks at a time when AFL-CIO unions were embarking upon a campaign to organize textile operatives. Race had always served as a wedge to divide the working class, with white solidarity between management and labor offered in exchange for worker support of a non-union shop. If blacks joined unions and unions organized workers across racial lines, employers had the most to lose. Significantly, it was the owners of Greensboro's largest companies who kept silent on the school desegregation issue. It was the same men who proved most reluctant to support the program of merit employment. As one small businessman observed: "these big companies could well have afforded to make changes. Who could hurt them? And yet they wouldn't do it. [They wanted] to remain in the upper social structure. And if [a Burlington executive hired blacks], people were going to criticize him. So when he goes to the country club, he's going to be behind the eight ball."

In all these ways, the politics of moderation provided an effective instrument for perpetuating North Carolina's "progressive mystique." At the foundation of the Pearsall Plan strategy was a commitment to the ethos of consensus. Since substantive desegregation would automatically create conflict, North Carolina's leaders refused to support state-wide compliance with *Brown*. Instead, integration would be permitted only where people in local communities were willing to "go along." Hence, justice for blacks would remain contingent upon prior consensus among whites. Yet the Pearsall Plan also sustained North Carolina's reputation for tolerance and openness. After all, the state had not defied the Supreme Court; it remained amenable to discussions about compliance. And communities that wished to take an innovative stance were free to do so, as long as others were not required to follow. Finally, suffusing the entire venture was the aura of paternalism. Whites cared about "their" blacks; whites were best equipped to supervise black education; and blacks themselves were welcome to cooperate as long as they accepted the established ground rules. Where problems arose, reasonable people could find a solution in a civilized manner.

By the last years of the 1950's, the politics of moderation had cast a chill over hopes for racial progress. In Greensboro itself, the city manager told an advocate of merit employment that he could not even consider the issue because the topic of race was untouchable. Even William Hampton could not secure election today, the city executive said. Although in the past business managers had at least been willing to listen to American Friends Service Committee staff presentations on economic discrimination, by 1956 it had become increasingly difficult even to secure appointments to discuss the matter. In 1958, community leaders placed so much pressure on the Greensboro Interracial Commission that it withdrew from participation in the United Fund, knowing that if it did not do so, the United Fund would in all likelihood cease its $250 annual support. Elsewhere in the state, the same mood prevailed. Jonathan Daniels of the Raleigh *News and Observer* refused to take part in a conference on black employment because he was not sure it was a good thing to attend, given racial tensions as they existed.

In the end, therefore, North Carolina's progressivism consisted primarily of its shrewdness in opposing racial change. The state's leaders failed to broaden the beachhead that the *Brown* decision had established. Instead, with the Pearsall Plan as its instrument and token desegregation in places like Greensboro as a primary defense, North Carolina set out to forestall integration. As one Little Rock school official wrote to an associate in North Carolina: "You North Carolinians have devised one of the cleverest techniques of perpetuating segregation that we have seen."

CHAPTER THREE

The Sit-Ins Begin

Somebody, a lot like myself, could run around another twenty years trying to take down the [Jim Crow] signs and plead with the Woolworth's to serve these people, and they would get nowhere.

Louise Smith, a Greensboro white liberal

Some Negroes say we're moving, but not fast enough. I say that if it takes two or maybe three months to gain equal service with white people in a chain store that has a hundred years of history behind it, we've done something pretty big.

Ezell Blair, Jr., a sit-in leader

On February 1, 1960, four young men from North Carolina Agricultural and Technical College set forth on an historic journey that would ignite a decade of civil rights protest. Walking into downtown Greensboro, they entered the local Woolworth's, purchased toothpaste and other small items, and then sat at the lunch counter and demanded equal service with white persons. "We do not serve Negroes," they were told. But instead of leaving, the students remained. The next day they returned, their ranks reinforced this time by fellow students. Their actions sparked the student phase of the civil rights revolution. Within two months, the sit-in movement had spread to fifty-four cities in nine states. By mid-April, the Student Non-Violent Coordinating Committee (SNCC) had formed in Raleigh, North Carolina, to carry forward the battle. Within a year, more than one hundred cities had engaged in at least some desegregation of public facilities in response to student-led demonstrations. The 1960's stage of the freedom movement had begun.

The Greensboro sit-ins constituted a watershed in the history of America. Although similar demonstrations had occurred before, never in the past had they prompted such a volcanic response. The Greensboro "Coffee Party" of 1960, one observer noted, would rank in history with the Boston Tea Party as a harbinger of revolutionary shifts in the social order. The Southern Regional Council—a voluntary agency supporting interracial progress—agreed. The demonstrations, the council declared, showed "that segregation cannot be maintained in the South short of continuous coercion." Not only was the South in for a time of change; more important, the terms of that change would no longer be dictated by white Southerners. The long road that would lead from Greensboro to Selma to Black Power and beyond had found its starting point.[1]

I

The sit-ins occurred against a backdrop of continued black frustration with Greensboro's racial policies. No issue provoked greater resentment than the minimal school desegregation that occurred in the years after 1957. Although Greensboro was no Little Rock,* word quickly spread that black children and black families suffered greatly during the desegregation experience. An American Friends Service Committee investigation concluded that six out of the seven families that had sought transfer to all-white schools in Greensboro in 1957 had experienced some form of harassment. The father of one student was fired; another family was forced to have its telephone number changed due to threats. As Brenda Florence walked to her first day of school at Gillespie Elementary School, hecklers yelled, "Go home, Nigger." A year later she returned to an all-black school, her family unwilling to have their daughter endure any longer the trauma of white rejection.

Josephine Boyd exemplified both the courage and the pain of these pioneers. An honor student at Dudley High, she decided to apply at Senior High because "I wanted to do what couldn't be done." Boyd's mother was a part-time domestic who also participated actively in the local NAACP. Her father worked as a cook in a large Greensboro bakery and for a time managed his own small business. Mrs. Boyd's application for transfer stated simply: "Since I live closer to Senior High School, I do not feel that my child should be subjected to the inconvenience of the extra travel distance to the Dudley School because of the mere desire to comply to unconstitutional custom."

Josephine's travail began her first day in school and continued throughout the year. One day a male student splattered her dress with an egg; another time a boy spat all over her sweater. On several occasions, Mrs. Boyd's car was pelted with rocks as she brought Josephine to school. White youths hurled stones through the Boyd's windows, punc-

---

*In Little Rock, Arkansas, during the fall of 1957, whites tormented black children seeking to attend Central High School under federal court order. Governor Orville Faubus used police and National Guard troops to block desegregation, forcing President Dwight Eisenhower to deploy federal troops to enforce the Court order. The black children in Little Rock became symbols world-wide of the suffering imposed on blacks by white segregationists.

Josephine Boyd entering Senior High School the first day of desegregation. Courtesy, Greensboro *Record*

tured their car tires with ice picks, and made obscene phone calls at all hours of the night. On several occasions, one teacher reported, Josephine was ready to give up, unable to take any more punishment.

Yet she endured. Two or three friends stood by her, invited her to lunch, and provided open reinforcement. Others confessed that they wanted to help but were afraid to. "I think you are a wonderful person," one girl wrote. "I wish I could be your friend, but I am scared what my friends would think of me." A few staff members also offered support and encouragement. But ultimately Josephine found the strength in herself. When the all-night phone calls came, she dismissed them as jokes. "One man kept calling and playing a trumpet," she told a reporter. "It was funny." She took courage from the fact that her experience might make it easier for others to follow after her. As a future psychology major, she even rationalized that the year's trials might provide insights for her later work. Still, there was the pain. Poignantly, as she was about to graduate (in the top 10 per cent of her class), she told the local newspaper: "I would like to talk to Vice-President Nixon about his trip to South America. The same thing happened to him there as happened to the Negro children in Little Rock. I'd like to ask him how he felt and what it was like."*

Although black parents were well aware of Josephine Boyd's experience, many continued to press for desegregation. In 1958, the parents of eighteen children applied for transfer to previously all-white schools—double the number of the previous year. Meeting in small groups with NAACP leaders, they rehearsed what responses they would make before the school board and prepared to cope with intimidating questions. But only two of the eighteen requests were granted, and in 1958 Greensboro had five children attending previously all-white schools compared with six the year before. The American Friends Service Committee decried "the atmosphere of caution and resistance to further progress" that had infected North Carolina. Nevertheless, given the reluctance of school boards to prepare students and teachers for desegregation, the social service agency found it "heartening" that the number of blacks attending previously all-white schools had not declined further.

These defeats coincided with the retirement of Superintendent Benjamin Smith, one of the strongest advocates of compliance with the *Brown* decision, from Greensboro's schools. Smith had fought against the Pearsall Plan, had convened human relations workshops for his staff, had encouraged parent-teacher meetings about human relations, and had invited Omar Carmichael from the Louisville school system to address Greensboro's teachers on how to desegregate peacefully. Smith, too, suffered for his convictions, with crosses burned on his lawn and windows broken in his house. Now past retirement age, he resigned once the first year of desegregation was completed.

Smith's place was taken by Philip Weaver. Nearly everyone agreed that Weaver would not "stick his neck out." Formerly Smith's assistant, Weaver evidently had concluded that it was not wise for school officials

---

*Nixon's car had been stoned by mobs in Caracas, Venezuela.

either to promote or discourage desegregation. He presided over a school board, moreover, that was moving rapidly toward a more conservative position. Mayor George Roach reported increasing pressure not to reappoint black school board member William Hampton, and, although the city council renamed Hampton by a four-to-three margin, the conservative pressure could be seen in the naming of more and more conservative spokesmen to the board.

The shift was palpable. In 1957, the AFSC had conducted a human relations workshop for more than forty teachers in Greensboro. One year later, a similar workshop was canceled due to insufficient registration, traceable, in the view of the AFSC, to a decline of support from the school administration. The commitment to old ways of acting was typified in a 1960 conference called by Weaver to discuss twelve-month utilization of the schools. White conferees met at Senior High School, black conferees at Dudley.

By 1959, conservative school boards across the state possessed an impressive arsenal of legal and administrative weapons to block widespread desegregation. The Pupil Assignment Act passed in 1955 served as a formidable barrier to desegregation. Two 1956 court cases upheld the validity of the Act, defining student assignments as an individual matter that precluded any class action suit before a school board or court. Under such rulings, not only was each application for reassignment a completely separate case; school boards also had the freedom to use a variety of administrative justifications other than race to turn down requests for transfer to previously segregated schools. Only when all administrative procedures had been exhausted and no other remedy existed could parents seek court intervention. Even then, the United States Fourth Circuit Court ruled in 1959, parents must prove beyond a doubt that race was the basis for exclusion. Within such a structure of judicial interpretation the total burden rested with the individual plaintiff, making a mockery of any notion of far-reaching "social" desegregation.

Not surprisingly, North Carolina's school districts used this arsenal of legal weapons with devastating effectiveness. A young black student in Raleigh, for example, tried to transfer from all-black Ligon High School, six miles away, to Broughton High School, within walking distance of his home. After the school board denied the request, the boy's parents and their attorneys appealed. The school board requested the parents and child to appear at a meeting. When only the attorneys went, the board dismissed the case, claiming that the plaintiffs had ignored the administrative rules.

Administrative hearings themselves were weapons of harassment. At one meeting in Carrboro, school board members repeatedly asked a black parent in accusing terms whether someone else had prompted her application for transfer. Failure to use correct forms provided another justification for rejecting parental requests. One story, frequently repeated, illustrates these obstacles: allegedly, a school board rejected the request of one parent because her child was a C student, hence not fit to go to a white school; the same board then denied reassignment to an A student because he was doing so well that it would be unfair to move him. As one AFSC staff member observed, "it is perfectly clear that the factors are so numerous and so vague that a school board determined to exclude Negroes . . . has no difficulty in finding some assertedly nonracial reason for doing so."

Such a system brought school desegregation almost to a total standstill. In 1959, only 53 out of 225 black requests for transfer were granted in North Carolina. Thirty-one of the fifty-three successful applicants were military personnel, all in one district. By 1961, only 89 out of 1000 black students had received a positive response to their applications. North Carolina reported a desegregation rate of 0.026 per cent—less than that in Virginia, Tennessee, Arkansas, or Texas. "We like the way you North Carolinians have solved the school desegregation problem," one Arkansas official wrote. "Why if we could be half as successful as you have been, we could keep this thing to a minimum for the next fifty years."

The effectiveness of the North Carolina approach was best illustrated in Greensboro itself. In the fall of 1958, Readall McCoy, a printer, took his children to the all-white Caldwell Elementary School—near their home—and sought to enroll them. James Tonkins, a milk delivery man, did the same with his son Michael. Both parents were told to go to a black school thirteen blocks away. Subsequently, the children were assigned to the all-black Pearson Street School—a building connected physically with the Caldwell School, where the parents had originally tried to enroll their children. At the same time, two other parents—Dewitt Simmons, a student at A&T, and William Cannon, an express handler—asked that their children be enrolled at Gillespie School, four blocks from their home. Instead, they were told to take their children to the all-black Bluford School, twelve blocks away. After the parents were turned down in yet another application for transfer, the NAACP initiated a suit calling for assignment of the children to the schools nearest their homes and asking the court to forever restrain the local school board, and the state board of education, from perpetuating a segregated school system. The Greensboro cases were filed simultaneously with similar motions made in Charlotte. The attorneys of record included Thurgood Marshall and Jack Greenberg from the NAACP Legal and Educational Defense Fund.

The NAACP action constituted a frontal assault on the entire structure of legal circumvention built so carefully by North Carolina authorities. Robert Moseley, school board attorney for Greensboro, called the court action "as important a suit of litigation as has arisen in North Carolina in the whole history of the state." Indeed, so seriously did the board view the legal action that it hired an outside law firm to assist in defending the board against the suit. The precaution was well-advised. Each of the plaintiffs had a strong case. The Cannon and Simmons families could argue effectively that the Gillespie School was seven blocks closer to their homes than the Bluford School was. The McCoy and Tonkins families, in turn, were able to use not only the issue of geographical distance, but also the Supreme Court's decision in *McLaurin v. Board of Regents* that segregation within the same physical unit—in this case the Caldwell and Pearson Schools—was just as unconstitutional as creating totally separate institutions. Both suits skillfully addressed the administrative and legal defenses that had been erected throughout the state to prevent desegregation. Each plaintiff had appealed individually to the appropriate authorities; all had been denied redress through administrative proceedings. The courts, therefore, were an appropriate avenue of appeal.

With equal skill, the school board responded. First, the board announced in the spring of 1959 that it would merge the Caldwell and Pearson schools, thereby making a single facility out of the two previously segregated schools. In so doing, it gave the appearance of accepting the four black applicants to the previously all-white Caldwell School; it also suggested—at least to the outside observer—that the resulting institution would be a truly desegregated educational facility. But in the meantime, Caldwell PTA leaders contacted every white parent in the community to explain how they might transfer their children from the theoretically integrated school to an all-white institution. White parents were told that approximately 450 black children would be assigned to Caldwell School, regardless of how many white students remained. The message, by no means indirect, was that white parents should seek transfer of their children to a near-by all-white school. Although the principal, the superintendent, and the school board supposedly were not parties to this operation, all tacitly supported it. Indeed, so clear-cut was the school administration's complicity in the transfer process that parents of white children were counseled by principals and other school officials on the reasons they could offer for reassignment. When the AFSC attempted to develop neighborhood support for creating a stable and integrated school community at Caldwell, it received a cold shoulder from every educational authority.

With this background, the school board met in July of 1959 to deal with the issues underlying the two court suits. On July 22, the board accomplished three objectives. First, it transferred the McCoy and Tonkins children to the Caldwell School, where they had initially applied for reassignment. Second, it transferred every white child from the Caldwell School to other all-white schools. Third, it removed every white faculty and staff person from the Caldwell School, replacing them with blacks. As a result, the board laid the legal groundwork for maintaining that the McCoy and Tonkins families had achieved the legal goal of sending their children to Caldwell, hence making the litigation moot. Finally, after approving 435 white reassignments out of Caldwell, the board approved—almost as an afterthought—the transfer of the Cannon and the Simmons children from the Bluford School to the Gillespie School. Thus, the school board had successfully taken care of the second lawsuit simultaneously with the first. Now, all the children who allegedly had been denied transfers on the basis of race were assigned to the schools they had initially sought to attend. As one observer noted, "one evaluation of the action might be that it is one of the cleverest legal maneuvers yet used in the desegregation field."

Temporarily, at least, the school board's tactics paid off. On October 26, 1959, Judge Edwin Stanley of the Middle Court dismissed the Simmons and Cannon suits, saying that their children were now in the schools to which they had applied. On the same basis, he ruled as moot the litigation initiated by the McCoy and Tonkins families. Furthermore, he refused to entertain a supplementary brief claiming that the school board had, in effect, continued segregation by making Caldwell into an all-black school with an all-black faculty. One year later, the Fourth Circuit Court of Appeals reversed Judge Stanley and recognized the legal circumvention that the school board had engaged in. By that time, however, the basic message of the school board's action had long since been received. If ever there had been hope that the white educational leaders of Greensboro were committed to genuine desegregation, that belief had now been killed and buried. The subterfuge surrounding the Caldwell School case provided a gravestone memorializing the bad faith of Greensboro's school board. As one black minister declared, "these folks were primarily interested in evading, and they weren't even embarrassed."

II

It was against this backdrop that the student sit-ins of 1960 occurred. All through the latter part of the 1950's, the accelerating pace of black protest activities bespoke a groundswell of grass-roots involvement. The NAACP in Greensboro had always boasted one of the largest chapters in the state, but prior to 1959 its peak membership had never risen above 1200. Now, amidst growing disillusionment over white indifference to black concerns, the NAACP's membership soared to 2300.

The leadership of the NAACP both mirrored and reinforced the trend toward activism. When Edward Edmonds arrived to teach sociology at Bennett College in 1955, he led a move to revitalize the NAACP. A veteran of the original March on Washington Movement in 1941 and a founder of the Southern Christian Leadership Conference, Edmonds was ready to assume the "risky' role of taking a front-line position against racial injustice. To at least some blacks, Edmonds wanted "to get things done faster than they could be done." As one protest leader observed, "Edmonds came on like a ball of fire." In addition to leading delegations of parents to the school board to protest inferior educational facilities and demand desegregation, Edmonds also insisted that the city open the formerly all-white swimming pool at Lindley Park to blacks. Although such bold action frightened some blacks and offended many whites, it had the effect of forcing people to think through their own positions and choose sides.*

Edmonds was not alone, however, in insisting on racial justice. Dr. George Simkins, his successor, had led the effort to desegregate the golf course in 1955, and through a series of court suits had established by the end of the decade the right of blacks to play as equals with whites on the city-owned facility. Over the next decade and a half Simkins persisted in the battle for desegregation of every public facility in the area, including Cone Hospital, the tennis courts, and the schools. To most

---

*After the pool desegregation effort, the city council voted 7–1 to sell both the white pool and the black pool to private sources in order to avoid integration. Spencer Love purchased the black pool and turned it over to the community for segregated swimming under the management of David Morehead, executive secretary of the Hayes-Taylor YMCA.

whites, of course, Simkins was just another "troublemaker." But even those who disliked his politics respected his commitment. "George and his group pushed all the time," one white liberal recalled, "and you just couldn't help admiring him. . . . He just went ahead and did things that he thought he should be entitled to." Other members of the NAACP exhibited the same energy. Ezell Blair, Sr., a shop teacher at Dudley High School, led a drive in 1959 to pressure merchants in a new shopping center near the black community to employ black sales personnel in "nontraditional" jobs. Others joined in the effort to recruit prospective parents for desegregation suits in the school system. And when a cross was burned on Edmonds's lawn, members of the NAACP led by James Tonkins, a milk delivery man, and Jay Banks, a Western Electric worker, coordinated an all-night protection effort.

The supporters of protest received a powerful impetus in 1958 when Martin Luther King, Jr., came to preach. Dr. King's visit dramatized the ambivalence between caution and activism within black Greensboro. Fearful of economic reprisals, A&T College and the black public schools refused to make their auditoriums available for King's speech. Many ministers also held back, unwilling to identify openly with the direct-action tactics associated with King's Montgomery bus boycott. But just as it appeared that there would be no place for King to speak, President Willa Player of Bennett college offered the Phifer Chapel. "I told them," Player recalled, "that this is a liberal arts college where freedom rings—so Martin Luther King can speak here." As if to show that the caution of some established leaders was not widely shared, the Greensboro black community thronged to the college, filling not only the chapel but a variety of near-by rooms where the sermon was piped in through loudspeakers. King's message—that American racism must be brought to the court of justice and eradicated through active, loving protest—affirmed a movement growing within Greensboro itself toward more and more direct challenge of the status quo.

The young men who would revolutionize the civil rights movement in 1960 grew up in this environment. Three of the original four sit-in demonstrators had spent their adolescent years in Greensboro. They had attended Dudley High School, where they encountered teachers like Nell Coley, who instilled a sense of pride and provided a model of strength. Ezell Blair, Jr., recalled an eleventh-grade English teacher who had taught him Langston Hughes's verse, "My Soul Runs Deep Like a River." The literature of black protest and history challenged students to carry the fight forward. Joseph McNeil, a Greensboro demonstrator who had been reared in Wilmington, North Carolina, also had encountered teachers who had been "dynamic and straightforward [and] who would tell you what your rights were as citizens, what you should have, what you don't have, how you're going to get them."

The same message came from parents and ministers. "I grew up in a home," Ezell Blair, Jr., commented, "where I had a father who was very strong on the issue of civil rights. . . . If anyone did him wrong because of his race or color, he stood up." Indeed, Ezell Blair, Sr., was known throughout the community as "very vocal, . . . very militant in the total scope of the movement." Two of the four initial demonstrators attended Shiloh Baptist Church, presided over by Otis Hairston, who had led the NAACP membership drive in 1959 and who provided mimeograph materials to the students when the demonstrations began. Two of the four had also participated in a resurgent NAACP Youth group. Each week the Youth Chapter met at St. James Presbyterian Church or one of the black colleges in Greensboro to discuss local and national protest activities. Students from Little Rock came to share their desegregation experience. The Montgomery bus boycott also provided a focus for discussion. "It was like a catalyst," one of the four recalled. "It started a whole lot of things rolling." When Martin Luther King, Jr., came to Greensboro, his presence particularly affected the young. Dr. King's sermon was "so strong," the younger Blair noted, "that I could feel my heart palpitating. It brought tears to my eyes."

By the fall of 1959, all four young men were freshmen at A&T. They became close friends and they spent evenings talking about the condition of blacks in America and the need to take action so that they might have a better life. As students, the young men read an anthology by Langston Hughes, with selections from W. E. B. Du Bois, Ralph Bunche, and Toussaint L'Ouverture, among others. The examples of black heroism in the past prompted discussions of what might be done in the present to achieve the age-old dream of freedom from white oppression. "We challenged each other, really," David Richmond remarked about the rap sessions. "We constantly heard about all the evils that are occurring and how blacks are mistreated and nobody was doing anything about it. . . . We used to question, " 'Why is it that you have to sit in the balcony? Why do you have to ride in the back of the bus?' "

All around were influences that reinforced the instinct toward action. One of the students worked in the college library with Eula Hudgens, an A&T graduate who in 1947 had participated in Freedom Rides to test local compliance with a Supreme Court decision ordering desegregation of the interstate bus system. Hudgens spoke frequently with Joseph McNeil about her own experience, and was not surprised when the young men acted. In that same fall and winter, the students talked with Ralph Johns, a white clothing-store owner who had long supported the NAACP and had been committed to the idea of demonstrating against segregated public facilities. Johns's involvement in the black community, Joseph McNeil noted, "was far greater than [that of] any other merchant." He was one of the few white people to show support for the college as well as for black protest, and he talked frequently about the need to mobilize students into a more active role. Because McNeil himself "felt a deep need to make a contribution," he responded to Johns's advice and support. Johns's support of black protest in the past generated the belief that the merchant would not abandon the students in a crisis. "In my heart," McNeil remarked, "I felt this guy was not going to leave me to the vultures."

Gradually, the resolve to act crystallized. The immediate catalyst for the sit-ins is unclear. Blair recalled watching a TV documentary on Gandhi that inspired him with its model of "passive insistence" on freedom. For McNeil the role of Johns was crucial. The Wilmington native also noted his own anger and "heightened sense of racial pride" when at a concert his black peers misbehaved and failed to show the self-respect and pride that he felt appropriate. The episode bolstered his own determination to exemplify the dignity that black Americans should manifest. Still others pointed to a December 1959 episode when McNeil returned from a trip to New York and was refused food service at the Greensboro Trailways Bus Terminal. Ultimately, though, the decision to act came when they found each other. "The thing that precipitated the sit-ins," Franklin McCain declared, "was that little bit of incentive and that little bit of courage that each of us instilled within each other."

The four young men gradually drew from their conversations a determination to take a direct step. McNeil initially suggested the sit-in tactic. One night shortly before the sit-ins he told his friends: "It's time we take some action now. We've been . . . people who talk a lot, but [with] . . . very little action." To people such as Hudgens in the library, Dr. George Simkins of the NAACP, and Johns at the clothing store, the four gave signals that they were ready to do something. On a Sunday night at the end of January, Ezell Blair, Jr., came home and asked his parents if they would be embarrassed if he got into trouble. "Why?" his parents wondered. "Because," he said, "tomorrow we're going to do something that will shake up this town." Nervous and fearful, afraid that someone might "get chicken," the four friends shored up each other's confidence until the next afternoon. "All of us were afraid," Richmond recalled. "But we went and did it."

The scenario had been well rehearsed. Stopping off at Ralph Johns's store, the students agreed that Johns would call a friendly reporter at the local newspaper at a pre-arranged time to alert her that the sit-ins were occurring. The four freshmen, in the meantime, purchased school supplies and sundry items at Woolworth's, being sure to keep their receipts. They then moved to the lunch counter. When they were refused service, Blair said: "I beg your pardon, but you just served us at [that] counter. Why can't we be served at the [food] counter here?" Customers walked by, noting the quiet demeanor of the students. The manager came and failed to persuade them to leave. Instead, the students stated their intention to return the next day and to stay until they were treated just as white customers at the food counter were. By that time, McCain noted, "We had the confidence . . . of a Mack truck. . . . I probably felt better that day than I've ever felt in my life. I felt as though I had gained my manhood . . . and not only gained it, but . . . developed quite a lot of respect for it." The same exultation permeated the group. They had done it! "I just felt that I had powers within me, a superhuman strength that would come forward," McNeil remembered. "I don't know how the crusaders felt, but [I got] a heightened sense of duty . . . once things really started to go."

The sit-ins expressed the young people's anger at the racial indignities they had suffered while growing up. The tactic had been chosen because of the moral contradiction in being refused service at one counter while being catered to at thirty others. But once chosen, the sit-ins became a vehicle for galvanizing sentiments that had been mounting for years. As McNeil remarked: "When you start growing up your environment expands and you start observing what's going on. Then you talk about it at home. In 1959, 1960, I don't know how many black babies had been born eighteen years ago, but I guess everybody was pretty well fed up at the same time."

Almost immediately, the students knew they were not alone in their struggle. That night the campus buzzed with word of their feat, as well as with discussion of their determination to return the next day. The sit-in leaders got in touch with the president of the student body and other campus leaders, seeking to coordinate transportation and assure discipline among the demonstrators. On Tuesday morning, twenty-five

Students sit in at Woolworth's, February 1960. Courtesy, Greensboro *Record*

men and four women students arrived at Woolworth's. Some of the men wore ROTC uniforms, the others coats and ties; the women wore dresses. All carried books and study materials, using the time when they sat at the lunch counter to prepare their lessons. That evening during its regular monthly meeting, the local NAACP chapter endorsed the students' actions and voted to give them legal assistance.*

By Wednesday morning, participation in the demonstrations surged as students occupied sixty-three of the sixty-five seats at the lunch counter. A Student Executive Committee set strategy, informed students about the latest developments, and recruited new demonstrators. "We did an hour-by-hour job," Richmond noted. "We had students to take each other's places at the counters. We had a carpool to transport everybody. We had a place where everybody would come and register for the whole week." In the meantime, newspapers across the state picked up the story, and a Woolworth's representative issued a statement saying that the company's policy was "to abide by local custom." North Carolina Attorney General Malcolm Seawell became the first state offi-

---

*The national NAACP criticized the sit-in tactic and refused legal or moral support for some time. As a result, Dr. George Simkins sought help from CORE, and a few days later a CORE field secretary arrived in North Carolina.

cial to comment, announcing that he knew of no law that would force a private business to serve anybody it chose not to serve.

The next three days revealed that a spontaneous action by a few had triggered a massive social movement. On Thursday, for the first time, three white women from the Women's College campus in Greensboro joined the demonstrations, as did students from some of the other colleges in the area. With most seats in Woolworth's occupied, many black students began demonstrating at the S. H. Kress store down the street. Also for the first time, white teenagers and young men mobbed the aisles in Woolworth's and heckled the sit-in demonstrators, greeting them with abusive and threatening language. With the New York *Times* and other national publications covering the story, the local newspaper reported that the incident could no longer be viewed in a vacuum. "If not solved amicably," the Greensboro *Daily News* declared, "[the sit-ins] could erupt into something worse and that would reflect poorly on the community, including Woolworth's and the colleges involved." By Friday, more than three hundred students were taking part in the protest. Three white men were arrested, one for setting fire to a Negro man's coat as he sat at the lunch counter.

The demonstrations Saturday brought the wave of protest to a crest. Hundreds of students, including the A&T football team, descended on the downtown area to continue the demonstrations. They were met by members of white gangs who waved Confederate flags and heckled blacks sitting-in at the L-shaped lunch counter. Carrying small American flags purchased in advance by student leaders, the football team then formed a flying wedge that moved through the whites to permit new demonstrators to replace those at the lunch counters. "Who do you think you are?" the whites asked. "We the Union Army," the football-players responded. "You could cut the tensions with a knife," Lewis Dowdy noted later, "because you had ducktails down there. . . . And our whole football team." Nell Coley, the teacher who had inspired so many students at Dudley High School, could not resist the urge to see the demonstrations for herself. "You aren't ever going to see this kind of thing [again]," she remarked, "and I'm always happy that I did that because here were these black kids lined around this counter with books in their hands . . . and the white kids had Confederate flags in their hands . . . and you could hardly get through [until finally] they had to close the store . . . and I was right there when the store was closed and when those black youngsters formed lines and yelled 'we won.' " Woolworth's had closed after a bomb scare, and Kress followed suit quickly.

The crowd convened on the street chanting, "It's all over! it's all over!" Single file the students walked back to campus, their ranks extending about two miles. That evening, sixteen hundred students participated in a mass meeting. Convinced by their leaders that a message had been delivered loud and clear, they voted to cease demonstrations in order to provide time for "negotiation and study."

By that time the revolutionary new tactic the students had discovered had already begun to transform student consciousness elsewhere. Even as Greensboro's black students temporarily set aside their protest actions, young people in other cities were taking them up. One week to the day after the demonstrations had started in Greensboro, black students in Winston-Salem and Durham held sit-ins at local lunch counters. The next day demonstrations began in Charlotte, and the day after that in Raleigh. By the end of the week students were sitting-in across the state. Although a national representative of CORE had arrived on the scene, there was no conspiracy or collective planning involved. Rather, each group had acted upon its own impulse, drawing on the example that had been set the week before. As one Charlotte demonstrator explained, the sit-ins were a "means of expressing something that had been in our minds for a long time." By the end of the second week, demonstrations had moved to other states throughout the South, while supportive picketing had begun in Northern cities against Woolworth's and other chain stores. After demonstrators were arrested in Raleigh, the *News and Observer* of that city noted that "the picket line now extends from the dime store to the United States Supreme Court and beyond that to national and world opinion." Starting with four students, a mass movement had flashed across the country. Was it not an irony, the New York *Times* noted, that the North Carolina cities where the demonstrations took root all were "liberal" or "moderate" towns that had supported policies of "token desegregation?"

III

In North Carolina white reaction developed along predictable lines. Governor Luther Hodges told a press conference that the sit-ins were counterproductive and a threat to law and order. Attorney General Malcolm Seawell urged store managers to invoke antitrespass laws and arrest the demonstrators. Seawell also encouraged municipal and college officials to use their residual powers to keep students on campus. When the American Civil Liberties Union protested Seawell's effort to suppress freedom of speech, the Attorney General responded that the

ALCU could "lump it." "It seems apparent," he declared, "that these incidents have been promoted, encouraged, and even supervised by persons coming into North Carolina from other states."

White liberals, by contrast, responded with strong support. Frank Porter Graham, former president of the University of North Carolina, declared that "in sitting down [the sit-in demonstrators] are standing up for the American dream." The North Carolina AFL-CIO endorsed black efforts to secure desegregated lunch-counter service in a resolution passed at its state convention. Some church leaders were also supportive. The president of the North Carolina Baptist State Convention told one group of ministers that "in order to reach the cross and solve the wave of sit-downs . . . the South . . . must be willing to pay the price of personal change." In a February 19 statement, the North Carolina Council of Churches not only endorsed the sit-ins, but commended "our Negro citizens for their self-restraint under provocation."

Within Greensboro itself, measurable support for the demonstrations appeared within white groups identified with liberal causes. Among those that favored desegregating the lunch counters were the Greensboro Council of Church Women, the YWCA, the Unitarian Fellowship, and the two local ministerial associations. The Greensboro *Daily News* added its support, declaring that a moral issue was involved. Even though the stores might have a sound legal position, the paper editorialized, they were on shaky ground in admitting customers to some parts of their stores and rejecting them in others. Most typical of the white liberal response was that of McNeill Smith, a local attorney and chairman of the State Advisory Committee of the Civil Rights Commission. Smith urged Woolworth's to provide equal treatment, offered his own services in arranging a gradual transition, and warned that the restrained and moderate behavior of existing student leaders might give way to more radical acts unless white leaders responded intelligently. In the long run, Smith warned, the issue was the future of the South. If no progress were made, "the keener Negroes will leave the South, [and] the remainder will continue to try to fill the white man's expectancy that they be thriftless, shifty, and given to a petty and occasional serious crime."

But liberals did not hold power in Greensboro, so their reactions, for the most part, played no significant role during the ensuing months. Much more important for white Greensboro were the responses of two men directly tied to political and economic power in the state and community. The first, Chancellor Gordon Blackwell of the Women's

College in Greensboro, spearheaded the effort to contain the demonstrations. The second, Edward R. Zane of Burlington Industries, moved to resolve the underlying issue in a manner that would preserve stability and promote the city's reputation for "progress" and moderation. Each effort, in its own way, illuminated the dynamics of racial interaction in North Carolina.

Chancellor Blackwell initiated the effort to control the demonstrations on Friday, even as the sit-ins approached a climax. The previous day three women from his campus had participated in the sit-ins. Their involvement had produced headlines across the state. The Women's College was one of the most prestigious campuses in North Carolina, and its students were generally considered to be the elite of white womanhood in the state.* Blackwell convinced the three demonstrators that they should not return to the sit-ins. The same morning he convened a meeting of leaders from the other colleges in Greensboro. That group, in turn, made contact with black student leaders and store owners and produced the first negotiations about the sit-ins. As a result, A&T leaders agreed to present the idea of a two-week cooling-off period to the student body. A mass gathering of some fourteen hundred students the next morning voted unanimously to continue the demonstrations. "Black Saturday," as the day of the largest protests came to be called, then took place with its bomb scare, the decision to close down stores, and the feeling of exultation among students who believed they had won. At that point, Blackwell initiated another meeting between Women's College and A&T students in a new effort to persuade them of the wisdom of a truce. This time, when A&T demonstrators brought the proposal to the student body, a moratorium was accepted.

Although his subsequent participation was never large, Blackwell played a pivotal role in the first stage of containing the demonstrations, revealing both a style and an attitude characteristic of the white leadership's response. Not only did he convene and initiate negotiations; he also coordinated the public presentation of the result, maintaining contact with newspaper editors, instructing President Warmoth Gibbs of A&T to alert the press about the moratorium, and securing from store managers a promise to close down their food service counters temporarily. In the meantime, on the following Tuesday, Blackwell went before his own student body and instructed them to refrain from further demonstration. "Your class jacket is a symbol of the college," Blackwell

---

*The Durham *Morning Herald* had headlined their participation directly beneath another story with the headline, "Negro Man Attacks White Woman."

declared. "Your actions bring credit or discredit to the college, [and] there is no blinking the fact that participation in this demonstration by several of our students . . . definitely resulted in increasing the inflammatory quality of the situation." Significantly, Blackwell's remarks became the basis for criticism of the sit-ins by Governor Hodges. A subsequent letter sent by Hodges to all state university and college presidents warned them against tolerating demonstrations and cited Blackwell as an example to follow.

The second stage of the white response, occurring almost simultaneously with the first, rested in the hands of Edward R. Zane, comptroller of Burlington Industries and an intimate associate of Spencer Love. A World War I veteran from Tennessee, Zane had worked his way through Georgetown University Law School and then had begun a career as an accountant for the Internal Revenue Service. Subsequently, he had come to Greensboro to work on a special investigation of city government and had stayed to become owner of his own firm and then an officer of the rapidly growing Burlington corporation. Like so many other high-ranking officers at Burlington, Zane had come to know Spencer Love almost as part of an extended family. Love had a genius for cultivating bright and energetic colleagues, and developing over the years ties of loyalty and devotion to them that were parallel only to those found in a strong and stable household. Zane was perhaps the closest to him of his corporate officers. Nor could Love have asked for a more dedicated associate. Deeply committed to the rule of law and the premises of the American Constitution, Zane exhibited the kind of patriotism that rejected—almost instinctively—any suggestion that citizenship rights could be compromised because of race or ethnic origin. In his travels, he had been angered at the indignities imposed on individuals because of race, whether they be Jews in Miami or Palm Beach, blacks in the South, or Italians and Poles in Northern cities. Although not a liberal politically, and certainly not an activist on social issues, Zane nevertheless believed that treatment of blacks as second-class citizens was "unconstitutional, un-American, [and] contrary to my concept of the American way of life as we portray it to the world."

Zane's involvement in the sit-in situation began as the demonstrations were reaching their climax. Mayor George Roach, a realtor and insurance agent who lacked experience in dealing with such a crisis, had gone to the editors of the local newspaper to ask their advice. The group decided that the man to see was Spencer Love and that his connection with national corporate officials might provide a way out of the crisis. First, though, they called Zane, who had been a member of the city council since 1957. It quickly became apparent that Zane would play a key role, both as a trusted emissary for Spencer Love and as a concerned citizen in his own right. With Love's wholehearted approval, Zane proceeded to lay the groundwork for a possible solution. First, he called David Morehead, executive secretary of the Hayes-Taylor YMCA and Spencer Love's primary liaison with the black community. Three years before, Love had introduced Morehead to Zane and had told the black leader that he should be in contact with Zane whenever a problem of mutual concern arose. Now Zane requested Morehead's advice and urged him to arrange a meeting with the administration of A&T as well as business leaders of the black community. After that encounter, a further meeting was arranged with the student leaders at the Hayes-Taylor YMCA.

Impressing his audience with both his strength of character and obvious sincerity, Zane brought to the students a dual message of support and chastisement. "I told them," he later wrote Love, that "the method that they had initiated for the attainment of their objectives was wrong and in direct violation of the owner's legal rights." Moral privileges, he emphasized, could not "be obtained by force or intimidation, but must be secured through the medium of orderly negotiations, reason, and mutual respect." On the other hand, Zane expressed his own strong moral commitment to the principles for which the students were demonstrating and his desire to find a way of realizing their goals. He made clear his deep respect for the students and his admiration of their discipline and restraint. In return, he believed, he was able to establish "outstanding communication" with the demonstrators. It was important, he noted, that the students have a white person they could trust. Throughout the discussion, he wrote Love, "the attitude of the students, faculty, and business leaders of the colored community were exemplary and would have done credit to any group, regardless of race."[2]

The students, in turn, trusted Zane. At least some believed that Zane was Jewish (he was not) and that his comments on the evils of discrimination reflected his own personal experience. "I studied him," Ezell Blair, Jr., noted. "I watched the way he moved . . . [the Jewish] people have always been for justice . . . I believed that and I trusted him."* Adults in the black community also were impressed by Zane's "character." Even if they did not know whether they could trust "the power

---

*For years afterward, Blair sent Zane Chanukah cards.

structure . . . he represented," they believed cooperation was worth the effort. Joseph McNeil, one of the four original demonstrators, noted that Zane had emerged "unsolicited on the basis that here is a problem . . . not just locally, but nationally, and it could have a detrimental effect on the image of the community." When Zane said he would try to solve the issue, the statement seemed credible. As McNeil observed, "we had no other person from the power structure to come forward. . . . When you're in an uphill struggle you tend to look for as much help as you can without giving up control."

Within the framework of trust he had established, Zane worked to secure a continuation of the moratorium and buy time for negotiations. Zane pledged that if the students accepted a cessation of demonstrations, he would secure the appointment of a city-wide committee to find a peaceful solution to the conflict. As a city councilman, Zane went to Mayor Roach and insisted that a special committee be appointed to deal with the crisis. As added pressure, he drafted a statement of resignation from the council in case the Mayor refused. The result was an agreement to name a body composed of representatives from the Merchants Association, the Chamber of Commerce, and the city council. In return, on February 20 the students announced that they would pursue their goal "through the peaceful channels of negotiations." In a statement heavily influenced if not totally drafted by Zane, the students announced that they had succeeded in calling the attention of people "of intelligence and goodwill to our plight" and now realized that "an atmosphere of ultimatum has been created [which] is not the best position under which favorable progress can be made." Hence, they declared, they would turn their case over to "the reasonable local bar of public opinion." The next day, the city's newspaper headlined the decision as "An Act of Maturity," and five days later Mayor Roach announced the formation of a special committee with Zane as its chairman.[3]

The first sign that the Zane Committee faced trouble occurred when the lunch counters re-opened on February 23, just a few days after the students had announced that demonstrations would be halted. From that time forward, the committee operated within a framework that automatically favored the status quo. Although the committee urged the community "as a matter of conscience to embrace a pattern of . . . equal treatment of all customers," the pressure for immediate action exerted by the demonstrations had now been removed. The businessmen were no longer suffering. Furthermore, the committee outlined a variety of compromises that appeared to provide the lunch counter operators maximum latitude. Among the possibilities Zane suggested were to have everyone seated equally, to remove the seats and have everyone stand at the counters, to reserve separate areas for blacks and whites to sit down, or to abolish food service altogether. Clearly, only the first option had any appeal for the demonstrators.

Perhaps most important, the committee defined the issue as one of mobilizing public support for integrating the lunch counters, thereby placing the burden of proof on the demonstrators and their supporters. In so doing, the committee members appeared to accept Woolworth's contention that the store should "abide by local customs," and not change its practices unless the vast majority of the community agreed. Even as Zane dealt with managers of various local businesses, his primary efforts were devoted toward recruiting as large a body of public opinion on the issue as possible. Beginning on February 27, the committee mailed more than five thousand letters to citizens asking for their considered judgment. The newspaper carried repeated requests that local citizens send their comments. The only problem, of course, was that the managers of the stores retained the right to interpret the results and define what would constitute a mandate for change. In turn, the committee appeared to be saying that only a consensus in favor of desegregation would warrant a change in the stores' practices.

Events moved quickly to a head at the end of March. By the middle of that month, Zane had received more than two thousand letters on the sit-ins, with 73 per cent favoring equality of service on some basis. The local newspaper also pushed for change. "Negro citizens," the *Daily News* editorialized, "no longer intend to be treated like messenger boys at the food counter, asked to take their food standing up or eat it outside. . . . As long as those who seek a change in Southern civilities seek it in a peaceful manner, their power (and their haunting image on the white man's conscience) will not diminish." But there was pressure on the other side also. In private conversations with Woolworth's executives in New York and Atlanta Governor Hodges angrily demanded that a solution be found, making clear his own inclinations to arrest the demonstrators and use trespass laws to quell the protests.[4] Unwilling to risk alienating customers, Woolworth's executives refused to go that route. But the end result was stalemate, especially given the absence of pressure from demonstrators to tip the balance.

On March 24, Zane called together managers of eight downtown stores to force the issue. Reinforced by an editorial that underlined the justice of the sit-in issue and the necessity of finding a compromise, Zane and his committee suggested that the dime store designate a section of each lunch counter for integrated service, and another section for whites only. After a two-hour discussion, the store managers rejected the proposal, arguing that it would lead to a major loss of profits and disaffection of white customers. The leading opponent was C. L. Harris, manager of Woolworth's. A Duke University graduate who had worked his way through college as a porter and stockroom man, Harris identified totally with the company that had employed him since he was a student. For him, the sit-ins were an attack on the institution to which he had given his life. "Actually," he wrote Governor Hodges, "we are fighting a battle for the white people who still want to eat with white people. . . ." Faced with such opposition, Zane felt defeated. Ironically, he seemed to share management's view that the response of letter-writers had been "too meager" to establish a "definite community desire to change existing customs." In the absence of complete consensus, a shift in racial customs could not occur. Although the committee would continue to work behind the scenes, it appeared that without counterpressure of a direct kind the initiative would remain with those supporting the racial status quo.

IV

On March 31, Edward Zane went to the students at A&T to tell them of the committee's failure. The next day, demonstrations resumed. More than twelve hundred students at A&T and Bennett resolved to place pickets outside the variety stores and to send representatives on a regular basis to test segregation at the lunch counters. Within days, there was further support. Thurgood Marshall, national counsel for the NAACP, appeared at Bennett on April 3 and warned the students against accepting any solution of "token integration." Two weeks later, at the organizing meeting for the Student Non-Violent Coordinating Committee in Raleigh, Martin Luther King, Jr., preached a rousing sermon urging students to prepare for jail and to form permanent organizations so that protest could continue after the semester ended. During early April as well, students joined with adult leaders such as Dr. George Simkins of the NAACP to urge blacks to stay away from stores that refused to serve blacks. Editorializing on the situation, the A&T newspaper declared: "It can never be said of the A&T students that they did not allow ample time for a solution favorable to these students." But once the time had passed, students were prepared to act.

The resumption of direct-action demonstrations struck home. Under orders from the Atlanta regional manager, Woolworth's closed its lunch counters rather than deal with the day-to-day crises posed by the sit-in students. For a period, the Kress lunch counter remained open, closing only when a black student approached. But the strategy hurt business and confused customers. Meanwhile, after hearing Martin Luther King, Jr., tell the SNCC conference in Raleigh to prepare for arrests, forty-five young blacks marched into the Kress store on April 21 and refused to leave the lunch counter, inviting arrest on trespass charges. Those were the only arrests of blacks during the entire sit-in demonstration in Greensboro, but they highlighted how far students were willing to go to demonstrate their resolute intention. Every day, pickets marched outside the stores where they were harassed by white counterpickets bearing signs reading "go back to the cotton fields Nigger." Through their courage the young black demonstrators showed that this generation would neither accept second-class treatment nor allow anyone else to define their rights.

Just as important, the economic boycott provided a means for mobilizing the entire black community behind the cause. Despite Greensboro's strong NAACP chapter, there had always been a tension between the caution of many and the activism of some. The sit-ins, more than any other event, resolved that tension in favor of activism. The students, many noted, were the only ones who could have begun the sit-ins. Ezell Blair, Jr., observed at the time that "as college students we have no jobs from which to be fired by people who don't like to see us assert ourselves. . . . We can speak up loudly now without fear of economic reprisal." Echoing the same theme, Joseph McNeil remarked: "We had shelter, we had food, and we could take risks that the others couldn't." But in acting, the students had also set an example for the entire community. "It shook the people up," Eula Hudgens, the A&T librarian, commented. "Some were happy about it, some were scared to death." Yet the demonstrations had raised the consciousness of the second group and had made them aware of the need no longer to accept injustice. "They learned something from those four fellows, that if you want something done you've got to go out and fight for it." The genius of the economic boycott was that—like the Montgomery bus boycott—it gave even those in the most vulnerable economic positions an opportunity to stand alongside the students in affirming their dignity and commitment. The community responded.

Significantly, groups and individuals who previously had adopted ac-

Pickets resume protest after negotiations fail. Courtesy, Greensboro *Record*

commodationist positions now refused to restrain the demonstrators. Warmoth Gibbs, the president of A&T, was generally perceived to be a disciple of President Bluford, a man who would never act contrary to the wishes of his white superiors. Indeed, Gibbs had been chosen in the first place because of his deferential manner. As the white chairman of the Board of Trustees at A&T wrote to Hodges in 1956, Gibbs was "not as brilliant as some," but he was "a very safe and sound person and his views on racial questions are more in line with our thinking than many of his race." Yet instead of capitulating to Hodges's pressure to rein in the students, Gibbs stood firm in their support. Throughout the entire period of the sit-ins, Gibbs and Dean William Gamble defended the students' freedom to express their own political views off campus. Indicative of the A&T administration viewpoint was the statement of one faculty member: "As long as [the students] don't cut classes and don't foul up in some way, I don't see that it's any of the college's business." The students understood such attitudes for what they were—acts of courage in the face of overt intimidation.

Nor was support for the students restricted to adults on the campus. The Greensboro Men's Club, one of the oldest and most prestigious organizations in the black community, released a statement arguing that any solution "which will provide for segregated facilities is neither satisfactory nor equitable." Undertakers, ministers, and business people pledged bail support in the event of arrests. "Various parts of the black citizenry of Greensboro," Joseph McNeil noted "offered to put their land up as our bail—and that's significant." The support of some ministers was no surprise. Otis Hairston, pastor of two of the original four demonstrators, made available his church building and mimeograph facilities. ("They took over the secretary," he recalled later, "used up all our paper, and said we'll pay you back.") But other ministers came around as well. They might have to be "put up on the altar," as Ezell Blair, Sr., noted, and, pressured into action by their congregations, but in the end nearly all responded, using their pulpits as vehicles for dispensing information about the boycott and protest activities.

In the meantime, the students had gone to a number of established leaders such as Vance Chavis, Dr. George Evans, and Dr. Hobart Jarrett, seeking their advice and support in the negotiation process. As a result of that initiative, the Greensboro Citizens Association was revitalized as the institution around which community support of the demonstrations could develop. Jarrett called a meeting of all civil rights groups, established a day-to-day liaison with the students, and prepared to assist in whatever way possible. "We never tried in any way to tell the students what to do," he noted. "What we did was to say, if and when you need us, come."

The strength of adult support was perhaps best exemplified by Willa Player, president of Bennett College. She had come to Bennett in the 1930's to teach, and then had become a dean. One of her faculty members described her as "an administrator with a capital A; she went according to the rules, and regulations were carried out to perfection." To at least some whites, Player represented a potential ally in the effort to control the movement. Shortly after the sit-ins began, Spencer Love wrote her "about certain disturbances about which I'm sure you're familiar." Assuring her that he, together with all broad-minded people, wanted to keep "our part of the South on top of the heap in becoming more and more enlightened and progressive," Love offered his view of the situation. "For people who are younger, progress may seem slow," he wrote, "but as long as it is there, and as long as it is sure, it seems to me best to be patient and not to try to rush the clock too much."

Though not an open request for restraint, the letter's message seemed clear. So, too, was Player's response. "We hope that you will have time to express in a letter to Mr. Zane and to Mayor Roach," she wrote, "your desire to see us work together in the community for provision of services for all citizens alike." (To his credit, Love conveyed exactly those sentiments to Howard Holderness, a powerful member of the community who was generally thought to be conservative.) Throughout 1960 as well as later, Player offered firm support to her students. In addition, she was the first black to turn in her charge card when Meyer's Department Store, a prestigious downtown establishment, refused to desegregate its dining room. As one white observer commented, "something happened to Willa Player when the students took the lead and went out. . . . She became real impatient. She may have been impatient in her own right all along; it may simply have been that front she was putting up. But then she no longer put up that front."

The combination of direct-action demonstrations and the economic boycott eventually took its toll on the managers of downtown stores. Although opponents of the sit-ins had hoped that the end of the college semester would bring a halt to student activism, the movement had already effectively organized high school students, as well as permanent residents of Greensboro, to carry on the day-to-day picketing. Bill Thomas, a high school student who headed the NAACP Youth Chapter, coordinated the summer activity, making sure that the pressure stayed on throughout the city. In the meantime, the boycott exacted a high price. Although the Woolworth's manager had estimated that only 5 per cent of his trade consisted of blacks, the loss of that business as well as of patronage from other customers scared away by the demonstrations cost the store $200,000 in sales in 1960. Woolworth's sales went down 20 per cent in Greensboro in 1960, with profits off by 50 percent.

Finally, one day in June, Harris came to Mayor Roach and said, "for God's sakes do something, my business is going to pot." Beginning in May, the regional office of Woolworth's in Atlanta had indicated its willingness to go along with desegregation if other downtown businesses did likewise, at least in part due to pressure from protesters in other stores in the South and North. Early in July, a group of blacks headed by Hobart Jarrett initiated a meeting with the management at Kress, seeking to arrange a time and procedure for desegregation. With Kress willing to integrate as well, that left only the management of Meyer's Department Store to join the "big three." Ironically, Joseph Martin of Meyer's protested that desegregating the downtown lunch counters would make "a kind of ghetto out of this section of the city." But he, too, eventually agreed. Through careful negotiations, it was agreed that without prior announcement a few Negroes at a time would be served at the local lunch counters. On July 25, the first black ate a meal sitting down at Woolworth's. After one week, three hundred had been customers. No one protested.

V

In the long view of history, the Greensboro sit-ins will justifiably be seen as the catalyst that triggered a decade of revolt—one of the greatest movements in history toward self-determination and human dignity. America would never be the same once students discovered the power of direct-action protest and others followed their example. As one participant in the sit-ins declared, "that dime store . . . was the birthplace of a whirlwind."

But the Greensboro demonstrations must also be seen as part of a continuing struggle to overcome racism. The first and most important theme to stand out from the Greensboro demonstrations is the extent to which they represented a continuation of protest within black Greensboro, a tradition grounded in all the Nell Coleys and Ezell Blairs who had "been teaching those kids those things all along." Here was the generational continuity that gave historical meaning to the events of the 1960's. Whether it was the determined NAACP chapter, the parents who risked economic reprisal by sending their children to desegregated schools, the demand for equal access to public facilities, or simply the effort to build the best churches and schools possible, Greensboro's black community had long participated in the effort to achieve dignity and a decent life for its people. Within this context, the sit-in demonstrations represented a dramatic extension of, rather than a departure from, traditional patterns of black activism in Greensboro.

The second theme to emerge from the sit-ins involves the inherent fallacy of permitting other people to define one's life and possibilities. Greensboro had long boasted of being a "moderate" and progressive city. By those words whites meant a willingness to proceed, with gradualism and good manners, to discuss issues of social conflict in an attempt to find consensus and compromise. One of the principal ingredients of Greensboro's "progressive" style was the notion that "good" whites could be trusted to deal honorably and justly with the demands of local blacks. Thus, white leaders boasted of their city's success in achieving token desegregation. After all, Greensboro provided a dramatic counterpoint to Little Rock, and therefore showed how peacefully social change could occur.

A central ingredient in this style was the form of discourse that prevailed between whites and blacks. As long as the amenities were observed and Negroes conducted themselves appropriately, it was assumed by whites that an equitable solution could be found to any dilemma. Yet the boundaries set by correct behavior or the "amenities" ruled out the possibility that white leaders could hear the full depth of black disaffection. Conversely, devotion to proper social forms caused whites to reject as unrepresentative any black who failed to obey the ground rules of "correct" behavior.

From a black point of view, of course, the ground rules, or "civilities," were often just a way of delaying action. No event better crystallized the gap between form and substance than the Greensboro school board's handling of school desegregation during the late 1950's. The brazenness of the school board's arguing in court that it supported desegregation even as it transferred all white students from Caldwell School was overwhelming. Yet if good manners prevented white leaders from hearing the resounding depth of black protest, perhaps another form of communication would be necessary.

In this sense, the fundamental contribution of the sit-ins was to provide a new form through which protest could be expressed. The very act of sitting-in circumvented those forms of fraudulent communication and self-deception through which whites had historically denied black self-assertion. The sit-ins represented a new language. Moreover, the language communicated a message different from that which had been heard before. A direct connection existed between style and content. In an almost visceral way, the sit-ins expressed the dissatisfaction and anger of the black community toward white indifference. From a black point of view, the protest may have been the same as that which had been conveyed all along. But it was expressed in a manner that whites could not possibly ignore—the silence of people sitting with dignity at a lunch counter demanding their rights. Thus, from a white point of view, the message was different, because for the first time, whites could not avoid hearing it.

The connection between form and substance was perhaps best seen in the interim period after the sit-ins ceased and as negotiations proceeded. Significantly, the major claim of the Zane Committee was that only in an orderly and proper atmosphere would people of goodwill and understanding be able to find a solution to the community problems. It was in this framework that the student decision to accept a moratorium was described as "an act of maturity" removing the spirit of ultimatum that supposedly blocked any possibility of a solution. As the Greensboro *Daily News* commented editorially, public opinion was now on trial and the progressive instincts of the city would have a chance to be manifested. Black students had shown their trust in the good faith of white leaders, and now it was up to those leaders to find an appropriate solution.

The history of the next six weeks, however, demonstrated vividly that once blacks had relinquished the initiative, they lost the ability either to control what happened or to make the white community fully aware of their demands. Although people like Zane worked with courage and integrity to find a way to desegregate, they were once again operating within a traditional framework of communication where whites controlled the ground rules and dictated how the situation was defined. Blacks were left out. In the end, only when blacks resumed the initiative and delivered their message once again in terms that could not be mistaken or misinterpreted did the prospect of a just settlement become real.

The underlying issue of style and content was strikingly revealed in a Greensboro *Daily News* editorial on the death of Dr. William Hampton one week after the sit-ins began. The editorial eulogized Hampton for never engaging in public argument, and for never forcing an issue when people disagreed with him. Hampton, it said, was a model for everyone to follow. Self-evidently, the sit-in demonstrators had violated that model; more important, by doing so they had threatened the racial status quo and the entire fabric of "proper" behavior that reinforced it.

In three weeks the newspaper returned to the same theme in an editorial entitled "Of Civil Rights and Civilities." The issue before America, the editorial declared,

no longer concerns civil rights (such as school attendance or use of public facilities); it concerns civilities—the right of businesses to invite their own customers and the fairness of business practices. . . . Somewhere a Southern community must find a way to deal with civilities as well as civil rights. Such an answer will not be found while management is under the gun. It will be found only where both sides are able to sit down and work out an answer unimpeded by the threat of force or the worry of economic reprisal. Greensboro, we think, can come closest to this ideal. It has a fine committee . . . dominated by a feeling of the need for moderation and give and take rather than inflexibility and closed minds.

Just three weeks later the Zane Committee—grounded in a commitment to civility—announced its failure.

Ultimately, then, the sit-ins provided the only vehicle through which traditional patterns of white domination could be attacked. In that sense, they were both a consequence and a cause of black activism. The sit-ins were consistent with, and grew out of, a tradition of protest; but they also helped to reinforce and extend that tradition to the entire community and to change the form through which old as well as young would express their demands for dignity and equality. In that sense, the sit-ins represented a new stage of black insurgency, reflecting the lessons as well as frustrations of past experiences with protest. Some might argue that by adopting "illegal tactics" black demonstrators were permanently alienating the goodwill of their white supporters in the South. But it had already become clear that not until blacks trespassed would their right to equal service be established. "Constitutional Amendments, Congressional enactments, and Supreme Court decisions" one legal scholar noted, "failed to achieve the desired purpose. It was inevitable, therefore, that a more direct approach would be sought."

The sit-ins did not bring final victory to the Greensboro black community. But they created a new method for carrying on the struggle. Despite the desegregation of lunch counters, white Greensboro did not give up its "cherished traditions" easily. In the battle between "civil rights and civilities," it appeared that most white leaders still believed in the priority of "civilities." Thus, it would be necessary again and again for black students and adults to take to the streets during the 1960's in order to seek change in the political and social structure. But if the struggle continued, it was now waged with new weapons and a different language. After 1960, the forms of communication between white and black would never again be the same.

CHAPTER FOUR
A Time of Testing

The best in us comes out if we give it a chance. These are days when Southern honor and pride cry out to us—asking what is right and decent. . . . Is it really so difficult to allow all qualified persons to vote, to use the parks, to go to school? Are we so weak and afraid we cannot trust ourselves to do what is right—to answer honor instead of shame?

> Ralph McGill, *The Atlanta* Constitution,
> *September 28, 1962*

With the breakdown of faith in the integrity of the white power structure, there is a concomitant loss of respect for the law as an effective means of social change. This, I submit, is the main reason why the Negro revolt has come now and as it has.

> *Louis Lomax*, The Negro Revolt

By the time John F. Kennedy was inaugurated as President in the cold, snow-covered nation's capital in January 1961, Greensboro had become synonymous with the start of a civil rights revolution. In the eleven months after the sit-ins began, civil rights demonstrations had spread to nearly every city in the South. More than one hundred towns had already desegregated their lunch counters in response to direct-action protest, and the violence-plagued Freedom Rides were about to begin. Within the next five years hardly a day would go by without some additional testimony that black Americans would never cease challenging American racism—no matter how great the sacrifice and pain—until equality under the law became a reality.

Appropriately, Greensboro remained a bellwether for the continuing struggle. Although the era of direct-action protests had started there, the city proved no speedier than most in recognizing the justice of black demands—in fact, it was slower. As one black college president in the community observed, "Greensboro and North Carolina had people believing that they were progressive, [but] when [the demonstrations] started they began to show their real feelings . . . they weren't nearly so liberal as they were cracked up to be." On fundamental issues of jobs, education, and equal access to public accommodations, Greensboro showed that the lessons of 1960 had not yet been learned. Thus, the city continued to be a microcosm of the battle waged by black people across the South for jobs, decent schools, and basic constitutional rights.[1]

I

With the election of Terry Sanford to the governorship in 1960, the voters of North Carolina appeared to be choosing the path of enlightened liberalism over that of political retrenchment. An early supporter of John Kennedy, Sanford had waged his campaign on the slogan "not massive resistance but massive intelligence." Because his opponent in the primary run-off was the segregationist I. Beverly Lake, Sanford walked a tightrope during the campaign, endorsing separation of the races and refusing to accept the "integrationist" label. But his underlying stance became clear when he declared in his inaugural address that "no group of our citizens can be denied the right to participate in the opportunities of first-class citizenship." Alone among Southern chief executives, the new Governor talked eloquently of his commitment to jobs and education as solutions to the South's social ills. With good reason, many viewed him as the champion of a better, more tolerant South. Sanford harnessed classic Southern imagery in a way that reinforced rather than impeded his own vision of the future. The South, he said, would "rise again and march again," only this time "it will make the march not with bayonets, but with textbooks. We will not be firing on Fort Sumter but on the dungeons of ignorance."

An examination of North Carolina's social and economic conditions reveals just how monumental a task Sanford had assigned himself. Despite its image as one of the most progressive states of the South, North Carolina ranked almost last by most social and economic criteria. The state was forty-fifth in the amount of money it spent on each school pupil, forty-fourth in housing, forty-second in per capita income, forty-eighth—that is, last—in rate of unionization, and forty-fifth in illiteracy. In most categories, only South Carolina, Alabama, and Mississippi scored lower. One out of every four applicants for a North Carolina driver's license could not pass a simple comprehension test.

Investigation by North Carolina's Advisory Commission on Civil Rights, meanwhile, disclosed that the black population had benefited hardly at all from the state's "progressivism" in race relations. Although more than eleven thousand North Carolinians received income from the $5 million National Guard payroll, not a single guardsman was black. There were no Negroes in the six-hundred-man highway patrol.

Nearly the entire $5.5 million Employment Securities Commission budget came from the federal government, but the central office in Raleigh had only ten black employees: one maid, five janitors, two elevator operators, and two janitor-messengers. In Raleigh's state government complex seven thousand people held jobs: only twenty-four blacks held positions above the rank of janitor or messenger. Negroes constituted less than 1 per cent of all prison guards, only 2 per cent of those appointed by the Governor to state boards, most of these as trustees of black colleges. Although North Carolina was generally thought to be moderate on the issues of school desegregation, by mid-decade only Mississippi, South Carolina, Arkansas, and Alabama had a lower percentage of blacks attending desegregated schools.

From the beginning of his term, Sanford recognized that the race issue, inextricably connected with the problems of jobs and education, would be the central challenge to his leadership. Unlike Hodges, Sanford welcomed consultation with black groups and organizations committed to Negro rights. Early in 1961 he met with representatives of the Durham Committee on Negro Affairs and the North Carolina Council on Human Relations. Both groups emphasized the importance of making the state a model employer; they encouraged the hiring of blacks for jobs not traditionally given Negroes, the creation of biracial committees in each community, pressure on school boards to file desegregation plans, and support for integration of hospitals, state parks, and other public facilities.

Instead of resenting or suppressing black demands for change, Sanford sought ways of resolving black grievances in a peaceful manner. "I wasn't trying to be a hero," Sanford later noted, "and I certainly wasn't trying to be a martyr. But I did see that my great contribution to the state . . . would be proving that we could turn around and start in the right direction [after holding] the wrong position on race for a hundred years. . . . We were attempting to do what needed to be done while being fairly cautious that we didn't overdo it."

Within this context, Sanford's greatest personal accomplishment was to provide an environment that encouraged racial protest by sanctioning its goals. At a time when less than one-fiftieth of 1 per cent of black children were attending classes with whites, Sanford sent his own children to a desegregated school. Although he later claimed that the decision had not even required discussion ("had we done anything else it would have been an obvious evasion, . . . a slap at everybody who stood up for the Supreme Court decision"), papers across the country carried pictures of the Governor's child entering an integrated public school. While every other Southern governor responded with outrage at President Kennedy's 1962 decision to send federal marshals to the University of Mississippi to ensure the enrollment of James Meredith, Sanford declared that he "had never been prouder of the President." Under constant prodding, Sanford appointed blacks to thirty state-policy boards and ordered the improvement of state-hiring practices, appointing a special coordinator to implement merit employment. Through such actions, symbolic and real, Sanford gave measured support for racial change. His objective, he told the *Christian Science Monitor*, was "to provide a climate of goodwill, counting on the local communities, local leadership, to establish lines of communication and work for proper solutions—the state giving whatever is asked by the localities."

The heart of Sanford's goodwill program was the creation of an interlocking network of Good Neighbor Councils headed by a state-wide committee and then replicated in each local community. Such biracial councils were to encourage employers to hire blacks and provide a forum for interracial communication in order to head off racial conflict. The idea had sprung from the precedent of the federal Fair Employment Practices Committee during World War II, and it reflected Sanford's belief that jobs were central to solving racial tensions. The title, in turn, came from Franklin Roosevelt's Good Neighbor Policy toward Latin America and the use of the same label in a Texas program to welcome dark-skinned diplomats from Africa, Asia, and South America. After consulting with an ad hoc group of black advisers and trying out the concept on a rural church gathering, Sanford was ready to take the idea to the general public.

Choosing the one-hundredth anniversary of the Emancipation Proclamation for his announcement, Sanford declared: "now is a time not really to look back for freedom, but forward toward the fulfillment of its meaning." Sanford urged North Carolinians to "quit unfair discrimination and to give the Negro a full chance to earn a decent living for his family." If local communities would create Good Neighbor Councils and encourage employers to hire on the basis of ability, the Governor said, North Carolina would have "a new kind of emancipation proclamation which will . . . set us free from the drag of poor people, poor schools, from hate, from demagoguery."

Sanford's declaration drew immediate praise. Ezell Blair, Jr., speaking to the A&T student body in Greensboro, commended the Governor for his moral leadership and courage. Adult black organizations in

Greensboro such as the Men's Club and the Ministerial Forum followed suit. A black protest leader in Raleigh said that Sanford's statement reflected "moral courage and integrity of character;" and Roscoe Drummond, the syndicated national columnist, praised Sanford for representing the social conscience of the South, "a voice of moderation and challenge." From the NAACP to the conservative white press, Sanford received enthusiastic endorsement of his proposals.

Yet the very strength of Sanford's message also constituted its primary weakness: no action would be taken unless people in local communities agreed. As the Fayetteville *Observer* noted, Sanford's plea was "basically sound, quite humane, and essentially conservative." It was the "conservative" quality of the concept that threatened the prospect of substantive change. The Governor had not called for a law compelling integrated employment, the *Observer* noted. Rather, he had urged voluntary compliance. Sanford relied on moral persuasion as his primary argument for merit employment. "I do not intend to force anybody," he told the press. "I do not believe in force. I do believe the conscience of North Carolinians will get this done."

Significantly, many conservatives believed that Sanford's plan placed the primary burden of action on blacks. According to such a view, Negroes needed to "recognize the responsibilities that fall upon them and their people" and take full advantage of educational opportunities; they had to prove themselves able to compete with whites. Those blacks who sought equal employment, one editorial noted, "must consider themselves missionaries, realizing that on their ability to fit in, the enlarged employment of their race depends . . . they will have to prove their professional skills competively [and to show] that they can avoid irritating racial incidents, even though occasionally placed under unusual provocation." Thus, a plea to end discrimination became in some people's eyes another occasion to ask the victims to bear the entire weight of change. Although this clearly was not Sanford's view, it was the opinion of many he counted in his camp.

In the end, Terry Sanford's positive contribution to North Carolina's race relations involved primarily the areas of atmosphere and leadership style. By conferring recognition and legitimacy on the aspirations of black protest, Sanford helped to reinforce the black struggle for racial equality. His own programmatic solution, however, produced little in the way of substantive change in the personnel and policies of state government. Although this was due in part to the failure of the state constitution to give the governor significant power, it also reflected how entrenched were the patterns of racism against which the forces of change had to battle. Even Sanford's own appointee in the area of merit employment found it impossible to move the state bureaucracy and alter traditional hiring practices. The state-wide Good Neighbor Council, in turn, had no administrative power to enforce its mandate of securing equal employment opportunities. Nor could the state shape the actions of local Good Neighbor Councils. As the Kinston *Free Press* said about the program, "the Governor is advocating a policy the principle of which is just, [but] it will not become generally effective at once." By relying upon conscience and persuasion, Sanford was depending, ultimately, upon the same forces that progressive Southerners had relied upon for more than a century, with practically no results. Control over race relations remained primarily in local hands and in individual communities. The question was whether those who exercised power in those communities wished to move voluntarily toward the principles of justice that the governor had enunciated.

II

On that issue, the initial response of Greensboro's white leadership offered little basis for optimism. When Negro citizens, led by middle-class women, demanded that Meyer's Department Store open its well-appointed upstairs dining room to black customers, store executives rebelled. Furthermore, those who had promoted the lunch counter settlement—led by City Councilman Edward Zane—supported management's insistence that it should not have to negotiate further. The agreement on the sit-ins, Zane noted, had specifically covered only lunch counter facilities. Therefore, he could not support blacks who sought to carry the issue further. Although Meyer's soon surrendered to the economic leverage exerted by well-to-do black patrons, the reluctance to move except under pressure accurately reflected the attitude of the larger community.

Nowhere was the absence of voluntary commitment to racial change more obvious than in the area of jobs, precisely the sector singled out by Sanford as most crucial to solving the state's racial problems. A 1958 survey of 402 employers in Greensboro had shown that only 13.2 per cent endorsed hiring workers without regard to race. Three years later, the figures were almost the same. At a national conference on "merit employment," Tart Bell, director of the Southeast Region of the American Friends Service Committee, called Greensboro an example "par excellence of tokenism." Although a number of job categories had been opened, Bell observed, the primary accomplishment of the merit employment program had been to assuage the conscience of the community, "[leaving] the lard bowl pattern of segregation . . . unmoved." At institutions like Western Electric, where one or two blacks had been hired in "nontraditional" jobs in the late 1950's, promotions had been few and far between; moreover, the initial ranks of black "pioneers" had never been enlarged. When the P. Lorillard Company established a new plant in Greensboro, it insisted on maintaining traditional employment patterns, turning away applications from blacks with M.A.'s and Ph.D.'s in organic chemistry. Even where Negroes had secured good positions, they met resistance. Geraldine Siler, the first black secretary at Burlington Industries, was told by the Personnel Department not to apply to the employee "Country Club" until she was fully accepted by others. In the meantime, she found "others" ignoring her. Despite a few breakthroughs, the number of successful black applicants for better jobs could still be counted on one's fingers.

The admissions policies of a local technical institute highlighted the "Catch-22" dimension of the employment struggle. Out of 1212 students enrolled at the Industrial Educational Center in Guilford County, only two were black. When the Greensboro Citizens Association, a black protest group, demanded to know why Negro applicants were being rejected, the staff responded that the institute accepted only those who could prove that they had a job waiting for them when training was complete. Since the Negro applicants could not secure promised positions from employers, they were turned down for training. The vicious cycle was completed, of course, when employers and editorial writers then explained away the black employment situation by saying that Negro young people had not taken advantage of the technical training available to them.

The same reluctance to act voluntarily appeared in the desegregation policies of the city school board. As the Greensboro *Record* noted in a retrospective story, the city's desegregation pace had "slowed drastically" after 1957. Although in the spring and winter of 1961 the Greensboro Citizens Association had petitioned the board of education to take the initiative in promoting integration, board members continued to restrict desegregation to the one school that had accepted blacks since 1957. Six years after the first five black children entered Gillespie School, there were only nineteen Negroes attending desegregated schools in Greensboro—all at the same facility. Nearly every other large city in the state had a better record. Even when the federal courts ordered that the children involved in the 1959 Caldwell/Pearson suit be admitted to the schools of their choice, the board insisted on sending them to Gillespie, notwithstanding their parents' demands that they be assigned elsewhere.

Although school board members later cited "prevailing community sentiment" as justification for gradualism, their own recalcitrance was the primary force at work. Surveys made at the time suggested little opposition to further desegregation. In comparable cities such as Chapel Hill and Charlotte, integration had occurred at ten schools and five schools, respectively. School leaders in Greensboro simply refused to move. Staff members of the American Friends Service Committee found that, although Superintendent of Schools Philip Weaver was "cordial and friendly," he believed adamantly that school officials should not promote desegregation. When some liberal white women approached him to discuss integration, Weaver became "fearful, very uneasy . . . impossible to communicate with in an open way. A chip went on the shoulder immediately." Under fire from one white supporter of desegregation, Weaver retorted: "Do you want your children to go to Dudley?"—a question, which under the circumstances, seemed designed to evoke the same racial anxieties as "Would you want your daughter to marry a Negro?" Chairman Thornton Brooks of the school board, senior partner in one of the city's most prestigious law firms, was equally unwilling to promote desegregation, preferring to avoid the issue as long as possible. As a result, one Greensboro black woman commented, the school board's "deliberate speed was mighty slow." By the end of 1962, Greensboro tokenism was at a standstill, and there seemed little reason to think that the pattern would change voluntarily.

Private institutions in the city proved no more sensitive to the issue of race. In 1959 the International Quota Club had commemorated "brotherhood and freedom" week by holding a luncheon at the Mayfair Cafeteria. The restaurant excluded blacks. Even after the sit-ins, organizations that professed to be inclusive persisted in barring Negroes. On many occasions, city-wide denominational meetings of churches failed to invite black congregations that were part of the denomination. A former clergyman at the prestigious First Presbyterian Church recalled that "in those days I simply did not have the freedom to invite [a black] to come to the church for weekends and [to share in the] service." On one occasion, he noted, an act of the "session" (the church legislative body) was necessary to approve a black minister reading Scripture. Even those most ostensibly committed to racial tolerance resisted desegregation. Guilford College, a Quaker institution that had long boasted of its international student body—including Africans—declared publicly that "our admissions policy does not permit us to admit members of the Negro race." The statement came the same day the college president left for a month-long trip to Africa and Asia.

The situation, of course, was not all one-sided. The YWCA continued to hold interracial activities and to move toward integration of its two branches. An informal group of church women, mostly Methodists, also met to find ways of promoting school desegregation that would benefit the city and at the same time protect the children from harassment. Some clergymen, such as Charles Bowles and Harold Hipps of West Market Street Methodist Church, spoke out for desegregation of public facilities. Yet in most areas of education, employment, public policy, and private associations, the two years after the first sit-ins witnessed an almost complete lack of progress toward equal opportunity or public desegregation. Rather than move voluntarily toward the goals Governor Sanford had endorsed, most of Greensboro's white leaders seemed intent upon clinging to the tokenism they had so grudgingly accepted at the end of the 1950's. The only problem with such a stance, Marion Wright of the Southern Regional Council observed, was that "token integration is like a man stopping at one-tenth of stop lights . . . and obeying one-tenth of the commandments." At some point, the ledger would have to be balanced.

It was against this background that protest rose again in Greensboro during the fall of 1962 and the winter of 1963. There was almost a pendulum motion in the history of Greensboro's civil rights struggles. Blacks wanted to trust in the good faith of whites. Only after frustration reached a peak did overt rebellion occur, to be followed again by quiet and patience when promises of change were offered. Then the spirit of rebellion would rise once more, set in motion by yet another betrayal of promises made in the heat of crisis.

Now the pendulum of protest was moving toward assertive action again. Part of the battle was legal and represented efforts by the professional elite in the community. Part of it reflected a new determination to mobilize the community for action on school desegregation. But all aspects of the new wave of protest drew inspiration from the direct-action demonstrations of students who insisted that public accommodations be opened to all citizens. In all their manifestations, the protests that began during the fall of 1962 signaled Greensboro's white leadership that tokenism would no longer suffice and that substantive change must come, by force if necessary.

III

Dr. George Simkins, head of the local NAACP, spearheaded the legal battle. During the 1950's Simkins and a number of his colleagues had been arrested and put on trial for attempting to play on the segregated public golf course. (They were convicted, sentenced, and fined, with their sentences later being commuted.) Since the golf course was subsequently closed by the city, the only satisfaction Simkins could take from that battle came when he won a city tennis championship from the man who had prosecuted him. Now, Simkins, other black doctors, and several patients sued the two all-white hospitals in Greensboro for equal admission of blacks to staff and patient facilities.

When Cone Hospital had first been constructed in the 1950's, its director spoke optimistically, at least in private, about plans to integrate staff and patients. But through both executive indecision and a negative response from several wealthy patients, neither plan was ever implemented. Although the hospital's original charter had pledged to serve indigent patients without regard to race, there were no equal facilities for blacks. Nor could black doctors practice there, being restricted to Richardson Hospital, a segregated, smaller facility in the black section of Greensboro. The exclusion of doctors paralleled the policy of the North Carolina Medical Society. "I am frank to say," the Medical Society's leader said, "I would want no social relations with some of the Negro delegation with whom I have conferred." According to spokesmen for the Medical Society, blacks wanted "the white physicians to do all the compromising." Simkins suit—initiated in early 1962—argued that Cone Hospital was an instrument of the state and therefore subject to the equal protection clause of the Fifth and Fourteenth Amendments. The plaintiffs' lawyers, headed by Jack Greenberg and James Nabrit, contended that as a recipient of funds under the federal Hill-Burton Act and as a tax-exempt facility the hospital was obviously a public agency. Since black doctors were prohibited from the hospital and black patients were admitted under conditions totally different from whites, the equal protection clause clearly had been violated. Although Judge Edwin Stanley initially upheld Thornton Brooks, the attorney for the defense, the case was decided on appeal in favor of the black plaintiffs. Another legal bastion of segregation had been destroyed, but only after decisive pressure from the black community.

Once again, however, it was young people who provided the cutting edge of protest. Ever since the sit-ins a small group of students had sporadically picketed downtown movie theaters, particularly during the fall and winter of 1961. The pace of activity quickened in the summer of 1962, when a CORE chapter was begun in Greensboro under the leadership of William Thomas, an A&T student who, while still in high school, had coordinated the summer picketing of Woolworth's in 1960. As CORE chapters in the South embarked on their ambitious "Freedom Highways" program in the summer of 1962 to desegregate interstate restaurants, members of the Greensboro chapter joined other protesters demonstrating at Howard Johnson's in Durham. With the re-opening of school, members of a rejuvenated direct-action move- ment returned to Greensboro ready to assault the barriers of segregation there.

By late September, hundreds of demonstrators were picketing the S&W Cafeteria and the Mayfair Cafeteria in downtown Greensboro on a daily basis. On October 13, the picket lines gave way to two successive Saturdays of mass marches. Fifteen hundred black students marched in the first, more than two thousand in the second. On each occasion, the marchers sang freedom songs and carried signs demanding a boycott of white merchants who refused to integrate their facilities. "Enter to cook, depart to eat," one sign declared. "If God is thy Father, man is thy brother," another read. Virtually all Bennett students and as many as half of the A&T students took part in the parades. The second march culminated in a mass meeting addressed by James Farmer, national chairman of CORE, who declared prophetically that "North Carolina should stop praising itself for being ahead of the Deep South [and] get moving again." Six months before demonstrators took to the streets of Birmingham in protests that would galvanize world-wide attention, thousands of Greensboro young people were giving notice that their patience was at an end.

Temporarily, the demonstrations were overshadowed by a charge that the marchers were communist-led. A police intelligence report claimed that Alice Jerome, a new teacher at Bennett College, had in the past participated in communist or communist-front organizations. Armistead Sapp, Jr., lawyer for the two cafeterias, accused Jerome and her hus- band, Victor, of being oustide infiltrators "schooled in the field of demonstrations," and together with Black Muslims—known for their "fanaticism"—coordinating the protests. (In fact, Mrs. Jerome had been a correspondent for the *Daily Worker* and her husband had served three years in prison after a Smith Act conviction for failing to register as a communist.) Stunned, CORE leaders declared that they would have nothing to do with communists. Within a few days, the Bennett Board of Trustees fired the accused woman. But as if to show that such tactics would not stop the demonstrators, the same day that the Board of Trustees met more than two thousand students marched downtown.

The fall demonstrations reached a peak in mid-November when forty-eight members of CORE were arrested for sitting-in at the two cafeterias. While some demonstrators sang hymns on the streets outside, others went into the Mayfair and S&W restaurants taking seats and demanding to be served. "If we can't be free entirely," CORE Director William Thomas said, "then we do not want superficial and hypocritical freedom." For too long, Thomas declared, "efforts at negotiations have proved fruitless, reflecting an attitude of 'nonchalance' by white participants." Led by Thomas on the one hand and by two Bennett faculty members on the other, the students had decided to "take things into our own hands." "It may take two weeks or two years," Thomas said, "but we are determined."*

The student demonstrations coincided with a growing interracial effort to force the school board's hand on desegregation. The new effort reflected the convergence of at least three separate groups. The first consisted of black and white women—most of whom were married to professionals—who came together in an attempt to avoid the pain and anguish of Little Rock and find a better way to build an integrated school system. In early 1962, the group decided to seek out blacks who might apply for admission to previously all-white schools. Concentrating on geographical areas where blacks lived close to white schools, the women sent interracial teams to recruit black parents willing to seek transfer for their children. This effort quickly became intertwined with another by the Greensboro Citizens Association (GCA), an all-black group that had been revitalized during the 1960 sit-ins. The GCA had carried two petitions to the city school board in 1961 demanding initiatives on school desegregation. Now it redoubled its efforts, emphasizing a survey of black schools and their inadequacies *vis à vis* white schools. Both these groups, in turn, became affiliated with the American Friends Service Committee school advisory body, which chose Greensboro as one of its primary focal points.

The coalition of school desegregation groups advocated two strategies. The first sought geographical districting, with everyone in a given atten-

---

*The 1962–63 demonstrations constitute the focus of the next chapter. Here they are introduced in conjunction with other protest developments to set the stage for the confrontation in 1963.

Young Greensboro blacks picket the Mayfair Cafeteria during the fall of 1962 demanding equal service. Courtesy, Greensboro *Record*

dance zone—regardless of race—being assigned to a neighborhood school. Such a system would eliminate situations in which black students were bused twenty-nine miles round-trip each day to attend Dudley High School. The GCA, in particular, emphasized the injustice, under the arrangement then existing, of placing the total burden for change on the pupil who wished to attend an integrated school. Too often, Otis Hairston noted, segregation had "so conditioned Negro parents and children as to inhibit their taking the initiative to obtain a desegregated education." Blacks were tired of occupying "the guinea pig status" of being a minority of one or two in a sea of whites. Furthermore, he declared, blacks justifiably feared economic reprisals if they did seek out an integrated setting solely through their own efforts.

The second strategy pressed by the coalition emphasized the gross inequalities already existing between white and black schools. Gladys Royall, a black professor at A&T, pointed out that less than one-half of 1 per cent of black students attended white schools in Greensboro. Yet in many black schools, textbooks were more than thirteen years old, cast-offs from white schools. While 95 per cent of school buses bringing blacks to school departed before 7:30 in the morning, only 3 per cent of the buses serving whites left so early. The same discrepancy existed in the afternoon. Black students were systematically excluded from programs for the academically talented, from participation in science fairs, from symphony instrument training, and from specialized courses preparing students for a mathematical specialty in college.

Throughout the winter and spring of 1962–63, the school coalition accelerated its campaign against the school board. At every meeting of the board, delegations appeared to present new evidence and petitions. While public meetings at churches and the YWCA sought to educate parents on their rights and to "smoke out" the school board, teams of interested citizens canvassed various neighborhoods seeking to build pressure from below. There were some conflicts. Theoretically, at least, those who urged parents to apply for reassignment of their children to previously all-white schools might be working against a program of mandated geographical zoning. But all in all, the mounting assault of petitions, together with the new campaign for open public accommodations, reflected a groundswell of protest against the racial status quo. Although not coordinated in any coherent manner, each campaign inevitably intersected with and reinforced the others.

Each of these endeavors proved instrumental in forging the first community-wide effort at interracial activity to develop in Greensboro during the 1960's. Stirred by the growing crisis in race relations, Warren Ashby, a white professor from UNC-Greensboro; John Taylor, the white realtor who had desegregated the Holiday Inn; Cleo McCoy, a black chaplain at A&T; and Dr. George Evans, the black member of the school board, came together to find ways of avoiding racial confrontation. Except for the YWCA and some women's church groups, liberals had lacked an organizational outlet for their political energies in the 1950's and 1960's. The American Friends Service Committee was a professional social service agency; the Quaker meeting required a religious commitment. Occasional informal conversations among liberals provided neither a sense of efficacy nor a base from which to build political influence. "There was a real lack of confidence that anyone anywhere was trying to resolve the problems," Warren Ashby noted. "[There was probably] some sense of guilt, too. We hadn't really done very much through all these years, just sort of drifting and letting things go."

Making contact with the GCA, the AFSC, and other liberal-minded civic groups, the interracial activists formed the Greensboro Community Fellowship (GCF) in early 1963. The new group had two goals: to

provide leverage for desegregation of both schools and public accommodations, and to serve as a study group to find answers to problems of
jobs and housing. As John Taylor recalled, "the Community Fellowship [reflected] the feeling of some blacks and whites that we ought to
create more dialogue and that by coming together in an integrated
group we could do something." The GCF circulated petitions seeking
school desegregation, convened community-wide meetings to discuss
school board policy, and solicited citizen support for those businesses
that opened their facilities to all customers. Meeting on a monthly basis
at the Holiday Inn, the group attempted to find an identity that combined elements of a non-sectarian church, a discussion club, and a
direct-action organization. Although ultimately it fell between the
cracks of these options, during the winter and spring of 1963 the GCF
represented the only embodiment of the biracial coalition that so many
liberals believed in as the ideal for their city.

IV

Despite such activities, none of the insurgent efforts that developed in
Greensboro during 1962 exerted direct influence over those wielding
power. Significantly, the Greensboro Community Fellowship spent most
of one meeting attempting to find a distinguished outsider who could be
imported to speak on its behalf to "the power structure." Clearly, GCF
members themselves felt out of touch with the wellsprings of power in the
community; yet if a group containing large numbers of "established" liberals experienced such difficulty, what would be the leverage of student
protesters, women reformers, or the average black citizen?

It was not surprising, then, that white economic and educational
leaders responded to the new protests with only minor concessions.
Faced with the pressure of school desegregation groups, the board of
education announced that parents could register first-grade pupils at any
elementary school in the city. Indeed, said the school superintendent,
such a policy had been in effect since 1959. (Needless to say, the
announcement came as a surprise to those who had been pushing
futilely for desegregation during the same period and now heard of the
policy for the first time.)* On the more important issue of geographical

---

*Other white leaders were also surprised. After McNeill Smith told a public meeting of
the "freedom of choice" plan for the first grade, he was accosted by a leading white
attorney who asked, "what in the hell did you open your mouth for?" In fact, the school
board no longer had a choice in the matter. The Sixth Circuit Court ruled in 1962 that
"Negro children [cannot] be required to apply for that to which they are entitled as a
matter of right," thereby invalidating Tennessee's Pupil Assignment Act.

assignment, however, the school board resumed its hard-line position. Although easing the process of seeking reassignment, the board insisted that there were no geographical school zones in Greensboro and that therefore the concept did not apply.

To supporters of school desegregation, the decision came as a heavy blow. As black school board member Dr. George Evans noted, the board had thrown away an opportunity to take "a giant step forward." It was unfair, Evans said, to continue placing the full burden for desegregation on the victim—requiring parents who favored integration to send their children into hostile environments—when desegregation could be mandated through zoning. Totally failing to understand Evans's point, Chairman Richard Hunter of the school board insisted that a parent should welcome the obligation to select a school for his child, and never see it as a burden. Indeed, Hunter said, juvenile delinquency was high precisely because parents were unwilling to assume such "burdens," implying, at least, some connection between juvenile delinquency and black complaints. There could hardly have been a more vivid example of how little most white leaders understood the black perspective.

In the area of public accommodations, the same pattern prevailed. Despite the mass arrest of students in November, city leaders refused to take decisive action. In the preceding summer the Mayor had appointed a Human Relations Commission (HRC) consisting of established business and educational leaders from both the white and black communities. The commission was to study racial practices in the city and "by quiet consultation with those involved, seek solutions to problems in' human relations as they arise." After the mass demonstrations of October and November, the HRC endorsed equal treatment of all people—but, at the same time, it emphasized the importance of maintaining private property rights, including the right of businesses to decide who should enter their premises. In effect, the commission had adopted the same formal posture on race relations as Governor Sanford; desegregation should occur, but only through voluntary compliance. Yet with no clout behind it and no real attempt to apply pressure, the HRC's quest for voluntary change produced nothing. Indeed, the plea for open access was almost totally diluted by the commission's equal emphasis upon private property rights.

Thus, as Greensboro approached the spring of 1963, the new wave of protest activities met a firm wall of resistance, made all the more effective by an appearance of flexibility. The various challenges to the racial status quo shared no common origin or organization. Those who concentrated on school desegregation had little contact with CORE demonstrators who besieged the downtown cafeterias, and the established liberals of the Greensboro Community Fellowship differed markedly in style and philosophy from the young college students. Nevertheless, it was clear that the time of patience was gone. The pendulum once again had swung toward open protest. Whatever their differences in focus and organization, many in the black community and at least some in the white community now insisted on substantive action toward desegregation. When the city's white leaders responded with only the rhetoric of good intentions, there was no alternative but to intensify the confrontation. As a result, the largest civil rights protests ever to occur in North Carolina took place in Greensboro during May and June of 1963.

CHAPTER FIVE
"My Feet Took Wings"

The students have set up a beachhead on the shores of freedom, and we're going to move in.

> Charles Anderson, a black minister, to a mass rally
> of twelve hundred people at United Institutional
> Baptist Church, 1963

In the past we have had to swallow the insults, smile at the pain, and quench the spirit of human dignity throbbing in our breast. We had to act in so many ways as though we believed in our own inferiority in order to get along and survive. This day is over.

> Inaugural Address, President Samuel Proctor,
> A&T University, 1962

Between May 11 and June 7, 1963, Greensboro was rocked by unprecedented demonstrations. For eighteen nights, black marchers numbering more than 2000 assaulted the bastions of segregation in the city's central business district. At one point 1400 blacks, most of them college students and teenagers from area high schools, occupied Greensboro's jails. The demonstrations shattered white Greensboro's confident self-image, shook the city's social and political institutions to their foundations, and emphasized as never before the conflict between racial justice and North Carolina's progressive mystique.

I

All during the spring signs of the impending crisis had appeared with mounting frequency. In addition to the insistent demands of school desegregation groups, Dr. George Simkins and the NAACP raised questions about city personnel procedures. In early March Simkins pointed out to Mayor David Schenck that no blacks were enrolled in Greensboro's police reserves. Of the five who recently had applied, three had received notices of rejection. A month later the NAACP leader was back, this time with a query about why a black truck driver for the sanitation department made significantly less than a white truck driver. Meanwhile, others expressed their anger more directly. Three times during early 1963 blacks picketed City Hall to protest discrimination in the hiring and promotion of policemen and other city employees. Beginning in April, new demonstrations erupted against restaurants that excluded blacks, and three students were arrested during a protest at McDonald's.[1]

The city's white leadership responded to the situation with a combination of anger that the issues were raised in the first place and a proclamation of good intentions to work out any legitimate grievances. Both reactions characterized the behavior of Mayor Schenck throughout the crisis. On the one hand, Schenck was offended that men such as Simkins would dare question the city's integrity or interfere in issues that, in Schenck's view, were none of his business. In an angry response to Simkins's complaint about the police reserves, Schenck wrote: "it would seem that the cause of equal opportunity of employment . . . would better be served by emphasis on meeting qualifications and evidencing sincere desire to serve, rather than on test cases or the publicity to be derived therefrom."

On the other hand, in his more dispassionate moments Schenck recognized the need to deal with "the churning and surging tide of events throughout the South . . . as individuals and groups seek to obtain, defend, and indeed define their civil rights. . . ." With the violent demonstrations in Birmingham, Alabama, as a backdrop, Schenck declared upon taking office for the second time on May 13 that "the tragic drama being enacted in other cities of our region could well have been staged on the streets of Greensboro. Though Greensboro has been widely noted as a city of liberal tolerance, . . . still we are yet to face the greatest challenges in this incredibly complex field of human relations." In an editorial praising Schenck's sensitivity, the Greensboro *Daily News* asked whether the city's leadership would "sit quietly on its hands, hoping trouble will go away, or whether it will rally to work toward solutions while there is still time. . . ."

Even as the newspaper asked the question, demonstrators on Greensboro's downtown streets proved that time had already run out. A new round of protest activity started on Saturday, May 11, when thirty students picketed McDonald's at the Summit Shopping Center. During the next two days the demonstrations expanded to other chain stores and then downtown to the S&W and Mayfair cafeterias. Ku Klux Klan demonstrators set up a counterpicket line on Sunday, May 12, and two whites were arrested when a can of beer was thrown in the face of a black picketer. By Tuesday night, May 14, three hundred and fifty demonstrators had gathered. After whites threw objects and heckled picketers at the shopping center, the crowd marched downtown to the central business area and held a kneel-in demonstration in front of a local theater.

From that moment, each day brought a heightened intensity of protest. The next night more than two thousand students from Bennett College and A&T descended on the S&W and Mayfair cafeterias and the Center and Carolina theaters. "They'd come marching uptown . . . in lines by the hundreds and sometimes the thousands," a local reporter noted. More than two hundred of the demonstrators chose to be arrested that night when they intentionally blocked the entrance of the S&W Cafeteria and the two downtown theaters after being refused admission. CORE leaders had decided to test the city's resolve by upping the ante.[2] Clearly, the demonstrations had moved to a new stage.

In an effort to head off further confrontations, the Mayor, together with his Human Relations Commission, sought emergency meetings with the Chamber of Commerce and the local Merchants Association. In both cases, the organizations responded on Thursday, May 16, with resolutions endorsing equal access of all citizens to government and business facilities within the city. Although not a breakthrough in itself (the resolutions carried no enforcement power), demonstration leaders nevertheless acknowledged the gesture. That evening, the one thousand students who marched downtown neither invited arrest nor confronted the business owners. Instead, they simply walked through the business area and back to campus. The next day both the S&W Cafeteria and the Center Theater rejected the recommendations of the Chamber of Commerce and Merchants Association.

Over the next two days the demonstrators made their own response, with more than seven hundred adding themselves to the list of those arrested. Filling the jails became a primary strategy for putting pressure on the city. Each arrest not only added to the logistical burden of police but also raised the political and psychological stakes for white leaders trying to find a way to defuse the crisis. As students thronged local churches for instructions, demonstration leaders offered advice on how to provoke arrest without incurring violence. On Friday evening, May 17, the strategy went into effect.

That night, more than five hundred highly disciplined protesters attempted to enter the downtown cafeterias and theaters. In some cases they went into the theaters without tickets and sat down; in others they simply blocked the entrances. The police made massive arrests and herded the students toward the courthouse to be arraigned. The students were jubilant. Suffused with a sense of hope and power, they sang, "freedom, freedom will come some day." By mid-evening the local courtroom was so jammed with singing and shouting demonstrators that later groups had to be taken to the county courthouse. The jaunty mood of the students was best summed up by one protester who told the cafeteria manager, "my father cooks for y'all, and I'd like to come in and eat some of his cooking." Only ten of the more than four hundred who were arrested accepted bond; the rest chose jail.

The next day brought still more of the same. Led by two husky A&T students carrying a cross bearing the sign "Equality, Justice," the students at first simply marched through midtown, but then headed once again for the Mayfair Cafeteria. The atmosphere, one reporter noted, now "seemed angry and militant," which it had not been a day earlier. Whenever a white customer appeared, the manager would unlock the revolving door, but each time black students would attempt to enter. A group of white youths carrying signs reading "go home niggers" and "jungle bunnies go home" roamed through the area. By the end of the evening, another 287 demonstrators had been arrested, bringing to 940 the total placed in custody over the previous four days. With prison facilities already strained beyond capacity, local officials had moved many of the students to county prison farms near Greensboro. On Saturday night, for the first time, they housed over three hundred of the demonstrators at the old polio facility, Central Carolina Rehabilitation Hospital. Unused for years, the hospital was—ironically—one of the first places to experience integration in Greensboro. But in this case, its use highlighted the underlying strategy of the movement—to pack the jails, exhaust the county, and compel action from local officials. When asked whether he was running out of demonstrators, the local CORE leader responded emphatically, "No!" and he warned that forty thousand Greensboro citizens would be willing to go to jail if necessary on behalf of racial integration.

The CORE leader was William Thomas, a twenty-year-old sophomore at A&T. A native of Greensboro, Thomas attributed some of his sensitivity to racial oppression to having grown up in a "relatively sophisticated place." Like so many others in Greensboro, Thomas was inspired by his teachers at Dudley High to accept nothing less than his full rights. "They cared," he noted. "They became personally involved with their students," especially teachers like Nell Coley. During the late 1950's, Thomas had been president of the youth chapter of the NAACP, making that group a focal point for protest activity in the city. As a high school student, Thomas had led the picket line during the

Student demonstrators confront police as protests intensify during the spring of 1963. Courtesy, Greensboro *Record*

summer of 1960 when college students left Greensboro, ensuring that the momentum of the sit-ins would not be lost. There he learned the skills of organizing, passing out leaflets, going door to door to recruit support for the economic boycott, and providing much of the impetus for continued pressure on downtown merchants. When the college students returned, Thomas was elected head of the CORE chapter. Not surprisingly, he saw the 1963 demonstrations as a direct continuation of the first sit-ins. "We had something going at the time; it developed from one thing to another, it expanded—we left Woolworth's and Kress and started going to S&W Cafeteria, Mayfair Cafeteria. We started economic action, we started political action, our demands broadened."

Although Thomas was neither flamboyant nor charismatic, he served as one of the two principal leaders of the movement. As David Morehead observed, "Bill was kind of the quiet type that would lay strategy like the quiet general of the army." He came from a good family, and he had been reared by a deeply religious pentecostalist mother who had taught him to be well-mannered and disciplined. Some viewed him as "a shy boy . . . not the sort of fellow you would think of as a leader." But shyness was simply an external guise that obscured enormous strength. Otis Hairston noted that although "Bill was a person that did not want to go out front . . . he called the shots." Early on, Thomas had learned the importance of building from the ground up, recruiting supporters through door-to-door canvassing. Above all, he had learned the importance of establishing credibility with both his allies and his enemies. "I'd tell [the police] that tomorrow we're going to have a thousand people down here blocking the streets," he recalled, "and I had a thousand people down there. That created respect for you. Next time a threat would do the same thing and I didn't have to do it." As Captain William Jackson, head of the Greensboro detective division, commented, "Thomas knew where he was going and knew where he had been."

Thomas's alter ego was A. Knighton (Tony) Stanley, a young black minister serving at A&T as part of a Reynolds Foundation program to provide a campus ministry for black institutions. Stanley, the son of a clergyman, had also grown up in Greensboro. Like Thomas, he shared a sense of pride in his Greensboro background. "We felt that we talked better than most Southerners and we attributed a lot of that to the two black colleges." Like Thomas, also, Stanley viewed his education in Greensboro as a mandate for accomplishment and self-realization. "I had a tremendous sense of awe and respect for the schoolteachers," he noted. "They were people who looked good and they smelled good and they had dignity." The teachers at Dudley had communicated a clear sense of direction. Vance Chavis, Stanley recalled, had "always said you can go where you want to go." And Nell Coley, through her stern and rigorous standards, had taught the students not to be dissuaded from their primary mission in life by getting caught up in trivial questions such as who had "good" (i.e., straight) hair. "What did they mean?" she used to say, "all hair is good as long as it covers your head."

Stanley responded to the civil rights movement with both impassioned commitment and ambivalent detachment. The direct-action demonstrations in the South had started while he had been a student at Yale Divinity School. The paradox struck him forcefully. "Here I am in the nice beautiful North and my people are fighting this revolution," he told his adviser; "the revolution will be over when I get back to North Carolina." (Prophetically, his adviser responded, "if you stay in school for one hundred years the revolution will not be over.") When Stanley moved back to Greensboro in 1962, the same sense of paradox remained. He heard of the outbreak of demonstrations in his native city while returning from a trip to Duke University, where he had been lecturing students on "what freedom means in a segregated society from a black perspective." Upon discovering that his fiancée had been jailed, he ruminated: "here I am drinking tea with the white folks . . . and these kids are really giving their bodies."

In effect, Stanley acted out his dual response of commitment and detachment by assuming the role of intellectual strategist for the movement. "I hated protest," he recalled. "I hated to argue with anybody, I hated to disturb the peace among those white folks." But no one was better at plotting the moves that forced the "white folks" to deal with the past and present of their relationships with blacks. Although Stanley was cautious in his tactics, his careful planning was instrumental in orchestrating the demonstrations in a disciplined manner. Together with Thomas and friends like Lewis Brandon and Robert Patterson, who helped the group stay together in times of tension, Stanley shaped the day-to-day battle plans of the student struggle, deciding when to invite arrest, when to back off, when to raise the level of tension. In his own words, "Bill Thomas was my guts . . . I was his brains, it's as simple as that."*

If Stanley was the intellectual strategist and Thomas the field general, Jesse Jackson was the hero who led the troops into battle and inspired the rank and file. Dynamic, flamboyant, a figure who thrived in the limelight, Jackson provided the charismatic attributes necessary to rally the movement and reinvigorate it if energy lagged. Jackson had grown up in South Carolina and had transferred to A&T from school in Chicago, quickly becoming a football star and campus leader. Thomas and Stanley recognized immediately the importance of recruiting such a person to their ranks. "We needed Jesse as a football player the girls loved . . . the president of the Student Council," Stanley noted. "We woke him up one day and told him to protest with us and he has been protesting ever since." Although initially recruited by Stanley and Thomas simply to act as marshal for the downtown marches, Jackson overnight became publicly identified as a demonstration leader. By the end, he had become a significant figure in his own right, shaping as well as being shaped by the movement's struggle to overcome the obstacles in its path.

Not surprisingly, those obstacles were both subtle and imposing. The first and most difficult to combat was the style of moderation that permeated Greensboro's response to the demonstrations. In contrast to Birmingham, William Thomas noted, there were no fire hoses in

---

*Significantly, there were no women in the inner circle of movement strategists, although women comprised, in many people's views, the backbone of the demonstrations, always ready to march and picket and get arrested.

Greensboro. "Nobody was beaten, so we had to create confrontation." Police strategy was coordinated by Captain William Jackson, head of the detective division. A wily, shrewd, and brilliant tactician, Captain Jackson proceeded on the belief that outlasting the demonstrators through patience was better than creating martyrs through overreacting. "I didn't want no heads busted," he observed. "Didn't want to see nobody get hurt . . . it was always my belief to treat people like I wanted to be treated as long as they would let me. And when they wouldn't, then I would treat them the way they wanted to be treated." He soon established rapport with demonstration leaders, devising an intricate etiquette for negotiating where protests would occur, how many students would be involved, and what response might be expected from the police. "We never had any trouble," Captain Jackson noted. "Jesse would tell me what he was going to do and I'd say you can't do that . . . or you can do it this way. And we had an understanding." As a result, the demonstrations became, in one observer's words, "a kind of ballet," acquiring the "highly stylized qualities of a formal Japanese dance." For reasons of personal character and temperament, Stanley and Thomas shared Captain Jackson's preference for avoiding violence; yet the police department's tactics clearly made it more difficult for movement leaders to crystallize the conflict in a dramatic way.

The strategy of inviting arrest provided one effective means of countering police moderation. By having hundreds of students violate the law, demonstration leaders created a confrontation even as they avoided violence. The physical presence of hundreds of students in overcrowded facilities challenged the city's physical resources, while dramatizing the extent to which students were willing to sacrifice to achieve integration. In flooding the jails with demonstrators, Tony Stanley recalled, we were trying to "break the back of the whole damn thing."

But if sending students to jail represented an effective way of overcoming one obstacle, it brought to the forefront two additional problems. First, it compelled a response from the administrators in charge of A&T and Bennett College. Serving in loco parentis, Dr. Willa Player and Dr. Lewis Dowdy were under considerable pressure to discipline the students or, at the very least, remove them from jail and prevent their re-arrest. Second, the presence of so many students in jail increasingly placed the burden of carrying the protest on the nonstudent population. When William Thomas told a local reporter that forty thousand blacks were ready to go to jail, he was referring to the total Negro population of Greensboro. But how many adults were prepared to support the student protest actively if it meant putting their own bodies on the line?

The "generation gap" presented a particularly vexing dilemma. Many whites believed that the demonstrations reflected the actions of only a few "outside student agitators" and would dissipate as soon as school ended. The very nature of power relationships within a traditional Southern setting created situations where at least some older blacks seemed to confirm this view, especially given the distortions of the white racial prism. *The Candle,* a student-movement newspaper, acidly portrayed the dialogue that might be expected to occur between some white employers and their black help:

MR. CHARLES: Tom, stop dusting a minute and come here. I want to ask you something. Tom, I don't see why you people want to eat downtown.

TOM: Me neither, Mr. Charles, Sir.

MR. CHARLES: And all that walking and singing. It doesn't make any sense.

TOM: No, Sir.

MR. CHARLES: A really educated Negro like you doesn't want integration, does he?

TOM: No, Sir.

MR. CHARLES: You'd rather be with your people, wouldn't you?

TOM: Yes, Sir.

MR. CHARLES: Tom, I always enjoy talking to you because I like to find out how you people feel about things. Wait 'til I tell ole Dave how you people really would talk if those communists didn't get you all confused.

Despite the first sit-ins, and the years of protest that came before and after, many whites continued to believe that black people—and older blacks, in particular—were contented.

In addition, real differences existed between students and adult black leaders, especially over strategy and methods. "Older blacks," Tony Stanley noted, "[were] prone to believe things would be all right. . . . There was tension in terms of who called the plays." In the minds of younger activists, too many of the traditional leaders believed that the very act of sitting down with the white "power structure" solved the problem. For the students, however, the act of negotiation signified nothing without substantive concessions. "We were not going to permit the old guard to take over," Thomas remarked. "They didn't have any bodies out there." Students were particularly angry at some deferential local pastors who seemed more concerned about the wear and tear on their churches than about winning the struggle. Indeed, so great was the potential split that students threatened to picket one of the most prestigious black churches because its minister was reluctant to have students meet there.

In an effort to alleviate the conflict, black leaders representing both generations acted quickly to establish a coordinating council. Headed by Otis Hairston of the Greensboro Citizens Association, the council included Dr. George Simkins of the NAACP; Father Richard Hicks, representing Greensboro's Ministerial Forum; and either Thomas or Stanley, speaking for CORE. The council spoke with a united voice on behalf of the protests and sought to prevent whites from using a divide-and-conquer strategy. By its very existence, the council conferred adult legitimacy on the demonstrations, and it also provided a forum to coordinate a strategy for negotiations. Hairston and his colleagues refused to act without student acquiescence and worked carefully to avoid any appearance of internal disunity. Reinforcing the same sentiment, the Greensboro Men's Club wrote Mayor Schenck on May 15 that its membership, comprising most of the male black establishment, supported actively "all groups who are in the vanguard" seeking civil rights. Still, the larger issue of adult support of the young demonstrators remained pivotal, especially with more than seven hundred students filling the jails and a limited reservoir of additional student protesters to be drawn upon.

Each of these issues came to a head during a tension-packed period from Sunday, May 19, through Wednesday, May 22. As national CORE Director James Farmer flew into the city to address a mass rally on Sunday evening, hundreds of students from A&T and Bennett marched to the old polio hospital to express solidarity with the four hundred students crowded inside. Others marched downtown for the fifth day in a row to protest the absence of equal service to blacks at the cafeterias and theaters; this time their ranks included more than fifty adults, some old enough to be grandparents. Meanwhile, inadequate food, bedding, and toilet facilities heightened the dilemma of college administrators faced with responsibility for the large number of their students being held in jail. As would happen repeatedly over the next four days, questions of adult involvement, strained prison facilities, student determination, and the response of university administrators came together, creating a spiral of events that brought the movement to the first of its two moments of climax.

II

Demonstration leaders received some good news when Dr. Willa Player, president of Bennett College, arrived at the Central Carolina Convalescent Hospital the same night that more than two hundred of her students were imprisoned there. Many observers believed that Bennett women were carrying the movement, providing pickets, marchers, and canvassers even when others were not available. When Dr. Player arrived at the hospital, Tony Stanley recalled:

She was very upset, obviously upset . . . she passed [me] in the little lobby but she hardly spoke. I knew she was hot . . . she wasn't angry because these girls were protesting or that they were even in jail, but in those days with the president of a small college, nobody did anything unless they said "do it" . . . and [here] you have placed two hundred of [her] girls in jail. She went into the barracks, the girls looked at her almost like hungry birds, you know, what are you going to say about this? And when she came out she said, "Mr. Stanley, I want you to get every girl's name in there and I will send a wire to all their parents, telling them that they're here and they're safe and that I'm going to stick with them and they need not worry."

That night, Dr. Player telegraphed her decision to the parents and proceeded to mobilize her own staff in support of the movement. In Player's view, the students were not rebelling against the law, but rather were carrying out the message of dignity and concern for others that the college had striven to teach them. "I didn't tell them that they were supposed to join the protest," Player said. "I just said to them: you will be expected to practice what you've learned; and that was it. . . . That reduced any tensions that the students had with me as the chief administrator." Gathering her faculty together, Dr. Player urged them to become involved as well and to establish an organization for distributing mail and assignments to the jailed students. Each day teachers met to coordinate the lessons students would be asked to study. Dr. Player, meanwhile, lobbied for better conditions and told Captain Jackson that it was illegal to put the girls in an uninspected building. Although she was not herself jailed, it was clear where her sympathies lay. "I had to explain to [the students]," she noted, "that I had to stay out of jail in order to be sure . . . they were sufficiently understood."

Conditions in the jails, in turn, served as a primary rallying point for the adult community. Although students were not brutally treated in the hospital or on the prison farms, the crowding and shabbiness they experienced shocked the black community. John Corry, a Bennett College professor and minister of St. Matthews Methodist Church, told more than twelve hundred blacks assembled at a Sunday afternoon meeting that as many as seventy-five students had been required to share seven beds in a fifty-foot by fifty-foot room, that some students had no beds at all, and that almost one hundred and thirty boys had to share two toilets. Student leaders emphasized that girls were denied privacy and were forced to undress behind makeshift curtains. It is difficult to imagine a set of circumstances more likely to generate support from the older generation.

That night James Farmer galvanized the mass meeting, exhorting black adults to go to jail "if necessary" to complete the battle begun by the young people. "The segregationists have found out," he declared, "that when they start putting our children in jail, then they'll have to get us too." Using the lesson of the Birmingham police dogs as his text, Farmer declared that a "second revolutionary war" had begun. "Our kids need us," he proclaimed, "don't stop now. . . . If you want [integration] bad enough, you'll get out into the streets for it." By the time he finished several hundred blacks were ready to march through the downtown streets. This time the march was composed of adults singing freedom songs, and proceeding, wave after wave, into the central business area. After the group sang hymns for an hour, Jesse Jackson addressed the throng. "No doubt about it," he proclaimed, "we're not going to stop. We'll be there tomorrow and tomorrow and tomorrow."

By the next night it was clear that events were reaching crisis proportions. More than one thousand blacks gathered at Trinity A.M.E. Zion Church, standing and shouting their endorsement of a resolution prepared by the black ministers urging a boycott of white-owned businesses. Following the singing of "We Shall Overcome," hundreds of demonstrators once again besieged the downtown area, at least four hundred and twenty—the largest number since the demonstrations had begun—seeking arrest. By the end of the evening more than a thousand Negroes crowded the city's prison facilities, bursting the capacity of the old polio hospital, the prison farm, and the National Guard Armory. For the first time numerous juveniles were arrested. An air of desperation was building. Law enforcement authorities searched vainly for bedding and food for the prisoners. Demonstrators were everywhere, and commercial buses had to be seized by police to carry them away. The protest had reached a fever pitch. There was no more jail space, and police as well as demonstrators were fast losing their patience.

As a mark of how critical the situation had become, Governor San-ford intervened directly for the first time. Sanford kept in close touch with the local situation, several times alerting the National Guard to be ready to move. His goal throughout was "to keep order" and "protect the demonstrators and the public from each other." Now, that goal appeared to be endangered. "Legitimate demonstrations we have always approved," he told a news conference, "but to deliberately invite jail is carrying the demonstrations too far. It is not necessary." Yet even as the Governor spoke, demonstration leaders were planning new protests. That night reports arrived of growing tensions in Greensboro, including a march past the polio hospital by a white group known as "the Little Hoodlums" demanding a confrontation with the prisoners. An intelli-gence report noted the presence of a large, unidentified man thought to be an explosives expert with the Ku Klux Klan. Undercover agents believed that unless something were done within forty-eight hours the situation would explode.

Sanford responded by calling Lewis Dowdy, acting president at A&T, and asking the black administrator to seek a return of the jailed demon-strators to the custody of the college. "It occurred to me," Sanford later commented, "that if instead of putting these kids in jail [we] take them back to campus . . . we would have broken up the continuity [of the protests]. . . . This was just a good piece of strategy, even if [some] ran back up [and got arrested again.]" Through such a move, the crush on jail facilities would be alleviated and the college would become legally responsible for student behavior again, including the prevention of fur-ther violations of the law. In effect, the Governor, as head of the entire university system, had directed his lieutenant, the head of A&T, to defuse the crisis. Although no actual orders were given, Dowdy was placed in a situation where refusal to comply would be tantamount to insubordination.

Caught in the middle, Dowdy searched desperately for a course of action consistent with his own beliefs as well as the Governor's request. One of seventeen children, he had grown up in a family proud of its independence and achievements. Even in the Jim Crow world of South Carolina in the 1920's and 1930's, his parents had sent most of their children to college, had built a large farm, and, in the countryside of South Carolina, had fought for better schools, better roads, and a de-cent life. Dowdy inherited their resiliency and strength; as acting presi-dent, he had moved effectively to build the academic excellence of A&T. Now, he faced the greatest crisis of his tenure. "He was terribly distressed," Dr. Willa Player recalled. "I think he was under such great pressure that . . . the only thing that he could do [was comply]." The A&T leader called other black spokesmen in the early morning hours of Tuesday, May 21, seeking some way out of his dilemma. Finally, at 2:00 a.m., Dowdy went to the polio hospital to ask the students to go back to A&T with him. They refused.

By Tuesday morning, however, the Sanford strategy had already found other outlets. That day the first court hearing was held for those retained in jail. After the first twenty-five defendants were remanded into custody, the judge suddenly changed tactics and immediately released the next seventy-two defendants called. Meanwhile, another two hundred and fifty demonstrators were removed from the National Guard Armory to the A&T campus under the sheriff's orders. That night Dowdy returned to the polio hospital, where eight hundred demonstrators were still being held. Whatever Dowdy said, law enforcement officials made clear, students would be returned to campus. Dowdy spoke movingly to the demonstrators about their compatriots in Durham, pointing out that black students there were still attending classes even while protesting, and that a return to college did not mean an end to the struggle. Whether he was persuasive or not, in the early morning hours of May 22 more than seven hundred A&T students were transported to A&T in fifty police vehicles. A dozen had to be carried forcibly.*

---

*The entire episode revealed the tensions inherent in the crumbling of the caste system. In refusing to leave the jail that first night, the A&T students were manifesting their determination to no longer accept traditional modes of authority imposed from above. Lewis Dowdy, in turn, was caught in a riptide, torn between his own identification with the students and his responsibilities to the Governor. Sanford recognized the dilemma he had created for Dowdy. He himself felt split between a commitment to existing structures of authority and sympathy for black demands. "I know damn well [Dowdy] didn't do it with glee," Sanford recalled. "He took it about as well as anybody in the state, and I've admired him ever since. He didn't ever get in the position of being the Governor's pawn or the Governor's 'Uncle Tom.'" On other occasions, Sanford acted very much in support of black college officials caught in difficult circumstances. During demonstrations in Elizabeth City, Dr. Walter Ridley, head of the black state college there, was told that angry whites from the countryside were pouring into the city to confront student demonstrators. To forestall possible violence, Ridley called student leaders and told them to use official college vehicles to transport the protesters to and from the demonstration site. Later, a Sanford aide called Ridley and blasted him for using state cars in support of the demonstrations. Ridley responded that he was the head of the college, it was his responsibility to protect student lives, and if the Governor's aide thought he could do a better job, he was welcome to try. Shortly after midnight Ridley's phone rang. It was Sanford. "I've just heard the tapes of the phone conversations," the Governor said. "You did exactly what you should have done and you have my complete support."

The one act of collective resistance came from the Bennett College women, 115 of whom were also in custody at the hospital. When Dr. Player was informed of the proposed Sanford strategy, she immediately demurred, instructing Tony Stanley to find a lawyer who could tell her how to keep her students in jail. "I was not going to let a private school be dictated to by a governor," she later noted. Going to the hospital, she told the students that if they returned to the college, they would still be in jail because they had not been released from custody. The college would become a jail instead of the polio hospital. "I said, 'I'm not going to have Bennett a jail,' " she recalled, " 'so we'll just stick it out.' " The girls sang the alma mater and stayed until they were freed under court order.

Nevertheless, Sanford's action struck at one of the key levers of the movement's strategy. If civil rights leaders could no longer fill the jails, they would lose their primary means of exhausting police energies and compelling action from Greensboro's leaders. Thus, when Dowdy officially assumed responsibility for student actions and on May 22 declared that any student seeking arrest would be liable to expulsion, state and local leaders appeared to have scored a crippling blow against the demonstrators. Local white leaders saw the release of the prisoners as a key turning point that would force a truce. In effect, they hoped to break the back of the movement.

The black response, in turn, was to organize the largest protest march ever attempted in Greensboro's history. Throughout the preceding weeks, McNeill Smith, a prominent white attorney and civil rights sympathizer, had kept black leaders informed about white attitudes toward the demonstrations. Early on, Smith reported, whites believed the demonstrations to be solely the product of outside agitators. That message had prompted the Greensboro Men's Club's May 15 letter declaring solidarity with the students. A few days later, however, Smith called again. Whites still "had not got the message," he said. In response, Farmer emphasized the importance of black adult participation in his May 19 sermon. The next night hundreds of adults endorsed the economic boycott of white businesses and took part in the downtown march. Never before, newspaper reporters commented, had so many older people been involved in the demonstrations. Now—in the face of the students' removal to the campus—leaflets flooded black neighborhoods calling upon the entire community to mobilize Wednesday night for "the granddaddy of all marches." Black adults would prove once and for all how Greensboro's Negroes felt.

The evening of May 22 began with a mass meeting of more than fifteen hundred blacks at the Trinity A.M.E. Zion Church. The rally was held at "Big Zion" because it had more space than any other church, but that night there was not enough room; loudspeakers had to be set up to broadcast to the hundreds outside. The service began with the singing of "Oh, Freedom," a lilting spiritual that connected the age-old quest for liberation from slavery with the new movement for equality. Like a circle without a break, the song showed young and old alike how much they were joined in common struggle. Greensboro's black clergy then told the congregation that it was time to show the white community how Negro adults felt about the protest demonstrations. The eyes of the city would be upon them.

Slowly, the adults formed lines in preparation for the march. Two by two, walking down the sidewalk, their ranks stretched more than eight city blocks. Without a word, they moved to the heart of the city, speaking with their silence more powerfully than words could convey the depth of their conviction. Over two thousand participated—every black school principal, twenty-six black ministers, all black doctors, and nearly every teacher, as well as hundreds of workers and average citizens. "I remember going in there," Nell Coley recalled; "I didn't know that they were getting ready to march and I had on heels about yea tall; but I got out there and I tell you, it seemed that your feet had wings really." All the way downtown whites lined the streets to watch. They could not miss the meaning of the moment. "In an eloquent but silent way," Cecil Bishop recalled, "that somber march dispelled once and for all the idea that this was only a student movement."[3]

The two events—removal of the students from jail and the silent march—created the backdrop against which the first attempt at a negotiated settlement occurred. If the return of students to campus had been the only significant event of those days, the movement's momentum might have been crippled. But the response of the black adults—"starkly impressive," the newspapers called it—more than outweighed the temporary setbacks suffered by student demonstrators. Belatedly recognizing the new state of affairs, the Greensboro *Daily News* declared that many whites had missed the impact of "this quiet revolution. They have been blind to the intense suffering which acquiescence to stigmatized treatment in public places . . . produces in human beings." No longer was it possible to say that a Birmingham could not happen in Greensboro. The "widening gulf" between whites and blacks left little time for delay. Jesse Jackson had declared that the silent march was "our way of showing that we are willing to negotiate." Only if the city's best leadership asserted itself in response, the newspaper replied, could the situation be saved.

The paper's hopes rested on a new human relations committee appointed on May 22 by Mayor David Schenck to find a solution and end the demonstrations. The committee's formation itself reflected tense behind-the-scenes conflicts between black and white leaders.* Early on May 22, Schenck had told a press conference that the city already had a human relations committee and that negotiations could not be carried on as long as the "inflammatory" actions of protesters continued. But in an angry afternoon meeting, black leaders from the Coordinating Council persuaded Schenck that anything less than a new initiative would be disastrous. Early in the meeting Schenck threatened to cut off all water supplies from A&T and Bennett. Otis Hairston responded that, if he were to do so, there would be ten thousand blacks on the streets. "Is that a threat?" Schenck asked. "Only if cutting off the water supply was a threat," Hairston responded. After two hours, the Mayor agreed to break the deadlock with a new committee, hoping it would become a *quid pro quo* for a cessation of the demonstrations. Black leaders, in turn, saw the committee as a vehicle for negotiating substantive concessions. That night the committee held its first session and elected Dr. George Evans, a Negro physician and a member of the school board, as its chairman. †

From the very beginning, the Evans Committee was caught in the vortex of conflicting pressures, seeking some formula for meeting black

---

*On Sunday, May 19, after most of the students had been placed in the polio hospital, Lewis Dowdy proposed to the city's white political leaders that a negotiating group be named to supervise a cooling-off period during which the city would drop charges against students. Some adult blacks suggested that if assurances were given that a committee could be formed, the students could be persuaded to accept a moratorium on demonstrations. Meanwhile, McNeill Smith was working with the Greensboro Community Fellowship as well as members of the "white establishment" to find a possible compromise. Smith played perhaps the most interesting behind-the-scenes role of any white during the demonstrations. Either in meetings at his office or over drinks in his home, Smith brought together representatives of the opposing sides. On the basis of his consultations, Smith presented the Mayor with a two-page list of possibilities, including calling for a moratorium on demonstrations, introducing a public accommodations ordinance before the city council, and having the state prosecutor take a *nol pros* on all court cases. Smith also proposed an exchange of symbolic statements, with the Mayor promising to endorse desegregation and demonstration leaders promising to avoid arrests and to bargain in good faith.

†Schenck and Hairston both subsequently became members of the Board of Directors of the Chamber of Commerce and when they met would frequently joke about their exchange of "threats" at that afternoon meeting.

demands in the face of continuing ambivalence and even resistance
from Mayor Schenck and other white city leaders. If any people thought
the demonstrations would end just because of the committee's appointment, the next day proved them wrong. On Thursday, May 23, more
than twelve hundred blacks—almost all adults and teenagers—marched
downtown again. Although the demonstration was billed as another
silent march, fourteen protesters were arrested when they sought admission to downtown hotels where they had made reservations. Very few
A&T students participated, at least in part because of Dr. Dowdy's
earlier statement that students might be expelled for leaving campus; but
it quickly became clear that Dowdy would not stand in the way of the
protesters, nor be a symbol of division within the community. When
asked whether students who did participate would be expelled, he responded: "such matters are left to the dean of students and we may
study the matter tomorrow." Conversely, the students had no intention
of criticizing their president. In a statement entitled "President Dowdy's
Dilemma," student leaders praised Dowdy and attacked Governor Sanford for placing the college leader in an untenable position.*

As if to punctuate black determination to press on, the Coordinating
Council of protest organizations presented its own "action ideal" of
programs to be implemented if racial justice were to be achieved. Bold
and far-reaching, the "action ideal" encompassed the full range of concerns that had driven blacks to the streets. Beginning with the demand
that all charges against the demonstrators be dismissed, it urged the city
to enact a public accommodations ordinance, fully desegregate schools
and staff by September, promote at least three black police officers to
the rank of detective if their records permitted, hire blacks in various
city departments, and appoint at least one Negro to each city board.
The "action ideal" challenged the city in virtually every public policy
area, exhibiting in the process a shrewd insight into the need for joining
the concerns of students and adults.

Facing such pressure, the Evans Committee implored the city to
issue a formal resolution of support for equal public accommodations.
Such an official statement, Evans believed, would provide the minimal
foundation on which further negotiations could proceed. Hence, his
committee urged the Mayor to convene a special city council meeting
to consider the resolution supporting equal treatment, and simulta-

---

*"We have sympathy for Dr. Dowdy," Jesse Jackson said, proclaiming that no govern-
ment or pressure groups would stop the movement for desegregation. A&T alumni leaders
also issued statements of support for Dowdy and the students.

neously requested demonstration leaders to assure that future protests would be conducted in "an orderly manner" without inviting arrest.

The Mayor's response reflected again his own deeply divided feelings about the protests. Clearly offended that demonstrations were continuing, Schenck declared that the city council possessed no "legal authority to pass laws regarding segregation practices." When he had named the new committee, Schenck said, he had expected a curtailment of mass demonstrations. Instead, "the size of the demonstrations has actually increased. . . . This has created in our city an intolerable situation. We will brook no violence, and . . . we intend, with aid from the state if necessary, to maintain the peace of the community." Although Schenck's statement included an informal endorsement of equal treatment for all persons, there could be no mistaking its tone of rebuke. The task of the Evans Committee, he concluded, was to "secure a cessation of demonstrations" and to cooperate with the Chamber of Commerce and the Merchants Association in working for a settlement. That afternoon, nine members of CORE sat in at City Hall demanding an official city council resolution. They were arrested and carried to jail.

During the impasse that followed, each side sparred with the other, seeking to find a point of vulnerability or common agreement which might provide the basis for resolving the conflict. Having established the precedent of continued demonstrations, protest leaders announced a temporary truce on Saturday, May 24. At the same time, the Evans Committee attempted to negotiate the issues. On May 27 and 28 it convened meetings of restaurant operators in an effort to hasten individual decisions to desegregate through the pressure and protection offered by collective action. A subcommittee on theaters did the same. Perhaps the most positive news was a meeting convened in Washington by Attorney General Robert Kennedy to urge theater-chain owners throughout the South to desegregate. A report also circulated that Governor Sanford had personally called all theater-owners in Greensboro requesting that they integrate their facilities before June 1. Amidst such activity the moratorium continued, but not without a warning. "We're going to wait," Charles Anderson told a mass meeting at United Baptist Church, "but we're not going to wait another hundred years."

Black impatience centered on Mayor David Schenck. From the perspective of protest leaders, Schenck's record during the conflict was infuriatingly ambivalent. On the one hand, he appeared sympathetic to the underlying goals of the demonstrations; on the other, he persistently refused to take a strong public stand on the issues and more often than not condemned the demonstrators for disrupting the city's calm. Furthermore, he frequently left town on weekends even in the midst of the crisis. "He was not worth a damn," one protest leader charged. "He had no personal backbone." Another black leader, referring to Schenck's statement that the demonstrations were a "roadblock" to peace, declared that Schenck himself was "the roadblock and . . . should resign."

In fact, Schenck was manifesting both his own deep qualms about the movement and the divisions within the white community. An insurance broker whose roots in Greensboro went back to the late nineteenth century, Schenck believed wholeheartedly in the city's reputation for progress, stability, and reasonableness. From his point of view the demonstrators were assaulting the institutions and processes he valued most dearly. Although Schenck personally favored desegregation, he believed that the issue should be addressed voluntarily by individual citizens in an atmosphere of reason and calm, not made the focal point of forceful public action. Furthermore, as a businessman, he agreed with those who argued on behalf of the inviolability of property rights. Hence, Schenck rejected the notion that the conflict could be resolved through "a wave of the hand by the city government"; at the same time he lambasted the demonstrators for making impossible a settlement negotiated by consensus. In a statement that perhaps best represented his underlying convictions, Schenck declared, on June 3, that the protest had "caused a serious erosion of the mutual respect and friendship that has existed between the races in Greensboro. This, regardless of the outcome of the present controversy, will cause all of our citizens of all races to be the loser, and Greensboro's progressive spirit to be replaced by animosity and bitterness."[4]

If Schenck hoped to find agreement in the white community that would relieve the need for executive leadership, however, he found instead a division of opinion that only highlighted the need for decisive action from the top. Opposition to the demonstrations came from all segments of white Greensboro. Ku Klux Klan members appeared at each march, and teen-age adherents of the Klan philosophy carried signs saying "nigger go home." But federal and local officials had thoroughly infiltrated the Klan's leadership, and the threat from that sector was less than it might have appeared. More important was the opposition that came from "respectable" middle-class citizens who protested the violation of property rights and the efforts of the "liberal establishment" to compel racial change. In the eyes of many well-off whites, the civil rights movement was a communist plot seeking to subvert the country's freedoms. "The formula for instant integration," the attorney for S&W Cafeteria declared, "is three measures government, three measures mob violence, season with communism to taste, top with committee icing to disguise the recipe, and force-feed the public quickly before it realizes what it is consuming." Others protested the hypocrisy of white liberals who demanded integration for others but refused to desegregate their own companies. Eugene Hood, leader of the local White Citizens Council, noted that on the various human relations committees were bankers who employed no black tellers, executives who would not hire black secretaries, insurance representatives whose company eating facilities did not admit blacks, and members of the local country club that practiced racial exclusiveness.

In fact, a significant number of highly placed corporate officials vigorously opposed desegregation. "The rights of the owners of business establishments should be protected equally [with] the rights of Negroes," one prominent businessman wrote Mayor Schenck. Another defended "law-abiding businessmen" who exercised their privilege to serve whom they pleased. Perhaps the dominant sentiment was expressed by the vice president of a steel company in Greensboro. "The problem is somewhat real," he wrote to Governor Sanford, "and some adjustments should be made, but such adjustments should not even be considered in a climate of what amounts to coercion. . . . I hope you will tell this minority group to go home and stay home and behave like first-class citizens; and if this is done, I think maybe the climate will in time become such that adjustments which are in order . . . can be made sensibly and carried out peaceably." For many of Greensboro's most powerful whites, manners continued to have a higher priority than substance in the political process; but then, manners had been a primary means of keeping issues of race out of the political process, so that in the end manners and substance were inextricably connected. In any event, Dr. George Evans appears to have had some justification for his belief that "Mayor Schenck did not act as early as he might have . . . because of pressure from higher up."

White liberals, on the other hand, mobilized what pressure they could in support of rapid desegregation of public accommodations. In May the Greensboro Community Fellowship circulated a petition declaring that "there is only one solution to the present racial problem—the immediate removal of the color bar in all places and institutions to which the public has access." By the beginning of June, the fellowship

had secured more than thirteen hundred signatures and enough money
to publish the petition in the local papers. At its May meeting the
YWCA endorsed desegregation, and the Episcopal bishops of North
Carolina circulated a pastoral letter urging church members in Greensboro to support civil rights for all.

Yet even liberals did not unanimously support the movement. As
Louise Smith noted, "the second sit-ins were not as clean a thing as the
first ones were . . . they got messier." Manners again were important.
Whites were especially disturbed by reports that some black demonstrators had torn up pipes, toilets, bedding, and furniture in the various
jails; indeed, at one meeting of the Greensboro Community Fellowship, more time was devoted to discussing damages to the jails than to
considering progress toward desegregation. When the YWCA endorsed
integration, the resolution embodying its sentiments was a substitute for
a more forthright defense of the demonstrations themselves, including a
plea for amnesty. With the exception of the Greensboro Community
Fellowship, very few white leaders or institutions were willing to take a
public stand. In the face of protests that challenged fundamentally their
assumptions about Greensboro's progressive ways, even white liberals
would go only so far.

The continuing ambivalence of white leaders eventually undermined
the prospects of a solution being found during the moratorium on
demonstrations. When Mayor Schenck insisted that the parties to the
conflict work out their own solution without city intervention, he in
effect reinforced the argument for voluntarism put forth by those resisting integration. For a period of time during the week of May 27, it
appeared that progress was being made, especially on the issue of theater
desegregation. But in a shrewd move, Armistead W. Sapp, Jr., attorney
for several of the segregated businesses, prematurely disclosed word of a
settlement, thereby interrupting completion of the plan and causing
numerous public denials. At the same time, Boyd Morris, the owner of
the Mayfair Cafeteria and a popular former mayor, insisted that he
would not change his practices, no matter what others did.

With the danger of momentum being lost, protest leaders issued a
new ultimatum for action by Monday, June 3. While cities such as
Charlotte and Durham were acting to resolve disputes comparable to
those in Greensboro, CORE leader Tony Stanley declared, "elected
officials here have not spoken out and given this whole matter some
direction." The time had come, the CORE leader said, for "a little
spunk." The demonstrations had not been mounted to "destroy the

image of Greensboro. . . . [But at] the same time, we are not in a position to restore the image of the city. This should come from the highest elected official." With trenchant insight, movement strategists had recognized that the only way to force a resolution of the crisis was through tightening the vise on the one man who could speak for the entire city—Mayor David Schenck.

On Sunday, June 2, the final crisis of the 1963 demonstrations started to build. Disgusted because "nothing ever happened in those [negotiation] meetings . . . except doing what . . . middle-aged folk do . . . we talked," black activitsts called a mass meeting on Sunday afternoon and commenced a silent march. This time, the police were not notified in advance. Jesse Jackson, meanwhile, began to play an increasingly important role, at times independent of other movement strategists. "We are concerned with actions," he declared, "not words. We won't stop until we get what we want." Most participants in the march were adults and high school students. Reflecting the mood of the evening, the movement newspaper declared that the time for waiting had passed. "What positive proof has resulted to cause Negroes to believe that other citizens of Greensboro sincerely want to effect a morally sound settlement of racial tension?" the paper asked. "After years of patience, Job regained his children and property; but if he had been sitting outside the S&W, he might be waiting yet."[5]

Simultaneously with the new demonstrations, the Coordinating Council of activist organizations presented a revised agenda for action to the city council. Different from the May 22 version in that it no longer made amnesty for the demonstrators a pre-condition, the new proposals focused on public policy toward equal access to public accommodations. Shrewdly, the Coordinating Council seized upon the Greensboro Community Fellowship's petition demanding equal treatment. Since the GCF petition represented the views of many Greensboro whites, the Coordinating Council asserted, the city council should endorse equal treatment of all persons and support the immediate removal of the color bar in every business to which the public had access. The Coordinating Council also asked the city council to provide an example by eliminating racial barriers in any publicly owned facilities, and by making the city a model employer through hiring workers strictly according to merit. As illustrations, the Coordinating Council pointed to the need for qualified black representation on city boards, the creation of a permanent biracial commission, and the promotion of black police officers. In effect the Coordinating Council was asking the city council to accomplish by public pronouncement what it, had said it could not do by legal authority.

The June 3 city council meeting represented a microcosm of the political forces striving for control of Greensboro. Coolly and effectively presenting the black agenda, George Simkins of the NAACP urged immediate action, since the consequences of postponement might "be extremely grave." Almost instantly, some city councilmen interpreted Simkins's statement as an attempt at blackmail. Meanwhile, attorney Armistead Sapp brought a counterresolution demanding that demonstrators pay $38,000 for the damage done to the polio hospital. Faced with such explosive divisions, Mayor Schenck announced once again that the city council had no legislative authority to act and appointed a subcommittee to study further both of the resolutions.

By Tuesday, June 4, events in the streets had assumed a life of their own, moving inexorably toward a final confrontation. There was fear on all sides. Tony Stanley worried that he could no longer control the demonstrators because so many were not students and had not participated in the training workshops that had given such discipline to the earlier demonstrations. On the other side, police tempers were frayed, threatening to erupt in violence against the protesters. Throughout the state a brooding sense of crisis developed, and intelligence reports from Charlotte, Greensboro, and other cities poured into the Governor's office telling of multiple situations at a flashpoint. Early in the week the theaters in Greensboro had publicly announced their readiness to work out a plan for desegregation, but that victory merely heightened the determination of the protesters to force a response from the man who had become a symbol of the resistance—Mayor David Schenck.

Events leading to the final clash were triggered on Wednesday evening, June 5, when Jesse Jackson led seven hundred demonstrators downtown. For more than an hour and a half the protesters covered the sidewalks of the main business area; then they suddenly moved toward City Hall. Under Jackson's orders the protesters filled the streets in front of City Hall and lay down in the street. Addressing the crowd, Jackson once again invoked the image of Birmingham and declared that the next night the demonstrators would return and "take over the city of Greensboro." After ten minutes in the street the demonstrators moved out and marched back to the A&T area. By that time, however, Jackson's bold foray had already struck a spark. That night police swore out a warrant for Jackson's arrest on the charge of inciting to riot.

The decision to arrest Jesse Jackson created the direct confrontation that demonstration leaders had so long been seeking. Police asked Tony Stanley and Bill Thomas where they might find Jackson. Seeming to cooperate, Stanley and Thomas in fact staged the arrest scene for maximum media coverage and symbolic effect. With cameras rolling and newspaper reporters surrounding the Church of the Redeemer, Jesse Jackson was brought forward to meet Captain Jackson and be taken to jail. In the meantime, ten thousand leaflets had been produced, broadcasting the headline, "Your great leader has been arrested." As the movement's popular spokesman moved to prison, where he would write, in emulation of his hero, a "Letter from a Greensboro Jail," movement organizers orchestrated the finale that would force city leaders into a showdown.

That night more than one thousand blacks gathered at Providence Baptist Church. Local ministers recounted the events of the day, accusing city officials of trying to intimidate blacks through the unjustified arrest of Jackson. The mood was tense, the situation fraught with danger, particularly if events got out of control and the confrontation led to armed retaliation by police. After singing the freedom songs that were the anchor of every meeting, there came the pointed message from Stanley and other demonstration leaders. In the past, Stanley told the congregation, he and others had counseled moderation in the protests. Now they were prepared to go to jail. "If something is not done by 1 p.m. tomorrow (Friday, June 7), we're going to jail and just sit back and let you radicals take over." Whatever momentary conflicts had existed with Jackson, movement leaders were now united in throwing down the gauntlet. Singing, dancing, and chanting, the demonstrators left the church and marched downtown. More than fifty state troopers were on hand in response to an urgent request made to the Governor by Greensboro's Chief of Police. Breaking into multiple groups, the demonstrators swarmed into Jefferson Square, the central business area of downtown Greensboro, and sat in the streets. "You are blocking traffic," the police said. "We're going to arrest you." Chanting in cadence, "we want to go to jail," the demonstrators remained, and police loaded nearly three hundred of them into buses. "I've never seen anything to beat this one," a veteran police officer said. The chaotic scene appeared, at least to one reporter, to be "explosive and dangerous." An hour later, the last demonstrators left the Square singing "freedom . . . freedom." If the meaning of the evening was not clear, a telegram the next day defined it in unmistakable terms. "We will continue our actions," CORE said, "until the walls come tumbling down."

Hundreds of protesters sit down in the street at Jefferson Square, the heart of Greensboro's central business district, as demonstrations against segregated public accommodations reach a climax. The individual in the foreground is John Marshall Stevenson, professor at A&T. Courtesy, Greensboro *Record*

No longer could Mayor Schenck avoid a decision. The news wires on June 6 carried two stories that defined his options. The first told of a race riot in Lexington, only forty miles away, where one white man was killed and another wounded when a crowd of two thousand whites threatened to invade the black community from which sit-ins had been initiated. The other told of breakthroughs in Raleigh and Winston-Salem toward desegregation in public accommodations. In those cities, as in Charlotte and Durham earlier, stong intervention by city political and economic leaders had brought peaceful acceptance of change. In effect, the demonstrators had placed Schenck in the position where he had either to opt for massive repression, including the possibility of martial law, or the kind of public intervention on behalf of desegregation that he had for so long abjured.

Schenck responded by convening an emergency meeting of twenty-three community leaders on Friday morning. Every prominent banker and influential corporate executive was invited. During almost the entire crisis, none of these men had been recruited to help. Nor had they volunteered. As the Greensboro *Daily News* noted, there had been "failures at the top of the heap in the white community," and the time had come for Greensboro's top executives to "assist the political leadership in meeting issues which [can] no longer be evaded." Although some of the most powerful executives (including Ceasar Cone of Cone Mills, N. P. Hayes of Carolina Steel, and Howard Holderness of Jefferson Standard Life) did not attend, the meeting provided legitimacy for the "prompt and decisive action" that Schenck said must be taken by people of influence to bring about a settlement.

What would Schenck do? The world he lived in, had grown up in, was being challenged. With all his heart he wanted to reject the pressures being mounted against his city by the demonstrators. The first draft of his June 7 statement gave voice to these instincts. The Mayor harshly criticized the demonstrators and asserted—erroneously—that progress had occurred only in those cities where no mass protest had taken place. In a tone that bordered on petulance, he argued that blacks had been named to a biracial committee, supposedly in exchange for a curtailment of demonstrations, and that the possibility of real progress during the moratorium had been sabotaged by precipitous resumption of protests. Defensive and angry, Schenck's statement, if released, would almost certainly have infuriated blacks and triggered the bloodletting that both sides feared to be imminent.

But instead, Schenck swallowed his instincts and declared forcefully that the city had no choice but to support desegregation of public accommodations. In effect, the Mayor had no choice. The progressive image Greensboro cherished so much would be shattered by resort to martial law; ironically, the only way to preserve the progressive mystique was through capitulating—for the moment, at least—to those forces that sought to burst free of its constraints. Moreover, business and political leaders in the state were pressing for compromise. "We were all over that situation," Sanford noted, "encouraging Schenck and trying to give him the necessary backbone." Black waiters at the country club reported the same concern: leaders from Cone, Burlington, Jefferson Standard, and the other economic giants in Greensboro were finally getting together and discussing ways of salvaging the city's good name. In response to all these forces the Mayor acted.

Schenck opened with traditional language, reciting proudly Greensboro's accomplishments in the area of race, pointing to desegregation of the golf course, the library, and playgrounds. He also called upon the demonstrators, in an act of good faith, to cease their protests. But the

Captain William Jackson and other police arrest hundreds of milling demonstrators after the Jefferson Square sit-down protest. Courtesy, Greensboro *Record*

heart of his statement was an unmistakable affirmation of human rights over property rights. To those who defended their right to serve whom they pleased, Greensboro's chief executive asked, "how far must your city government and fellow businessmen go to protect that [property right?]. . . Must the city be brought to a point of serious explosion; must extra policemen, sheriffs, highway patrol, and even the National Guard be kept on alert to enforce your private business decision?" The answer, said Mayor Schenck, was no. "Now is the time to throw aside the shackles of past custom. Selection of customers purely by race is outdated, morally unjust, and not in keeping with either democratic or Christian philosophy." For the first time, Schenck publicly questioned the right of businesses to threaten the public good through private decisions. In his official capacity as Mayor, he called on all places of public accommodations to "immediately cease selection of customers purely on the basis of race." As if to underline the historic importance of his statement, Schenck adopted an almost Lincolnesque cadence: "This city cannot long endure the impasse of inaction, nor can it expect to progress half climbing to the future, and half shackled by outdated prejudices of the past." Finally, he returned to home base—the reputation of the city he so deeply cherished. "When our image in the nation is damaged, for whatever reason," he concluded, "our citizens of all races suffer. Let us now move to restore to Greensboro the progressive spirit which is rightly ours."*

Although the crisis was not over, a decisive victory clearly had been won. For the first time the black community had succeeded in forcing the city's political leaders into forthright endorsement of desegregation. The Mayor gave businesses one week to respond to his request for desegregation. Guardedly, but with renewed high hopes, protest leaders agreed to suspend demonstrations. "I pledge my support to restore the image of our city in the eyes of the nation and the world," Tony Stanley announced to a cheering mass meeting. Echoing the same theme, Jesse Jackson, just released from jail, announced that "if Greensboro wants another Birmingham, that's what Greensboro gets," but in the meantime, he urged the audience to give "the new Schenck" a chance to do "what he should have done a long time ago." The day's meaning was best summarized by Isaiah Reynolds, a national CORE field representative. Recalling the downtown demonstrations the evening before, he said: "We opened their eyes and ears last night." Dramatically, vividly, through persistence and massive struggle, the issue had been drawn. Now would come the much more difficult task of solidifying the victory and defining its meaning.

III

As events turned out, black protest leaders were correct in focusing on Mayor Schenck. Although the Mayor wielded little power in his own right, his support for the movement's objectives caused a number of business leaders finally to speak out. In effect, compliance with Schenck's request had become the most conservative policy business leaders could follow if they wished to avoid further instability. By June 13 eight additional restaurants had decided to desegregate, making 25 per cent of the city's total restaurant capacity open to blacks. Three additional motels pledged to cooperate, as did four indoor theaters.

From a movement perspective, the most impressive aspect of Schenck's new statement on June 13 was his endorsement of an activist stance toward civil rights. In language nearly identical to that used by the

---

*Many people subsequently claimed authorship of Schenck's speech. "We just about wrote it," Sanford later said. Others suggested that Greensboro's business elite had controlled the content. While there may be an element of truth in these assertions, the handwritten drafts of the speech and earlier notes indicate that the themes, as well as the words, were Schenck's.

Coordinating Council in its June 3 proposals, Schenck declared that "government has the responsibility not only to lead but to reflect the best examples set by others." With that starting point, Schenck declared that race would no longer be a criterion in hiring or promoting city workers, pledged to appoint black representatives to all city boards, and espoused development of a city "merit employment" program. He also promised creation of a permanent human relations commission as soon as possible. Although black leaders criticized the absence of greater progress in desegregating hotels and restaurants, the tone and content of Schenck's statement warranted continuing the moratorium on demonstrations.

Over the next few weeks and months, white leaders boasted of continued progress in race relations. On June 18, the S&W Cafeteria quietly opened its doors to blacks. Two weeks later the city council created a permanent commission on human relations which included prominent black activists such as Otis Hairston and Dr. George Simkins. By the end of summer, the city's four bowling alleys had desegregated, two black policemen were promoted to the rank of detective, and a black employee in the tax office was raised to the position of assistant cashier. In addition, a black family for the first time moved into an all-white public housing project. By the summer of 1964, the Human Relations Commission claimed that 60 per cent of nonagricultural jobs were available on a nondiscriminatory basis as against 20 per cent the summer before. Finally, Greensboro officials pointed to the more than two hundred blacks who were attending schools with whites in 1963. There had been only nineteen a year earlier.

But if such statistics offered a basis for optimism, there was reason for skepticism as well. Almost all the children in desegregated schools were there because of the dedicated efforts of the biracial school coalition, and the sacrifice of black parents willing to risk reprisals in order to send their children to integrated schools. The school board gave *no* support to desegregation during this period. Although the board boasted of "staff integration," it turned out under questioning that the phrase referred to the use of the same building for city-wide teacher meetings. When a Committee for Improved Attendance in the schools was created in August of 1963 it included no blacks, and it held its first meeting in a segregated restaurant. Only after the YWCA protested did the committee broaden its membership and change its meeting place.

In addition, Greensboro's rate of progress lagged considerably behind the pace set by other cities. By the fall of 1963 Charlotte officials had achieved complete integration of all hospitals, hotels, and restaurants, as well as of Chamber of Commerce membership. Durham reported that 95 per cent of its restaurants were completely open, as well as 100 per cent of its motels. In Greensboro, by contrast, less than 40 per cent of the restaurants and motels were desegregated; hospitals still discriminated against black patients and doctors; and the Chamber of Commerce remained "lily-white." It was only after the passage of the 1964 Civil Rights Act that Greensboro reached the same degree of integration that other North Carolina cities already had achieved.

The issue of jobs proved particularly troublesome. Although the Human Relations Commission declared that 60 per cent of nonagricultural positions were now open to blacks, the change was more in theory than in practice. Again, Durham served as a counterpoint to Greensboro. Black leaders pointed to the significant number of Negroes in retail sales positions in downtown businesses there. "You can walk in any midtown store [in Durham]," William Thomas noted, "and see plenty of Negro salespeople to wait on you. They are not hidden in the basement." In Greensboro, on the other hand, only three or four downtown stores had begun to train blacks for retail positions. Although white leaders complained about the lack of black applicants, CORE spokesmen pointed out that in light of past discrimination white employers must take the initiative in establishing their credibility and sincerity.

In fact, Greensboro's economic and political leaders displayed less than 100 per cent devotion to the goals of desegregation. In Durham and Charlotte, business executives had applied pressure on their peers to fulfill the agreements made during demonstrations. In Greensboro, on the other hand, the white elite withdrew to its former position of silence once the immediate crisis had passed. Most white leaders viewed blacks as the source of the problem and hence ignored their own responsibility to find solutions. The city council reflected this attitude in its official response to the demands for change submitted by Negro leaders on June 3. Although a city council committee supported naming blacks to city agencies, it blamed Negroes for straining the good race relations in the city. The council's underlying assumption about where responsibility for the crisis lay was obvious: "Negro leaders and Negro citizens of our city are hereby challenged . . . to show faith in the Greensboro City Council by agreeing to work through a permanent biracial commission . . . for the solution to peaceful relations in our fine city."

It soon became clear that city leaders were concerned primarily with preventing further demonstrations. Just two weeks after his strong, if belated, affirmation of racial justice, Schenck wrote Governor Sanford: "We desperately need to use this period of relative calm to devise means to prevent the recurrence of mass demonstrations." Two months later, Schenck invited Sanford to attend a meeting with A&T officials to accomplish "some effective disciplinary control of this mass of college students." Sanford declined, writing his aide Capus Waynick that "Such action could be justified only in a riot situation which occurred one day in the spring. . . . We can not substitute force of this kind in place of creative leadership in solving the problem." Yet the correspondence revealed how obsessed city leaders had become with avoiding protest. The mere mention of sit-ins could evoke hysteria. Although the fear of demonstrations could on occasion be used by protesters to bring about concessions, ultimately the singular focus on preventing protest worked to the detriment of substantive racial progress. First, it directed the energies of political leaders to problems of social control rather than social change, and, second, it led to an emphasis on doing only the minimum necessary to prevent demonstrations, rather than the maximum necessary to achieve racial justice.

The ultimate irony, of course, was that Sanford's formula for "creative leadership" necessarily depended upon the voluntary cooperation of local leaders for its effectiveness. The Governor's policies could only work if in every town and hamlet there were people committed to bringing about major change. Yet the events of the 1960's showed that even where such individuals were present, they lacked power. Thus, although Sanford's leadership proved more enlightened and more imaginative than that of any other Southern governor, his strategy for change foundered on its own premise of voluntarism. Good Neighbor Councils had the power to suggest; they lacked the power to implement.

In the end, therefore, the story of Greensboro and North Carolina between 1961 and 1963 highlighted how profound and interlocking were the obstacles to racial change. The progressive young Governor spoke boldly of erasing prejudice, and reassuringly of his "faith in the intrinsic goodness of the children of God." But even as Sanford sanctioned black demands and raised black hopes, he proved unable to alter the underlying structure and substance of race relations. It would be a mistake to underestimate his contribution, particularly given the importance of "psychological space" to the emergence of a protest movement. Even so, on issues of substance the record was less impressive. Significantly, the program of "merit employment" in state government produced only slight change. Although the program coordinator sent the

names of 225 blacks to the state personnel office for jobs not traditionally held by blacks, only seventeen placements were made.

The story of white Greensboro, in turn, suggests how reluctant local
leaders were to initiate voluntarily the kind of changes Sanford requested. If consensus were necessary for racial justice to occur, there
was little likelihood of change ever taking place. School officials repeatedly refused to support those seeking desegregation, instead devoting
most of their energies to circumventing the law. Employers engaged in
the same pattern of delay and intransigence. Throughout the early
1960's, the most powerful economic figures in the community opposed
any substantive change, either in their businesses or in their private
associations.

Thus, blacks found again that they had no alternative but to take to
the streets. The process of petition and patient verbal protest had proved
fruitless. Led by students who refused to accept the constraints prevailing among the older generation, civil rights demonstrators provoked
arrests and insisted on a confrontation. Stunned, white leaders found
that the "responsible Negroes" whom they had created—and manipulated—no longer had control. As William Thomas, leader of CORE,
told one reporter: "[City leaders] are going to have to talk with me—not
the so-called prominent people. CORE is representing the grass-roots
people." Through brilliant organization and consummate tactical skill,
student protesters forced the city's hand and seemed once and for all to
have communicated the message that blacks would no longer accept
second-class treatment. "Anyone who hasn't received this message,"
Governor Sanford declared, "doesn't understand human nature."

Yet the ultimate lesson of Greensboro in the early 1960's was that the
message, even if heard, was not acted upon. Over and over again, those
who held power refused to make racial equality more than a temporary
verbal commitment. Whether intentionally, or simply through acting
on inherited assumptions, most white leaders substituted promises for
performance. At a moment of crisis, in order to forestall disaster to the
city's progressive mystique, Greensboro's corporate leaders might temporarily endorse concessions to the protestors. But once the crisis had
passed, the old ways returned. With the good name of the city re-
deemed, concern with manners, reasonableness, and civility could once
again prevail. Only direct-action demonstrations, it seemed, could
move people with power from their complacency. In the words of
William Thomas, "the Negro won't ever get any more than he pushes
and presses for."

But if such a conclusion seems incontrovertible in light of the evidence, it also boded ill for the future. No group of people, no matter how dedicated, could reasonably be expected to sustain the energy or the hope to wage endlessly a war of non-violent direct action. As Tony Stanley was later to recall, "we knew full well in the summer of 1963 that we were revolutionaries without a cause that we could handle so well; . . . we were physically exhausted. We could go anywhere in Greensboro that we wanted to go, but we were already raising the question, 'what the hell, if people can't afford food on their table at home, it matters not that they can eat at the fancy little restaurants in Greensboro.' " Yet those were the concessions that the movement had been able to extract. In effect, the failure of white leaders to initiate more substantive programs toward racial equality carried a dual message: not only would renewed direct-action protest be necessary for further change; the next time such protests would be fueled by the anger that came from knowing how little past rhetoric had accomplished. What would happen when there no longer existed the dramatic objective of gaining entry to the S&W Cafeteria? Where would movement energies go when symbolic enemies and victories were no longer available?

If one looked back at Greensboro and North Carolina in the early 1960's from a white perspective, it would not be difficult to perceive a rosy picture. The state boasted a creative and sensitive Governor who was praised by NAACP President Roy Wilkins at the March on Washington as a model of executive leadership in the area of civil rights. Greensboro, in turn, was led by a Mayor whom President Kennedy singled out for his moral leadership in urging business leaders to "throw aside the shackles of past customs." Yet by the standards of historical accuracy, both judgments would miss the point. The surge for racial justice in North Carolina came not from the City Hall in Greensboro nor from the State Capitol in Raleigh; it emerged from a thousand streets in a hundred towns where black people, young and old, acted to realize their vision of justice long deferred. Furthermore, despite their sacrifice, most of the underlying problems remained, largely because those in power felt no compulsion to alter established patterns once token concessions had been made. Only when such causal relationships are understood will it be possible to appreciate the real history of these years, and the achievements—as well as the limitations—of the Negro freedom movement.

PART II
Years of Polarization

CHAPTER SIX
"WE WILL STAND PAT"

As a metaphor, the color line is not . . . represented by a single, sharply drawn line, but appears rather as a series of ramparts like the "Maginot Line" extending from outer breastworks to inner bastions. Outer portions of it may be given up only to hold fast to inner citadels.

> Herbert Blumer, "The Future of the Color Line," in John McKinney and Edgar Thompson (eds.), The South in Continuity and Change

With the demonstrations of 1963, Greensboro's blacks had carried direct-action protest to a new peak of effectiveness. Over the preceding twenty years different strategies had been developed to cope with white modes of control. Beginning with tha patron/client relationship of Tarpley and Bluford during the 1930's, blacks had moved toward a more direct assertion of their demands in the political elections and school board campaigns of the 1950's. The sit-in movement had addressed the shortcomings of all these strategies through its genteel but forceful rejection of the existing structure of interaction between the races. Now the 1963 protests raised this form of collective self-expression to a new level of confrontation. Never before had the progressive mystique of Greensboro been challenged so frontally. Through besieging restaurants and theaters that excluded blacks, Negro demonstrators both exposed the hypocrisy of Greensboro's claim to be racially enlightened and threatened to destroy the fabric of civility so central to the city's self-image.[1]

Yet the very success of direct-action protest revealed its limitations as an ongoing strategy. Once the demonstrations ended, control over negotiations reverted to those who exercised power in the first place. They set the rules; they determined the framework for discussion. Nowhere was this power of definition more clearly revealed than in a letter from W. O. Conrad, the Western Electric executive who was the chairman of Greensboro's new Human Relations Commission, to William Thomas of CORE. In order to solve the problem of jobs, Conrad wrote, Greensboro must attract new industries. Yet,

because of the world-wide press coverage of the strife and riots
throughout the nation, the Negro has developed an image among
many people that looks like this—he can't be trusted—he is the
benchmark of strife, riots, and civil disobedience—he doesn't
display a responsible attitude—he is uneducated—he is lazy.

Although Conrad disassociated himself from such views, he insisted that
blacks must change the image by foreswearing demonstrations, cooperating with city leaders, and establishing self-improvement programs.
Once before, Conrad noted, blacks had brought their plight to the
attention of the nation. During Reconstruction some positive changes
had occurred, but then, "by continuous pressure and outbreaks, the
nation became tired and disgusted and the Negro took a long step
backward." Now, Conrad concluded, just as in the nineteenth century,
"the challenge is up to you. . . . [The Negro must show] that he is a
responsible element." If friends adopted such an attitude, what could
one expect from enemies?

As Conrad's letter suggests, the crisis of 1963 had meant very different
things to black people and white people. For most Negroes, victory in
the struggle signified a new beginning, the opportunity to build on the
momentum already established to attack other manifestations of racism.
To most whites, however, the 1963 demonstrations were a trauma,
never to be forgotten, certainly never to be tolerated again. Under
intense pressure, white leaders of Greensboro had capitulated on the
issue of public accommodations. But that was the final straw. They had
gone as far as they would go. The time had come to stop all demonstrations. "No more," they seemed to say. As Conrad wrote, it was now
time for the Negro "to take a responsible position."[2]

After the euphoria of victory faded, black leaders began to realize the
dimensions of the problems still remaining. It took time and organization to build a movement; only once in a generation, perhaps, could a
people sustain the sacrifice and psychic turmoil of constant demonstrations. Mass protests could not be revived overnight, especially given the
evidence of some progress in desegregating restaurants and motels.
Without a dramatic, vivid, and overriding goal such as voting rights,
black protest leaders found it almost impossible to mobilize recruits for
direct-action protests. Never again would black activists in Greensboro
be able to achieve the mass outpouring of community support manifested in the 1963 demonstrations.

Even more important, the issues had changed, compounding the
problem of finding an effective strategy. Desegregating restaurants and

motels represented a monumental achievement, but the larger dilemmas of structural and institutional racism remained. With the passage of time, it became more and more clear how deep, perverse, and intractable these problems were. How could one demonstrate about the absence of decent apartments in black Greensboro? Where did one protest the refusal of a bank to make a loan for a new house? How could civil rights leaders sit-in over the city council's lethargy in responding to a Human Relations Commission report? These were not dramatic issues with a symbolic point of conflict. They reflected the nuances of built-in racism rather than the glaring inequities of overt discrimination. Yet they were the issues that became more and more oppressive at precisely the time mass demonstrations became outmoded.

The years after 1963 thus became a new time of testing, a period of discovery. The issues were different, the struggles more subtle. How would Greensboro's white elite respond to the continuing insistence of blacks on eliminating racism in housing, education, and politics? How would blacks, in turn, deal with the new challenges posed by the complexities of institutional racism when demonstrations were no longer available to punctuate their demands? And what would happen to the progressive mystique in an era in which massive sit-ins no longer posed a mortal threat to civility, consensus, and paternalism?

I

The issue of schools continued to provide an accurate barometer of the attitudes of Greensboro's white elite toward many of these issues. Much more than the city council, the school board was dominated by individuals from the largest corporations and law firms in the community. Its decisions, in turn, affected schools that over the years had come to symbolize class and status differences in the community. In addition to the question of how many blacks and whites went to school together, school desegregation was connected with problems of housing, political power, and the assessment of worth attached to white and black institutions. Thus, although in many respects it was a separate issue in its own right, the question of school desegregation led to, and became intertwined with, every other manifestation of racism in Greensboro.

Initially, advocates of school desegregation had hoped that victories on the public accommodation issue would have a positive impact on school board policy. Largely through their own efforts, members of the education committee of the Greensboro Community Fellowship (GCF) had recruited the parents of more than one hundred black children to apply for enrollment in previously all-white schools during the school year 1963–64. The school board claimed, as evidence of its compliance with desegregation, that all first-graders were free to choose their own schools; now, in September of 1963, some 239 blacks registered in desegregated school settings. Supporters of the GCF school program established a special summer kindergarten to prepare the first-graders for their new schools, and organized a tutorial program to assist those who experienced difficulty. In addition, school desegregation advocates hoped for a more cooperative attitude from school board authorities in light of Title VI of the 1964 Civil Rights Act, which required each school district to submit a plan for desegregation.

As in the past, however, the Greensboro school board resisted, adopting the most minimal steps toward desegregation, and then only under pressure. Although supporters of integration invoked federal-court decisions requiring neighborhood schools (a concept which at that time would have entailed significantly more desegregation than was occurring in Greensboro), school authorities argued that the cases did not apply to Greensboro. Only under federal compulsion did the school board make freedom of choice available for all grades, and then just for the first ten days of the school year in September 1965. Charles Davis, an American Friends Service Committee staff member, agreed in early 1965 to serve as a liaison between the black and white PTA's, doing so with the understanding that the two groups would eventually merge and work toward student and teacher desegregation. But he quickly discovered that the two bodies were far apart, with the white PTA believing that any discussion of "mixed" schools would be too controversial. Over-all, little progress occurred. While 1200 students requested transfer to desegregated schools in near-by Forsythe County, only 120 students did so during the ten-day period provided in Greensboro, and the number of blacks attending desegregated schools in Greensboro during 1965 fell appreciably below the totals in comparable cities such as Charlotte, Durham, and Winston-Salem.

Over the following three years, the lines on school desegregation only hardened. Although by 1967 more than one thousand blacks attended integrated schools under HEW pressure, the number still fell significantly below that in other cities. Furthermore, the school board offered no incentive for change. When white children lived close to a black school, the board of education provided buses so that the children could attend a predominantly white school. When black children wished to attend a predominantly white school, however, the board offered no transportation unless 50 per cent of the children in the black neighborhood wished to transfer. Thus, freedom of choice was more a myth than a reality. Blacks wishing to attend white high schools—the only places where Latin and advanced calculus were offered—had to provide their own transportation, rising early in the morning to make their journey. The school board refused even to provide passes for riding on city buses.

When pressed to defend this policy, school board officials argued that segregation was a housing problem, not an educational one. More than 90 per cent of the black residents of Greensboro lived in the southeast quadrant of the city, they pointed out. Hence, residential living patterns were the primary source of racially separate schools, with education officials having little if any ability to change the situation. On its face, the argument seemed to have merit; on closer examination, however, it lost credibility, especially when seen in the context of public policy. From 1914 to 1929 there had been a city ordinance prohibiting blacks from living on streets containing a majority of white households. Ever since, an informal pattern of segregation had continued. Although the law no longer required geographical separation of the races, both school and housing segregation represented a system of racial duality more than tacitly supported by leaders of the white community.

Housing, in fact, represented the most striking example of a racial double standard in Greensboro. Although blacks comprised 26 per cent of the population, they lived in an area covering only 14 per cent of the city's physical space. Bordered by an interstate highway on the south, stateowned land on the east, an industrial zone on the north, and the downtown area on the west, the black section of town literally had no room to expand. In 1966, there were 1437 new family units constructed in Greensboro—seventy-seven in Negro areas. Because of racial segregation, Negroes from all economic classes lived in the southeast quadrant, albeit in distinct neighborhoods. The black area contained far more than its share of substandard and deteriorating housing. The three poorest census districts in Greensboro were in the black community and 5000 families in the city—most of them black—lived in substandard housing or outright slums by 1969. More than 1000 of these units were in such bad condition that they could not be repaired economically. "Horton's row" illustrated the infamous conditions that existed in such neighborhoods. Presided over by an absentee landlord who collected rents with a pistol on his hip, the dilapidated shacks stood side by side, unmaintained, with broken glass all around, and abandoned refrigerators in the backyards. In the eyes of at least one white liberal, such houses were "terrible symbols of what was wrong with Greensboro—kids playing in the glass with the rats and snakes and the condoms."

The housing situation highlighted at least two problems. The first involved the poor conditions that were allowed to persist within the ghetto itself. Streets in the southeast were less likely to get paved than those in the northwest. Only one through-street traversed the black area of town—itself a fact, the Greensboro *Daily News* noted, that "may tell us more than we care to recall about the historic attitudes at issue." Yet in 1967 that single street was allowed to become a detour for interstate traffic, a development hardly likely to happen in richer, white sections of town. In black Greensboro a sanitary landfill and sewage-disposal plant sat in the midst of a residential area, while a polluted creek flowed through the neighborhood. Although few people argued that such circumstances represented a calculated conspiracy by white racists, the more subtle and basic point was that similar conditions would never have been tolerated in areas populated by middle-class whites.

The second problem was the inability to move out. Newspaper ads carried the designations "For colored" and "For white." Nearly all banks refused loans to black applicants who sought housing in white areas. In fact, such housing rarely could be found. There were no black realtors, and only one or two white realtors would consider renting property to blacks in or near white areas. One 1967 survey showed that rental housing units became available at the rate of eight a day for whites and two a day for blacks, with one of the two likely to be substandard. In 1965 and 1966 a few black families moved into Woodmere Park, a middle-class development of $13,000 to $15,000 homes. Yet almost as soon as the first Negroes appeared, a block-busting realtor swept in, exploiting the situation and seeking to push whites out. Despite concerted efforts by the Greensboro Community Fellowship, the Human Relations Commission, and a local church, it became impossible to maintain a racial balance in the area. By 1969 the Woodmere Park area had become 80 per cent black, with the city council permitting a zoning change to allow commercial and multifamily construction—another example, from a black point of view, of official complicity in destroying black efforts to build decent single-family residential neighborhoods. *

*The zoning change had the impact of turning a suburban area of small houses into a neighborhood with business and apartment houses. Not only would such a change materially alter the environment, it also would lower property values. It would be unheard of for such a shift in policy to occur in a white middle-class area.

In 1967 the tension over housing burst into public view. A young black family seeking larger quarters found a small house to rent not far from where the man in the family had grown up. They told the landlady that they were black; since she wanted "to do right," she invited them to sign the lease. The next day a For Sale sign went up next door and vicious phone calls began. One week after moving in, the new renter returned from work to find a life-size dummy hanging by the neck on a tree in the front yard. A sign attached to the dummy read: "This is what happens to niggers." The next week the young man's mother received word from a white woman that her husband—a Ku Klux Klansman—was going to "kill this nigger to teach a lesson to all others." The landlady finally asked the young couple and their small child to move. Reluctantly, they did so.

Four months later, the scene repeated itself, this time at a parsonage purchased by members of the Mt. Zion Baptist Church for their minister, Frank Williams. A charismatic evangelist, Williams had been a subject of controversy for refusing to disclose to a court hearing information about a labor walkout against Boren Clay Products Company in which some of his parishioners were involved. After serving a jail term for contempt of court, Williams moved into his new $22,000 home in a white neighborhood. Immediately, harassment began. Rowdies fired guns near the house, shone bright lights through the front windows, and shouted obscenities from passing cars. On July 8 bricks and bottles were hurled through the garage window, and eight of Williams's parishioners moved in to protect the house. One neighbor told a reporter, "They'll move, [and] if they don't move I've got a gun that will move them." Another yelled at the newcomers, "Go back to Coontown." Although sheriffs' deputies doubled their patrols, police would not station anyone on the premises.

By the next week the state-wide Good Neighbor Council had become involved in the situation. Bringing together local authorities, it sought to guarantee Williams's safety and stabilize the controversy. Far from subsiding, however, the harassment accelerated. On July 15 Ku Klux Klan members gathered on a vacant lot beside Williams's home, burned two crosses, and parked a pickup truck from which a black effigy was hung. That night three hundred people gathered to hear an address from leaders of the local Klan headed by George Dorsett. Six carloads of policemen were required to break up the crowd.

The violence at Williams's house was important for two reasons. First, it revealed the increasing strength of the Ku Klux Klan both in

George Dorsett and other Klansmen picket outside the home of Frank Williams in protest against the black minister moving into a formerly all-white neighborhood in 1967. Courtesy, Greensboro *Record*

Greensboro and across the state. In the years after 1964 the Klan experienced a remarkable revival in North Carolina. During some months as many as fifty meetings occurred across the state, always with fifty to a hundred people present. Dan K. Moore had been elected Governor of North Carolina in 1964 as a conservative law-and-order candidate. (I. Beverly Lake, the staunch segregationist, had been eliminated in the first primary and had thrown his support to Moore against Richardson

Preyer, a liberal.) But despite his law-and-order posture, Moore failed to crack down on the Klan, even permitting the right-wing organization to operate a booth at the State Fair from which vicious anti-black taunts were broadcast over loudspeakers.

The resurgence of the Klan could be traced in large part to the efforts of George Dorsett of Greensboro. As the Imperial Kludd of the United Klans of America, Dorsett spoke at most rallies. He was a powerful orator as well as a brilliant organizer. An aide to Governor Moore characterized Dorsett as "by far the most inflammatory speaker who regularly appears on the Klan's agenda." As head of the Greensboro Klan, Dorsett helped to direct the harassment at Williams's home. A year later he took it upon himself to organize a break-away wing of the Klan. Throughout these years, according to later newspaper reports, Dorsett served as an FBI informer, using his demagogic skills and aggressive behavior to gain access to the Klan's inner circle.[3]

The second notable fact of the Williams episode was the reluctance of many Greensboro whites to become overly concerned. Although the Greensboro *Daily News* condemned the Klan, it balanced its criticism with equal attention to what it implied was Williams's hunger for headlines. "[The newspaper] suspects that . . . Frank Williams . . . enjoyed the publicity surrounding his recent privileged communications trial," the editorial began.* "Mr. Williams' taste for notoriety, which apparently led him to call in the Governor before he summoned the Guilford County sheriff, in no way obscures the central issue [of Klan harassment]." But having denounced the Klan, the paper resumed its attack on Williams. "Whether . . . Mr. Williams dealt fairly with the sheriff's office and gave it a chance to do its duty before summoning the Governor and the Good Neighbor Council we don't know. It would seem to be a controversial question. If the answer is no, it is not to Mr. Williams' credit." Through such comments, the paper appeared to suggest that the minister was partly to blame for the violence against his own home, his quest for publicity having helped to cause the crisis in the first place. Even after the massive Klan rally, some law-enforcement officials still claimed that the black minister was just seeking publicity, as if he had created white racism.

In response to the housing outrages, the Greensboro Ministerial Fellowship set out to develop public support for open housing. Deploring

*The newspaper was referring to Williams's refusal to tell a court hearing about conversations he had held with parishioners who were striking against Boren Clay Products Company.

the "indifferent attitude of the citizenry which allows such threats to take place," the ministers' group demanded in March 1967 that the city council act on the issue of fair housing. The council, in turn, requested the Human Relations Commission to conduct an in-depth study of the problem. After more than two weeks of hearings, the Human Relations Commission found—not surprisingly—that racial discrimination was a pervasive problem for black residents in Greensboro. Documenting the deteriorated state of black housing, and the pernicious tendency toward block-busting whenever blacks attempted to leave the ghetto, the commission proposed a detailed agenda of action. The city council, it declared, should adopt a resolution favoring open housing, enact an ordinance prohibiting discrimination on the basis of race in buying or selling, enforce housing codes, eliminate substandard conditions, and pass legislation prohibiting block-busting techniques.

The response of city officials was hardly designed to bolster black hopes. The city council delayed any reaction through the summer and fall. When two days of public meetings were held in July to protest conditions at a local housing project, only one city councilman appeared, and then for only one day. Another councilman dismissed the complaints, saying that many were insignificant problems that the tenants could handle for themselves. In the meantime, the president of the local board of realtors attempted to discredit the Human Relations Commission, arguing that because 55 per cent of the membership was black, in contrast to 26 per cent of the city's population, the commission's recommendations could not be representative.* Six months after the Human Relations Commission issued its report, Mayor Carson Bain called the council and commission together for a dinner meeting, presenting them with an elaborate description of the housing dilemma. When some HRC members protested that they were looking for answers, not just more words, the meeting fell apart.

To Greensboro's blacks, the city council's lack of response simply dramatized the need for direct black political representation. How could Greensboro's Negroes expect fair treatment, black leaders asked, when all seven councilmen came from the wealthy and white northwest quadrant of the city? Not since the term of Dr. William Hampton (1951–55) had blacks been strongly represented in city government. Although Waldo Falkener, a black bondsman, had served on the council from 1959 to 1963, he had maintained a low profile. Since 1963 no black

*The realtor did not mention the fact that the entire city council and almost all city officials were white and hence even more unrepresentative.

had come close to winning. The absence of political representation compounded the sense of injury generated by the school and housing situations. If blacks were to be kept segregated in their own small section of the city, at least they should have representation on city bodies.

As had been true so often in the past, the issue of political recognition served as a barometer of black status, aspirations, and frustrations. When John Marshall Stevenson inaugurated a new black newspaper in 1967, he protested the fact that "Negro citizens of Greensboro have had their hope of achieving political representation . . . dumped unceremoniously to the ground." Over and over again, black leaders demanded that Greensboro institute a ward system of city council elections so that her 35,000 black citizens could have their proportionate share of political power. Such a system, Dr. George Simkins told Guilford County's state legislators, would not only be "just and right . . . but also in keeping with the Christian ethic which this fair city likes to think is one of its foremost characteristics." When state legislators refused to support the measure, citing opposition from the white city council and Chamber of Commerce, their action confirmed the growing sense of powerlessness and isolation in Greensboro's black community. As if to illustrate how deep the alienation ran, the Greensboro's Men's Club, the most "establishment" body in black Greensboro, announced in December of 1967 that it would not support a bond issue for a new courthouse and coliseum until the city took some action to recognize a black political presence in the city. At the very minimum, the Men's Club said, Greensboro should create a ward system of government, appoint blacks to appropriate boards, and respond to the glaring housing and transportation needs of the Negro community.[4]

II

Perhaps appropriately, events in the winter and spring of 1968 brought the circle of racial tension back to its starting point—school desegregation. As one way of dealing with the severe housing crisis in southeast Greensboro, city leaders had belatedly applied for assistance from the Model Cities program initiated by President Lyndon B. Johnson. With a waiting list for public housing three to five times longer than the availability of new units, it was hoped that federal money could provide a partial answer. Instead, the Model Cities agency rejected Greensboro's bid, pointing to the absence of a city commitment to end racial discrimination in education and housing. Nothing could have better illustrated the interlocking nature of Greensboro racial problems. At almost the same time, the Department of Health, Education, and Welfare started a crackdown against Greensboro's school policies. One of the fruits, it appeared, of Greensboro failures to address the continuing legacy of racism was to be a confrontation between the city's white leadership and the federal government.

The Supreme Court set the stage for the battle in mid-1967 when it ruled, in *Green v. New Kent County*, that local freedom-of-choice plans were invalid if they did not lead to successful integration of schools. The decision had the effect of shifting emphasis away from freedom of choice as a constitutionally viable means to an end and toward integration as the substantive goal to be achieved. Henceforth, attention was to focus on the result rather than the process. After the Court's decision, in February 1968 the Office of Civil Rights informed Greensboro officials that their progress toward desegregation was "below the degree normally expected." Freedom of choice, the federal administrator wrote, was only an "interim procedure," and the burden now rested on the school board to produce "a terminal plan" for dismantling the dual school structure.

On a *de facto* basis, there could be little question that the city's schools fell into racially identifiable patterns. While continuing pressure from black parents and the federal government had increased the number of blacks attending desegregated facilities, eleven schools had an all-Negro student body, five were totally white, and in only one school were whites part of a predominantly black student body (one white student out of 800). In February of 1967 the United States Commissioner of Education had called for a minimum of two full-time teachers assigned across racial lines to each school. By that criterion 24 of 45 Greensboro schools were not in compliance. Five schools, moreover, had no staff integration at all. Even where desegregation had occurred, blacks typically comprised less than 10 per cent of a total student body. In the best schools, they were hardly present at all. Grimsley High School, viewed by many as the elite educational facility in the city, had only seventeen blacks out of 1925 students. Claxton, a similarly prestigious elementary school, claimed only one black among 830. Clearly, "freedom of choice" had not fundamentally altered the dual school system.

An April 1968 site visit by HEW vividly illustrated the gap between the two sides. From the beginning, tension and acrimony marked the encounter. The HEW team arrived a day prior to their scheduled meeting with Superintendent Philip J. Weaver, and some members went to

interview black students at Dudley High School to compare their learning experience with that of students in integrated settings. Subsequently,
Superintendent Weaver accused federal officials of acting in an unprofessional, unethical manner in going to Dudley without prior notice.
When representatives of the two sides did meet, they seemed intent on
talking past each other. Repeatedly, the head of the HEW team asked
whether the school system's transportation policy did not discourage
integration by failing to provide buses for individual blacks who wished
to attend white schools. The Superintendent refused to agree. Weaver,
in turn, asked for a definition of a dual school system. When an HEW
official responded by saying it consisted of schools and faculties that
immediately could be identified by race, Weaver found the definition
vague and unsatisfactory. Furthermore, he argued that staff desegregation was difficult to acocmplish because "good teachers don't always
come in these set proportions."

By the end of the visit, the two sides had grown even further apart.
From the point of view of federal officials, it seemed obvious that "these
11 Negro schools will [continue to] be about as they are today" unless
an additional plan for desegregation was devised. Although school board
officials accused HEW of vagueness, the federal officials felt that they
had suggested a number of concrete options, including curriculum reor-
ganization to make subject matter, rather than race, the basis for a
school's identity. Another possibility was pairing schools in black and
white neighborhoods to make grade level the basis for attendance. Both
positions were rejected. "The board's position is to stand pat with freedom of choice," Weaver announced. The Superintendent denied that
he could arbitrarily assign teachers or alter school populations. From his
point of view, there was no reason to change school practices, despite
HEW's power to withdraw almost a million dollars in federal support
from the school system.

A confidential evaluation of the HEW visit by school officials revealed the near-paranoia that had begun to characterize school leaders'
perceptions of the federal government. Confusion over establishing the
date of the visit was seen as evidence of either federal incompetence or a
conscious effort to discomfort local officials. When HEW representatives failed to read thoroughly all the material the school board had
prepared, local officials interpreted the action as evidence of either
ignorance or intentional disregard of Greensboro's efforts. According to
the confidential analysis, "it was rather obvious that the [HEW] team
was somewhat disappointed to find that all the schools in Greensboro

were of high caliber and quality. . . ." The analysis then went on to question the propriety of six visitors renting two cars, when all could have traveled comfortably in one. Both sides appeared to be hardening their positions in preparation for all-out battle. As one federal participant commented: "The door wasn't open the tiniest crack. We'd say you aren't in compliance, they'd say they were. We'd suggest, they'd reject. No dialogue was possible."

Not surprisingly, HEW soon notified the Greensboro school system that it must submit additional integration plans. "The freedom of choice procedure has not been an effective means of desegregating students," Dr. Eloise Severinson wrote Superintendent Weaver, "and the dual school system remains virtually unchanged in your administrative unit." But Weaver continued to insist that no adequate definition of a dual system had been provided. Greensboro, he declared, was in compliance. Indeed, he said, "I would take a solemn oath that a desegregated education has not been denied any child in Greensboro since 1957." Although HEW officials had suggested zoning, pairing of schools, and curriculum change as ways to proceed, Richard Hunter, chairman of the school board, declared in September that "We asked them to tell us what to do and they wouldn't. That's contrary to their own guidelines." Obviously, a problem in communication existed.

However one viewed the conflict, the underlying issue remained the school board's refusal to do anything about the glaring presence of all-black and all-white schools. "Those schools were built for Negroes and are used now for Negroes," an HEW official declared. In the face of that reality, Greensboro's claim that it no longer operated a dual system ran "contrary to the facts and to all competent legal precedent." Even school board supporters acknowledged that the city's failure to provide transportation for black children to attend schools outside their neighborhoods constituted a damning piece of evidence. Given the board's reluctance to even discuss compromise, HEW had little choice but to declare the city in noncompliance. As the only black school board member later recalled, "the powers that be . . . were determined to fight a last ditch stand and to maintain the status quo as long as they possibly could."

To a remarkable extent, the personalities behind the policy were united in their hard-line posture. Superintendent Weaver genuinely believed that "freedom of choice" was the only educationally sound alternative for the city. Repeatedly he fought efforts by blacks and white liberals to inaugurate more far-reaching desegregation plans. If anything, Chairman Richard Hunter outdid Weaver in his conservatism. A strong leader, Hunter viewed any criticism of the board as tantamount to treason against Greensboro. Along with these two men, Robert Moseley, the school board's attorney, was perhaps the most influential figure on the scene. At every point, Moseley advocated resisting HEW and appealing decisions adverse to the board. The remainder of the white school board members were convinced that they were acting in the best interests of the whole community, including "the colored folk," as one board member said. Against such an array of forces, the only black school board member, Dr. George Evans, was virtually powerless. Although he dissented on most key votes on freedom of choice, Evans lacked the personality of a fighter. As one white observer noted, "He did the best he could. Dr. Evans is one of the most polished gentlemen of the Southern woods, but he never did get really angry."

When other black leaders protested, they ran up against a stone wall. Reflecting growing black impatience and frustration, the NAACP demanded in December 1968 that Superintendent Weaver resign. The Superintendent, the NAACP said, had shown "an attitude of indifference, contempt, and arrogance toward the rulings of the Supreme Court." The school board's response dramatized the polarization that had taken place. The NAACP's resolution was "so obviously wrong," said Chairman Hunter, that he would not comment upon it. Instead, Hunter charged that the NAACP action was motivated by a desire to get continued publicity after it had lost a vote to create a ward system of representation on the city council.

During 1968, events moved quickly toward a final courtroom confrontation. Predictably, HEW started enforcement proceedings in the summer of 1968, citing Greensboro's transportation policies, insufficient staff desegregation, unequal course offerings, and the perpetuation of racially identifiable schools. All new federal funds were placed in a "deferred status," with existing programs having to terminate when their funding period ended. The federal action threatened to cut more than a million dollars from the school budget, most of it for innovative programs for the disadvantaged in mathematics and reading. Early in 1969, an HEW examiner ruled that Greensboro was not in compliance with the 1964 Civil Rights Act because "under its freedom of choice plan . . . there has been no diminution of the dual school structure." Two weeks later the school board threw down its own gauntlet, accepting attorney Robert Moseley's recommendation that it appeal all the way to the Supreme Court if necessary so that the policy of HEW would not be adopted "unless we are forced to by the highest court in the land."

III

If nothing else, the years after 1963 revealed how interconnected and entrenched were the problems of institutional racism. Segregation in educational facilities was reinforced by segregation in housing. Both these problems, in turn, were related to a lack of political representation by and for blacks. None of these institutional inequities was the result of an accident; all were products of deliberate policy commitments made in the past—policy commitments that could be reversed only through concerted action by policy makers in the present. Yet exactly the opposite response occurred. Instead of moving against these forms of discrimination, white leaders used one issue to excuse another. They rejected black efforts to secure enactment of an open housing ordinance, refused to support a ward system of representation, and resisted school desegregation.

By their position on all of these issues, Greensboro's white leaders signaled a determination to stand fast in support of the status quo, refusing even to concede that justifiable grievances existed. More than any other body, the school board embodied this intransigence. In deciding to appeal the HEW ruling, the school board totally ignored reality. School leaders insisted that "there was no evidence of any economic or social pressure to maintain the segregated school system," a claim that could only cause dismay among blacks who had witnessed repeated setbacks in the areas of housing, school transportation, and political representation during the 1960's.

Various Southern communities had different ways of saying "Never!" to racial change in the 1960's. Greensboro was not a Philadelphia, Mississippi, where law enforcement officers believed they could use violence and terror to hold off the entire United States legal system. But in its own way white Greensboro, too, said "never" in the years after 1963. Deeply convinced of the moral virtue of their position, Greensboro's white leaders believed they could win the war of the courts. They were progressive, enlightened, and smart. They had a monopoly on superior legal talent. In 1954 and 1957, they had passed—in their own eyes once and for all—the test of moral and legal compliance with desegregation. No one had the right to question their credentials. No matter what others might say or do, they had justice on their side and would win.

Through such positions, Greensboro's white leaders revealed how solidly intact the progressive mystique was. The protests of 1963 had been traumatic. The concessions made then were as far as Greensboro's whites needed or wished to go. At every point of conflict in the five years thereafter, white leaders seemed to say: "how dare these blacks now bring up something else! We've done all we're going to do. They have no right to bother us any more." The response of the Greensboro *Daily News* to the Williams housing episode typified this attitude. It was as though blacks were asking too much, behaving improperly, stepping out of bounds. After all, overt discrimination in restaurants and theaters had been corrected. White Greensboro had paid the price for past errors. What right did blacks have to continue pushing when the city's whites had already done their part to remedy historical injustices and restore civility to the community?

Faced with this North Carolina version of "Never!" black activists experienced a profound crisis of purpose and direction. Even had protest demonstrations still been possible, there were no dramatic or symbolic issues around which to mobilize the community. The days of being able to take to the streets in mass numbers against visible enemies had passed. Yet high expectations remained—expectations that when frustrated could only turn into festering alienation. Traditional patterns of political action were not working. Not only were blacks turned down when they resorted to normal methods of pressure and petition; even the federal government was ignored. Fighting an elusive enemy—especially a "progressive" enemy—presented a problem of immense proportions. How black activists solved the problem—whether they could forge a new strategy for attacking institutional racism—would in large part determine the future of white-black relations in Greensboro.

CHAPTER SEVEN
Black Power

After 1965 it's a brand new day. New tactics had to be devised. I
think the turning point in the movement was when Stokely said
we're just tired of turning the other cheek, which is true. . . .
And there are only three ways to get power. You can request it,
demand it, or take it. And the alternative was trying to take it.
David Richmond, one of the four original Greensboro
sit-in demonstrators

The late 1960's were a fiery time in America. Black Panthers and
Students for a Democratic Society tried to organize ghetto dwellers into
a revolutionary phalanx to overthrow capitalism. Thousands of other
young people, fed up with United States hypocrisy in Vietnam and the
country's failure to solve problems of poverty and race at home, condemned "the system." Millions of adults, in turn, began to suspect that
everything they cared about was being undermined by dissidents from
another world—people who smoked marijuana, punctuated every other
sentence with "Motherfucker!" and held middle-class propriety in contempt. Violence became part of the language of political discourse.
Students with automatic weapons took over a dining hall at Cornell;
battle-garbed soldiers tear-gassed anti-war demonstrators at the Penta-
gon; and police brutalized demonstrators at the 1968 Democratic National Convention. Whether one came from the left or the right, the
country seemed under siege: for radical activists it was the brutal ham-
mer of government repression; for "middle Americans" it was the intol-
erance of self-righteous radicals.

In Greensboro many of the same forces were at work, nowhere more
clearly than in relations between black and white. Black activists felt
hemmed in and powerless before an intransigent opposition that was
proficient in using sophisticated forms of obstruction to frustrate black
demands. In the past, each new stage of insurgency had brought forth
new modes of white control. But never before had the constraints
seemed so difficult to attack, so invulnerable to conventional weapons
of protest. Clearly, new approaches were needed—approaches that

would address not specific instances of overt discrimination, but the structure of racism that pervaded the routines of everyday life.

Spearheading the search for these new strategies was a group of young blacks who came to maturity during the halcyon days of the civil rights struggle. For most of them, remembered history began in 1960, not in 1954 or 1945; thus the sit-ins represented a starting point, not a culmination, of protest. What had seemed radical and bold to those born ten years earlier appeared tame and ineffectual to a new generation. Attitudes, too, had changed. The initial sit-in demonstrators had believed profoundly in the goodness of America. They had trusted white people such as Ed Zane, and they had been convinced of the intrinsic workability of the system. The new generation believed none of these things. Betrayal, subterfuge, and frustration constituted their perceived experience. With no reason to trust traditional channels of authority, they set out to battle "the system" as an enemy with which they shared nothing in common.

Appropriately, the new generation of black activists began by attacking the cornerstone of white supremacy—its ground rules for racial interaction. In the past, white leaders had exerted ultimate control by shaping the pattern of dialogue between the races, dictating the terms of exchange. Now, young blacks seemed intent on overturning those modes of interaction. They would overcome the progressive mystique by operating outside of it, insisting that blacks seize control of their own lives, define their own rules, compose their own agendas, shape their own culture, language, and institutions—in short, take power for themselves, at least to the extent of determining their own priorities and methods of proceeding.

The vehicle for achieving this power was to be community organization. By mobilizing tenants around issues of slum housing, bringing workers together in unions, and "turning around the heads" of young people in high schools and colleges, the new activists hoped to establish a base of operations independent of control of influence from white Greensboro. They then would have a foundation, rooted in black institutions and controlled by black interests, from which to strike at the cultural and economic heart of white racism. In effect, the new generation of activists aspired to accomplish what Booker T. Washington had attempted eight decades earlier—to organize blacks for their own self-development and definition. But, unlike Washington, the new strategists wished total liberation from white control, not accommodation to it.

The very nature of such an approach, of course, invited bitter opposition. In part, the antagonism came from within the black community. The "young turks," as established black leaders called them, sometimes treated older activists as part of the problem, an enemy rather than an ally. The younger generation were "revolutionaries," the older generation "reformers." But the real opposition came from those white leaders whose values and control were under frontal assault. Influenced by events in the nation at large, most of Greensboro's white leaders believed that violent revolutionaries were at work in their community, too, threatening everything they had been taught to cherish. Like others in the nation, they found the thought intolerable. Their response, in turn, was to crush the incipient rebellion with massive force. The option that they had rejected in 1963 was now invoked—harshly, brutally, with neither debate nor uncertainty—a reflection perhaps of how far Greensboro's leaders would go to defend the progressive mystique from those seen to be beyond its reach.

I

Leading the new insurgency was Nelson Johnson, a native of eastern Northern Carolina who had entered A&T in the fall of 1965 after three years in the Air Force. Despite participating in one or two demonstrations before coming to Greensboro, Johnson had never considered himself an activist. "I had gone along with the thinking in the society that you try to do good," he noted, hoping that eventually justice would prevail. But while in the Air Force Johnson had started to question those basic assumptions. Although he defended Martin Luther King against supporters of Malcolm X, the idea of non-violence became less and less creditable. "It really got to be clear that turning the other cheek, trying to convince the enemy through moral persuasion . . . didn't really accord [with what the enemy] was about." Still, when Johnson enrolled at A&T, his primary extracurricular activity was with Youth Educational Services (YES), a white-dominated tutorial program very much in the New Frontier/Great Society tradition of helping individual blacks to "make it" within the existing system.

Gradually, however, Johnson began to question reform and integration. "A lot of the children I worked with," he remarked, "asked for white tutors, which bothered me at a time when social consciousness of our own history as [an Afro-American] people was rapidly on the rise." As he thought about the issue, Johnson began to see larger ramifications:

The question of why we had the tutor in the first place was linked to what the school wasn't doing and what the society wasn't doing . . . like how could a kid read if the lighting in the house is not proper, and how can the light get proper if his father isn't making enough money . . . and [the questioning] went into the [social root of things]. And the more you raise those questions, the more the hypocrisy of the society starts to come out.

During the same months, Stokely Carmichael raised the cry, "Black Power," telling his audiences: "it's time we stand up and take over."[1]

Some of Johnson's classmates were also questioning the efficacy of working through traditional channels of authority. Tom Bailey, who had taken a leave of absence from A&T to work for an antipoverty agency in Winston-Salem in 1966, concluded after his experience there that "the system had no real intention of bringing about any appreciable change." Like other antipoverty workers, Bailey had gone to work in a poor neighborhood. After living with the people and learning their concerns, he started to organize protest groups to demand improvements in housing and recreation. But before his efforts could reach fruition, he was attacked as an "outside agitator" working for Stokely Carmichael. (He had never met Carmichael.) Forced to retreat by his superiors, Bailey, too, began to doubt the sincerity of those who preached from a distance about social reform.

Nelson Johnson, in the meantime, was moving quickly toward a more radical concept of community organizing. Although continuing his tutorial work during 1966–67, he developed much closer community ties with black Greensboro, speaking at local political and social gatherings about the problems of schooling and housing. In the summer of 1967 he went to Fayetteville, North Carolina, where an effort was under way to organize poor blacks around issues of housing, rent, redevelopment, and jobs. During these months, he and Bailey became involved with the Foundation for Community Development (FCD), a statewide organization seeking to develop political activism among the poor. The FCD was an offshoot of the North Carolina Fund, established in 1963 by Governor Terry Sanford to lead a local war against poverty. "It is not enough to have the most powerful nation in the world," Sanford had said in 1963, "and then to admit that we are powerless to give our young people training in job opportunities." The FCD was to provide part of the power that was missing, but under the direction of Howard Fuller, its chief community organizer, the FCD became more and more an advocate of Black Power as well as community mobilization.[2]

By the fall of 1967, Johnson, Bailey, and Fuller had become convinced that white leaders would respond to black needs only if the entire black community—poor and middle class, high school and college students, average workers and professional people—joined hands to build an independent Black Power base from which to deal with the white community. The key ingredient was to be a coalition between campus and community. On the one hand, Bailey noted, "there was a lot of energy on campus that could be mobilized to assist the community-at-large in redressing its problems." On the other hand, the average black worker could teach students "what was going on in the real world as opposed to academia." The young activists sought ways of welding an alliance between the two forces against those institutions that were most oppressive, particularly housing agencies, the welfare system, and traditional political organizations. Although there appeared to be only limited support among students for protest in the winter of 1967–68, Greensboro's black newspaper warned that "things are happening a lot faster than a lot of people realize. . . . Considerable revolutionary activities are taking place in our city."

Johnson demonstrated his organizing skills with students after the Orangeburg Massacre of February 1968, when three South Carolina State students were killed by police during an attempt to desegregate a bowling alley. News of the tragedy arrived during a meeting between Johnson and FCD staffers, profoundly depressing the group but also triggering a determination to respond. "I came back here," Johnson said:

And we asked the funeral home director to give us a coffin to carry and we went to the cemetery and took some flowers and put them on the thing, we made an effigy of the governor, and just came to the student union and started to ask people to go and without any permit or anything we just lined up and started walking and when I looked back I just couldn't see the end of the line. That was a massive activity, it was one of the biggest activities, and it was the most spontaneous, it just happened . . . nobody knew who was organizing the thing, because I was nobody, I was just somebody, I wasn't even helping carrying the casket.

That Johnson's organizing ability extended to the community-at-large became clear the following summer (1968) when black activists formed the Greensboro Association of Poor People (GAPP). Directed toward the poorest, most oppressed blacks in Greensboro, GAPP sought to build a political base by sitting down with ten or twelve people in a housing project, talking about their problems, and then mobilizing the group to act. City redevelopment plans provided one focus for organizing efforts because of inadequate relocation procedures; housing conditions offered another rallying point. GAPP quickly acquired a reputation as a community ombudsman, fighting for people's welfare money, going downtown to protest official intimidation whenever local blacks felt aggrieved. No one with a problem was turned down. The GAPP approach, Johnson noted, "was just crude pressure tactics; [but] it won the hearts of the people [because they saw] us as an organization that they were part of." By the end of the summer a viable community base existed from which to work toward a coalition with students from Bennett, A&T, and Dudley High School.

Through such activities, Johnson quickly earned the enmity, as well as the grudging respect, of his white foes. "Johnson was the master organizer," one Greensboro white leader observed. His eloquence in public, together with his effectiveness behind the scenes, made him a powerful threat to those seeking to keep the black community under control. Moreover, because Johnson acted outside the traditional parameters of racial interaction, he was impossible to deal with in customary ways. Johnson seemed to go out of his way to disturb traditional white sensibilities. "If you're trying to persuade people to see things your way," one dismayed city official commented about Johnson, "what better way to start off than to be on time and be half-way pleasant to people you're trying to persuade?" Yet Johnson would not play by those rules. Consequently, most whites believed that he was not really seeking constructive change, but rather wanted "strife" for its own sake. "He was trying to stick a pin in the whole balloon, and he didn't care."

The same radical approach, of course, created problems with older black leaders. Existing black protest organizations dealt with only a limited range of issues. Almost never would they go into the poorest areas of town and agitate around problems like welfare. Moreover, the cry of "Black Power" challenged the politics of interracialism, threatening to undercut the deepest philosophical premises of the older generation. Simple issues such as dress and hair styles could pit old against young in a cultural war. When two young girls at Dudley High School wore their hair in an "Afro," the principal suspended them. "We want to create an atmosphere which is conducive for learning," he said. The girls, on the other hand, saw the issue as one of affirming their African origins and defining their own identity. Divisions over such questions sometimes threatened to drive a wedge between the new activists and their more conventional forebears.

Yet in the end the two sides had more reason to unite than to split into opposing factions. Nelson Johnson believed in a multi-class constituency; repeatedly, he went out of his way to avoid alienating potential black supporters, working on voter registration with the NAACP, cooperating with black ministers on social welfare projects. Johnson saved his most militant rhetoric for white audiences, intentionally adopting a more moderate stance before blacks, at least in part to discredit those whites who denounced him as reckless and dangerous. More importantly, black middle-class leaders recognized the value and effectiveness of Johnson's efforts. They shared his objectives, even if they did not always endorse his style. If leaders such as George Simkins of the NAACP or B.J. Battle of American Federal Savings & Loan did not initiate the same kind of community organizing campaigns as Johnson, they inevitably supported such actions after he took the first step.[3] Despite internal tensions, therefore, the potential existed for the kind of coalition that Johnson sought. All that was missing was a spark to move that potential toward actualization.

II

As in countless other cities, the assassination of Martin Luther King in April 1968 provided the occasion for the broad resurfacing of black anger and activism. "When the announcement came on the radio, everybody was shocked," one A&T student recalled. "Some people started crying, then all of a sudden the next thing I heard, kids were out on Market Street throwing bottles and rocks at passersby." As word of the tragedy spread, more than three hundred black students marched into downtown Greensboro. Chanting "Black Power," the students massed at the county court house for a moment of silent prayer, then marched on, yelling, "We shall change the white society!" After the crowd started to smash car windows and throw rocks, riot police responded, armed with tear gas and shotguns. Although the violence never got out of control, Mayor Carson Bain requested the mobilization of National Guard units.

The morning and afternoon of the next day were relatively calm. More than five hundred students, most of them from Bennett, walked peacefully to the courthouse for a noon service addressed by Nelson Johnson and others. Almost four thousand gathered for another service at the A&T gymnasium, where they heard a telegram from Jesse Jackson pleading for students "to be non-violent . . . [and] to help heal this sick nation." To defuse the situation, President Lewis Dowdy announced that the spring break would start five days early, with students returning home immediately to be with their families "during these hours of sorrow."

But at nightfall the calm ended. Shooting broke out when two white men fired into a crowd of blacks from a passing station wagon. As police and National Guardsmen arrived in Armored Personnel Carriers, students became enraged and joined the battle, throwing stones and bottles at white motorists. After sniper fire came from the A&T campus, National Guardsmen reciprocated. Three policemen were wounded by shotgun blasts, one of them seriously.

No one knew who was involved in the shooting once the first gunfire came from the station wagon. Some students said all the snipers were outsiders. Others described the campus as "gone wild," with students rushing the ROTC arsenal, grabbing guns, and organizing into platoons. Police estimated that there were no more than one to three snipers. But the shooting went on through much of the night, with five shots being fired at local firemen responding to an alarm, and repeated gunfire exchanged between Hodgins Hall—an A&T dormitory—and National Guardsmen below. Shortly after midnight, police and guardsmen used tear gas to assault what appeared to be a major source of sniper fire, and the violence came to an end. All in all, there had been six injuries.

In an act destined to become controversial, Mayor Carson Bain the next morning declared a 7 p.m. to 6 a.m. curfew and banned all marching and demonstrations. The Mayor declared his action was necessary to preserve life and safety, even though more than a thousand guardsmen were in the city and Lewis Dowdy had sent home all A&T students. That night, as an army surveillance plane circled over southeast Greensboro, National Guardsmen atop the city's tallest buildings looked down upon a deserted central city. Although some arrests were made for curfew violations, the city was eerily quiet. "What's going on right now," Councilman Jack Elam said, "illustrates that there aren't any civil rights for anyone when there is no law and order."

During the next four days peace prevailed. Conditions were described by authorities as "static" and "excellent." At white churches throughout the city, ministers pondered King's tragic death, one calling it an example of "the radical wrongness of human nature," another declaring that "we who have power in our society" must respond with "true freedom and opportunity." In the black community more than one thousand people gathered at "Big Zion," the rallying point of the 1963 Civil Rights Movement, to express their grief. Meanwhile, the Greensboro *Daily News* declared that the clearest lesson of the riots and curfew was that "the political process cannot remain free, and certainly cannot be normal, when any large group despairs of its stake in it."

To blacks, however, the way the crisis was handled exhibited just how small a "stake" they had in government. At no point did any white city leader consult black leaders about the call-up of the National Guard or the imposition of the curfew. A&T officials first learned that law enforcement officers had invaded the campus when shots were heard. Such actions, one black minister noted, displayed total contempt for the black community. Black leaders were willing to discipline dissident students; but whites bypassed them, undercutting further the channels of authority within the black community. When black leaders sought permission for a downtown march to commemorate Dr. King, city leaders rejected the request. Instead, Mayor Bain proposed that only ministers march. Cecil Bishop, the black chairman of the Human Relations Commission, could barely contain his rage. "It doesn't [sit] very well with me," he told the Mayor, "to have to always do something on someone else's terms." John Marshall Stevenson, professor at A&T and editor of the black newspaper, echoed the same theme. "Your hearts may be good," he told city officials, "but the structure is rotten to the core. You may feel you can represent all the people fairly, but the people on the other side of the tracks don't believe you can."

Predictably, the use of force to impose calm actually triggered a revitalization of protest. Most blacks questioned the necessity for the curfew, pointing out that serious violence had occurred only after the National Guard had arrived on the scene. From their point of view, the curfew functioned primarily to keep workers on the second and third shifts away from their industrial jobs. In protest against the city's indifference to their sensibilities, the blacks gathered at "Big Zion" formed a Citizens Emergency Committee (CEC). By Thursday, CEC pickets were spreading leaflets throughout the downtown area, urging blacks not to spend money where they were not given a "fair shake." As one younger activist recalled, King's death caused people "who had not been involved since the sit-ins [to be] pulled back into activity." The CEC demanded the appointment of blacks to important policy-making posts in the city, especially on the Board of Health, the Alcoholic Beverages Commission, the Draft Board, the Airport Authority, and the Housing

Authority. It also requested enactment of an open-housing ordinance, stronger building-code enforcements, more enlightened police practices, enactment of a ward system, the development of a Negro history curriculum in public schools, and more frequent appointment of blacks to municipal and school administration jobs. If the agenda sounded familiar, it was. Five years earlier the same demands had appeared on the "action ideal" of black protesters. In the intervening years, nothing had been done.

On the campus, meanwhile, Nelson Johnson became the focal point for renewed efforts to build a student-community coalition. Despite the Orangeburg Massacre demonstrations, most students at A&T did not engage in sustained protest activities. To alter that pattern, a Johnson supporter later recalled, "the decision was made that the most politically expedient thing to do was to take over [the campus]." GAPP was to be "the instrument for bringing together the community and the campus," with Johnson wearing the dual hats of student leader and founder of the community-action agency. As a result of that strategy Johnson became a candidate for student-body vice president, winning election in the spring of 1969 on a platform of Black Power and community organization.

Although police subsequently portrayed Johnson as heading a revolutionary conspiracy to overthrow authority, he was—on the scale of radicalism present at A&T in 1968—a relatively moderate figure. On one extreme was the Black Liberation Front (BLF), a group described by an A&T official as "well armed and planning for armed insurgency." By most black accounts, the BLF represented a dedicated cadre committed to Black Power and violent revolution. The BLF openly allied itself with Black Panthers from near-by Winston-Salem, a group characterized by one student as "walking around with their tams and black shirts and pants—everything was black—urging students to join the Panthers." "A kind of blacker-than-thou thing was developing," Nelson Johnson recalled. "People came together around frustration and hatred for what was going on." Yet the BLF offered no program for constructive action, turning inward upon itself and ultimately becoming an alienated clique. At the other end of the scale were the traditional sororities and fraternities. Students in such organizations were willing to get stirred up about campus issues such as grades or college rules, but not to engage in prolonged social activism.

Johnson represented a third alternative, closer to one group than the other, but basically seeking to build a coalition that would draw from all the factions on campus. Although committed to community organizing and Black Power, Johnson was clearly distinct from the BLF. Most students feared the latter's potential for violence and its reckless rhetoric. Johnson, by contrast, appeared responsible. This image, in turn, enabled Johnson to build bridges to the more conservative students who, with the correct approach, and under the appropriate circumstances, might be recruited for community action on schools, housing, or wages. The problem was to find the right issues.

The tactical difficulty of harnessing campus energies to broader political concerns became manifest when Stokely Carmichael spoke on campus in December 1968. As 4000 students thronged the A&T gymnasium, Carmichael exhorted blacks not only to be willing to die for freedom but to be willing to kill for it as well. Asked who he had voted for in the recent election, Carmichael responded: "I didn't vote, I stayed at home and cleaned my guns." Carmichael's call for black revolution, however, led neither to mass demonstrations downtown nor to greater student involvement in community issues; instead, students boycotted classes to protest "unprofessional and unethical conduct" by certain of their professors whose grading practices and teaching skills were under attack. Thus, those concerned with campus questions had seized the momentum created by Carmichael's visit to generate action on behalf of their own demands. Although Johnson and his allies would rather have seen student energies devoted to community action against the city, they still lacked the clout or persuasiveness to make that happen. "We didn't know how," Johnson said. "Only later would the two focuses come together." In fact there was an inevitable cultural logic to the progression. Students had to experience a new sense of power and rebellion over questions immediate to their own lives before moving outward to issues that tied those questions to others.

Campus problems continued to dominate student dissent during the early weeks of 1969. On February 5 student activists occupied A&T's central administration building to follow up on the December boycott. They demanded the abolition of pop quizzes, review of instructors who failed more than 25 per cent of their students, dismissal of six faculty members characterized as "incompetent and undesirable," and liberalization of dress and "visiting" regulations for female students. Clearly, students were developing a heightened sense of their own rights; by demanding a larger voice in controlling their own immediate environment, they were also discarding traditional habits of deference toward authority—a trend with far-reaching implications beyond the campus. Still, the only avowedly "political" demand was their insistence that the humanities department adopt courses in black history and culture. Moreover, President Lewis Dowdy was able to handle the disturbance with minimal trouble. An administration-faculty committee negotiated a settlement which both recognized the legitimate grievances of students and maintained existing lines of authority. No police were called. Nearly everyone agreed that Dowdy had handled the situation with skill and fairness.

The first confrontation with city police occurred two weeks later, at a memorial service for Malcolm X. Sponsored by GAPP and held at a black community center about a mile from A&T, the service was attended by approximately four hundred blacks, mostly students. Its sponsors hoped that the service would spread black pride and solidarity, but they planned no further demonstrations. Almost immediately, however, the occasion became a stand-off with authorities. Nine police cars appeared at the community center with a bus full of reinforcements standing by. As students approached the community center, police blocked the sidewalks, forcing repeated breaks in the line of march and a series of mini-confrontations before students arrived at the community center. After the service started, a tear-gas canister suddenly detonated, spreading gas through the entire area. Police called the episode an accident; most students believed it to be an intentional provocation. "There was a feeling," one activist noted, "that certain elements of the police department had a point to prove." Although organizers of the service kept the crowd under control, another layer of tension had been added to relations between the black community and the police.

That tension increased after students at A&T massively supported a strike by university cafeteria workers on March 13. The walkout provided the vehicle Nelson Johnson had been looking for to merge campus and community issues. At colleges all over the state, cafeteria workers had been protesting management exploitation. Paid less than the minimum wage, given no fringe benefits, and compelled to work overtime without extra pay, cafeteria employees represented a prime example of the black "under class." Now that exploitation was brought home to A&T students, many of whom realized for the first time that the people who served them "that awful food" were also victims. If Nelson Johnson's primary tactical problem was "how to plug [students] into" the issue of worker oppression, here was the answer. "These were really the closest poor and oppressed people [you could find] . . . an immediate group." As soon as the strike began, students rallied in support, organizing alternative sources of food so that fellow classmates would not be tempted to cross the picket lines. With the support of the adult Citizens Emergency Committee, students secured food donations from local merchants. They also distributed leaflets to the community in support of the strike. "It was one of the more successful things I helped organize," Johnson noted.

The tension with police exploded into violence after more than two thousand five hundred students marched to President Dowdy's home to express their support of the cafeteria workers. According to police, rowdy students disrupted traffic and stoned cars once the rally was over. In the melée that followed, gunfire was exchanged, with one student shot in the shoulder. Students, however, insisted that the police had precipitated the violence when they had attempted to force the crowd back to campus after it left Dowdy's home. Becoming angered, the students began to throw stones, with police shooting tear-gas canisters in response. According to students, no gunfire came from the campus, and police shot randomly into the crowd. In the disruptions that followed, three students were arrested for ransacking a local grocery store whose owner had refused to contribute food to supporters of the strike.[4]

Although the cafeteria walkout lasted only two days, the episode proved to be an important barometer of racial conflict in the community. For the first time, virtually the entire campus had become engaged in a protest that involved community as well as college issues. The police response, following hard after the Malcolm X memorial service, exacerbated the hostility already existing between law-enforcement authorities and black students. Among those arrested during the disturbance had been Eric Brown, one of the few avowed Black Panthers in the community. Brown's association with GAPP staff members, in turn, persuaded police that the community organizing effort was a Black Panther operation.

Events built rapidly toward a full-blown confrontation. Police received intelligence reports from the FBI warning that insurgents were plotting to ambush police and blow up buildings. Although the reports appear in retrospect to have reflected primarily the work of an agent provocateur planted by the FBI to incite illegal activities that would warrant a crackdown, Greensboro police at the time accepted without question the veracity of the information. Indeed, during the weeks following the cafeterial workers' strike, a mood of near-paranoia swept through the city's white leadership, as Greensboro, like so many other locales in the nation, mobilized to do battle once and for all with what it perceived as a black conspiracy to topple established authority.[5]

III

The issue that transformed Greensboro into an armed camp was both stark in its simplicity and devastating in its ability to crystallize racial tensions. Claude Barnes was a junior at Dudley High School. He had been president of his class, vice president of the school service club, an honor student, and a member of the student council. Barnes had also participated in a student group organized by GAPP around the theme of black unity. In April, a joint faculty-student election committee ruled that Barnes lacked the qualifications to be a candidate for student council president. The committee gave no reasons. When the election was held on May 2, Barnes received six hundred write-in votes—four hundred more than the runner-up. But since write-in ballots were "illegal," the runner-up was declared the victor. That day Barnes and four other students walked out of the school in protest. The episode set in motion a series of events that three weeks later led to more than six hundred National Guard troops occupying black Greensboro.

In part, the Claude Barnes controversy reflected simple divisions over authority. Dudley had always been run with a strong hand. It was the only high school in the city that maintained rigid dress regulations and prohibited students from leaving school premises during the lunch hour. Four months earlier a male student had been suspended for wearing bib overalls to school. Before that the same punishment had been meted out to girls who wore "Afros." Indeed, many Dudley faculty members saw the ideas of Black Power and culture as undercutting traditional academic standards. Nell Coley debated furiously with Claude Barnes about the relative merits of Shakespeare and Franz Fanon's *Wretched of the Earth.* "I don't think I really convinced Claude," Coley recalled, "and I know he didn't convince me." Later, when the Dudley students walked off campus, Coley refused to support their action.

In a larger sense, however, the issue was Barnes's association with Nelson Johnson and GAPP. Culture and politics were thus connected. When Barnes and his allies received no recognition from the Dudley administration, they sought advice from their friends at A&T. Johnson, in turn, offered full support, never denying that the school constituted a crucial component of his plans for a community/campus alliance. "As soul brothers," he later said, "we were very active with Dudley students." GAPP circulated literature at Dudley and invited high school students to meetings held at A&T. As a result, both black and white educators saw Barnes as a Johnson puppet, refusing to acknowledge that he might have a legitimate grievance in his own right. Because of this attitude, they also viewed actions by Johnson as part of a plot to foment rebellion.

Within this context, almost no room existed for common sense or compromise. A week after the election, twenty-five students walked out of Dudley in protest against the school's failure to explain why Barnes had been denied a place on the ballot. An additional seventy-five students joined the group after lunch. Meanwhile, Owen Lewis, the white public relations director of the school department, was sent by the central administration office to oversee the Dudley crisis. In the early afternoon, students from A&T—including Nelson Johnson—arrived to speak with the protesters. School authorities closed the building and dismissed all the students; police warned the "outsiders" that they were subject to arrest for disturbing the peace.

In the ensuing days, the situation at Dudley deteriorated quickly. Nelson Johnson and his associates claimed that they had come to Dudley "to cool off" the students rather than incite them, a version supported by an A&T chaplain who had asked the Johnson group to go to the school. But police and school authorities insisted that the "outsiders" had come to inflame the situation. At the request of school authorities, police arrested three of the visitors, Nelson Johnson among them. In the meantime, school officials rejected any sort of concessions. When some of the most respected adult blacks in the community pleaded with Principal Franklin Brown to negotiate the issues, they found him adamantly opposed to even meeting with those who questioned his stand. "He was really afraid," one minister recalled. Local NAACP leaders joined with members of the Dudley PTA and black ministers to ask for a meeting in a local church to thrash out the dispute. But again the Dudley principal failed to appear. Later, it was revealed that school board authorities had prohibited Brown from meeting with community representatives. Indeed, Owen Lewis, the white representative of the school board, had for all intents and purposes taken charge of Dudley.

During the seven days starting on May 16, the verbal controversy over Dudley escalated into a paramilitary confrontation. After school authorities insisted again that there had been no "irregularity" in the election, nearly four hundred students boycotted classes, calling for a "return of our exiled president." Violence erupted three days later when police arrested those seeking to persuade their classmates to stay away from classes. More than seven hundred students were involved in the fracas. Several students accused the police of brutality, one girl testifying that she had been "thrown to the ground and dragged in the mud." Police responded that they had been struck by rocks and umbrellas and had been acting in self-defense. Reflecting the attitude of most white leaders, the Greensboro *Daily News* bitterly condemned the protests. "The business of schools is to educate," the paper said, "not to serve as laboratories for experiments in student anarchy."

Events came to a head on May 21, Approximately seventy-five pickets circled the school demanding the dismissal of Owen Lewis and the calling of a new election. After lunch, the students agreed to leave if the police would withdraw, but then rushed the school and began to hurl stones at the humanities building. Police riot squads fired tear gas to disperse the crowd. After school authorities dismissed the rest of the students, hundreds of innocent bystanders became victims of the violence. As one parent told a reporter, "The gas was awful . . . this woman tried to get across the street to get her children from the school, and the gas was so bad that she fainted." Anger spread like a brush fire through the black community as reports of injured children circulated. At Dudley, protesters moved toward A&T, college students and community people became involved, and further rock- and bottle-throwing occurred. That night, at six, Mayor Jack Elam told the people of Greensboro that "we no longer have good order in our community."

From that point forward the battle scene shifted to A&T. Throughout the evening crowds gathered and were dispersed. A number of cars carrying white motorists were stoned. At approximately ten o'clock Mayor Elam requested National Guard support from the governor. Lewis Dowdy was not consulted. Indeed, communications with the campus appeared to be nonexistent. The city's policy was consistent with a hard-line stance toward campus demonstrations taken by Governor Robert Scott, son of a former "liberal" governor and a man viewed by most political observers as a typical North Carolina progressive. In February, the Governor had announced that colleges "are not places of refuge or asylum" and that law enforcement officers need not secure permission from university officials before entering a campus to enforce the law. To show that he meant what he said, Scott himself had ordered the clearing of a student-occupied building at the University of North Carolina in Chapel Hill against the wishes of officials there. The attitude of city leaders—and that of state authorities, who quickly gathered in Greensboro—clearly reflected Governor Scott's tough position.

Young students from Dudley High School march in protest against the refusal of school officials to permit Claude Barnes to be chosen as president of the student body because of his political beliefs. Courtesy, Greensboro *Record*

That night, at 1:30 a.m., Willie Grimes, a student at A&T, was shot in the head and killed. Throughout the evening police had been successful in routing crowds, but events appeared to worsen as the night wore on. At 10:17 a patrol car radioed for an Armored Personnel Carrier to come to the A&T area. Thirty-five minutes later the first report of gunfire came from the campus. A second Armored Personnel Carrier was alerted. Police radio messages of sniper fire intensified, and at 12:31, according to a police log, officers started to return gunfire. In the meantime carloads of white youths were seen riding through the area, apparently looking for trouble. At 1:14 a.m. a radio car reported a group of twenty-five people in the campus area. They appeared to be carrying something. Gunfire was reported at the same time. Fifteen minutes later another radio message announced the chase of a convertible. At 1:43 a.m. the convertible arrived at Cone hospital. It was carrying Willie Grimes, dead on arrival.

No one knew who killed Grimes. A student leader later charged that Grimes had been wounded in the leg, and then, while pleading for mercy, was shot in the head by an officer; police pointed out that there had been no leg wound. They also claimed that Grimes had been killed by a weapon whose caliber was smaller than that used by the police. Subsequently, observers told police that Grimes had been part of the group moving across campus to head off a group of whites throwing bricks at cars. Although the eyewitness accounts differ in details, all agree that a car pulled up near the students and that one or more men started firing. One witness identified the car as a police vehicle with a blue light; another said it had been white and looked like an unmarked patrol car. The autopsy showed the murder bullet to be less than .32 caliber. Although police repeatedly denied using ammunition of that type, news reporters subsequently revealed that officers had used both .30 caliber rifle ammunition and buckshot measuring about .30 caliber. The fatal wound could have come from either weapon. In addition, physical evidence at a greenhouse near the scene of the shooting suggested that buckshot was fired in the area where Grimes died. Who fired the fatal bullet has never been discovered. But at that time most blacks in Greensboro believed the police were responsible, and they still believe so.

The next morning the A&T area resembled a fortress under seige. Heavy gunfire had continued through the night until police withdrew from the campus shortly after three a.m. to await further instructions. Additional National Guard units were called out, and Mayor Elam declared a state of emergency, imposing an 8 p.m. to 5 a.m. curfew. As National Guard troops circulated through the area in trucks and jeeps, episodes of rock-throwing continued. One white truck driver was taken from his vehicle and beaten before being rescued and taken to a hospital by black residents. In the meantime, President Lewis Dowdy announced that school would close and that all students should leave their dormitories by six p.m. Friday, the next day. As night fell, State Attorney General Robert Morgan and State Bureau of Investigation Director Charles Dunn were on the scene. SBI officials claimed that outside agitators had been at work deliberately provoking disruptions in the state's high schools.

That evening the crisis built to another climax. Earlier in the day, according to a police informant, a student government officer had told a rally that no students should come to Scott Hall that night unless they were prepared to die. At one a.m. Friday morning a police car was attacked and four officers were wounded, one seriously. Immediately, police concluded that the plans for ambush so long rumored in intelligence reports were now being put into action. In retrospect, that judgment seems problematic. As one white observer commented:

> I can't shake the question from my mind that it wasn't one of the
> National Guardsmen [who shot] the policeman who was most
> seriously injured. The wound was described as a hunting rifle
> type wound and either somebody got him with a high caliber
> rifle . . . or he was hit by a stray bullet from a National Guard
> weapon. I don't think we ever really faced up to that. . . . The
> police didn't want to talk about it.

In the emotional intensity of the moment, though, such questions were not asked. Indeed, to have raised them would have been viewed as traitorous. Instead, city and state leaders decided to clear the campus, using the National Guard to sweep through A&T's dormitories beginning at 6:30 a.m. Lewis Dowdy was not part of the meeting (he could not be reached, city leaders said), nor was there any black person present at any of the discussions leading up to the decision.

While most students still slept, the National Guard operation began shortly after sunrise. President Dowdy was informed as the sweep commenced. Swiftly, the Guard moved through the buildings searching out weapons and evacuating students. Although Governor Scott declared that the National Guard displayed "remarkable restraint," news reporters noted that almost every door in Scott Hall had been shot through from the outside. Guardsmen, out of fear or anger, shot the locks off more than eighty doors before rushing the rooms. Confusion reigned because Dowdy had warned students to remain in their dormitories for purposes of safety until they left town. Some residence counselors also told the students to stay, even as Guardsmen ordered them out.

National Guard Armored Personnel Carrier moving into the area surrounding A&T to suppress black insurgents. Courtesy, Greensboro *Record*

That afternoon hundreds of students moved silently toward the bus and train terminals seeking ways of leaving the city. They were orderly. Most seemed noncommittal about leaving, although many expressed concern about what would happen to their grades if they were unable to take final examinations.

In the aftermath of the National Guard sweep, city and state officials repeatedly emphasized both the seriousness of the threat they had confronted and its conspiratorial origins. According to police, eight high-powered rifles had been seized during the National Guard sweep. Pointing to the semiautomatic and high-powered weaponry, Governor Scott asserted that the violence had been caused by "hard-core militants." A small group of troublemakers, he said, "used a frivolous issue—that of a high school election—to seek out and find confrontation." Others sounded the same theme, blaming outside agitators for fabricating a controversy, then manipulating it for purposes of sparking violence. Although refusing to name names, police declared that it was "general knowledge that this was too organized to be spontaneous."

At times the talk of conspiracy seemed to draw upon an international frame of reference. Endorsing the official point of view, the Greensboro *Daily News* editorialized:

> high school students of unripened years and judgment could not embark on such quasi-revolutionary behavior without sophisticated inducement. . . . What has confronted Greensboro police and school officials . . . is not a mere protest over a student election that miscarried, but a form of—let us say it—guerrilla warfare, characterized by manipulation of the silent or terrorized majority.

With logic remarkably parallel to that of State Department officials who claimed that the Viet Cong could not have started a civil war without guidance from Peking, the city's leading newspaper thus rejected any possibility that the Dudley conflict might have reflected home-grown, legitimate issues. Instead, the protesters were outsiders—foreigners— engaged in "guerrilla warfare" and, like the Viet Cong, manipulating a "terrorized majority."

The tragedy of adopting such a view was twofold. First, it caused white leaders to explain away or suppress contradictory evidence. Days after the sensational disclosure of high-powered weaponry, for example, it was revealed that only three of the guns seized at A&T were operable, the others being "dummy" rifles used in ROTC drills. Most of the weapons in Scott Hall had been taken out through heating conduits prior to the "sweep"; yet only after going public with a significant falsehood for a crucial period did police acknowledge that fact.* Second, the insistence on "outside" intervention prevented city leaders from recognizing the nature of the actual war that was going on. Polarization had reached the point of open conflict—including the use of arms—but the war was inside Greensboro and over real grievances, not over extraneous issues fabricated by foreign revolutionaries.

Nevertheless, the charge of outside conspiracy emerged even more clearly within the week as the centerpiece of the city's indictment of black insurgents. Not only had A&T students plotted insurrection with Dudley students, the police claimed; that effort was but one element in

---

*One high police official explained subsequently that all police were removed from the A&T area in the early morning hours before the sweep so that they could be briefed on the impending operation. As a result, he said, all the guns were removed without ever encountering a police roadblock or police surveillance. According to black sources, however, the guns that were inside A&T were taken out through the heating tunnels after some students learned from monitoring a police radio that the attack was forthcoming.

a state-wide scheme by the Foundation for Community Development (FCD) to foster rebellions against white authority. Beginning on May 27 the Greensboro *Daily News* printed a series of stories based on police intelligence information purporting to establish a link between various FCD personalities and the violence in Greensboro. The first story noted that while four new tires were being put on an FCD staff car in Greensboro on May 9, a mechanic observed three high-powered rifles in the trunk. The same car, the story said, was being driven by Franklin Williams—an FCD staffer—when he was arrested during the A&T disruptions for violating the curfew and possessing beer and firecrackers. (Williams had been arrested at 6:30 p.m. The curfew began at 8 p.m.). Finally, the story reported that FCD staffers had been barred from Dudley High School, and that the organization was under attack by Senator Strom Thurmond of South Carolina for its activities as an antipoverty agency. Although brief, the newspaper report strongly implied a relationship between the discrete facts it reported and the subsequent trouble in Greensboro. Other stories published a few days later reinforced the implication. One noted that on the day he had been arrested Franklin Williams had purchased 150 rounds of ammunition in Durham. It also pointed out that three members of the FCD staff— among them Howard Fuller and Franklin Williams—had earlier purchased high-powered rifles.[6]

FCD spokesmen responded angrily, arguing that police were concocting a plot out of unrelated facts and racist assumptions. Fuller and others had purchased rifles because their lives had been threatened, Nathan Garrett, head of FCD, asserted. Why had news reports described Franklin Williams's purchase of ammunition in Durham, another FCD staffer asked, and then failed to say that he left the ammunition there before coming to Greensboro? Pointing out that beer and firecrackers were not dangerous weapons, the same critic charged that the police were harassing Williams and had even threatened to accuse him of intending to use the golf clubs in the trunk of his car as "deadly weapons." To establish his own innocence Garrett came to the Greensboro police to volunteer information about the FCD, and then requested OEO in Washington to investigate his agency to determine whether any wrongdoing had occurred. Nelson Johnson, meanwhile, demanded an inquiry by the United States Civil Rights Commission, and, specifically, an investigation of his own involvement and that of other non-Dudley students.

Official commitment to the conspiracy theory only deepened, however, culminating when Chief of Police Paul Calhoun told a Senate Investigating Committee in July that the entire episode had been a plot of the Black Panther Party. Starting with Carmichael's speech in December, Calhoun traced every episode of protest to Panther influence. Without directly saying so, Calhoun implied that Nelson Johnson and GAPP were Panther agents. After the December boycott of classes, he charged, Eric Brown—a known Panther—had brought back with him to campus Harold Avent (alias Nunding), a Panther leader from New York. "This was the first concrete knowledge of Black Panther Party infiltration into . . . Greensboro," Calhoun told the Senate Committee. Thereafter, he charged, the Panthers had held training sessions at the home of Nelson Johnson, had taught guerrilla tactics on the A&T campus, and, in every way possible, had insinuated themselves into the community. Calhoun denounced Johnson as "one of the most militant Negroes in Greensboro for the past two or three years," describing him as the chief architect of the ensuing disturbances. From the Malcolm X memorial service to the cafeteria workers' strike, the Chief charged, Johnson and the Panthers had orchestrated a series of protests consciously designed to climax in the Dudley episode led by Claude Barnes, "an active militant who has attended some Black Panther Party meetings." As Calhoun saw it, each protest contributed to a master plot, with FCD, GAPP, Nelson Johnson, and the students at Dudley all operating under the influence, if not direction, of the Panthers.[7]

Calhoun's testimony met with an enthusiastic response from the Senate Investigating Committee. "That's what I call living under a reign of terror," Senator John McClellan of Arkansas said. Only A&T President Lewis Dowdy dissented from the prevailing view, telling the committee that the violence would not have occurred had police not used tear gas at Dudley High School. One of the lessons of the disturbance, Dowdy declared, was that college students were as concerned about what happened in their community as they were about what happened on their campus. But the Senate committee seemed little inclined to consider that perspective. When reporters asked why Nelson Johnson and other protesters had not been invited to give their side of the story, a committee spokesman said: "They've made their point already. . . . I don't believe in giving these people a forum, a lot of free publicity."

Only when the North Carolina Advisory Committee to the United States Civil Rights Commission held hearings in the fall of 1969 did the protesters receive a sympathetic response. Looking first at Dudley High School, the committee concluded that "the prevailing system was unjust," that dissent had been suppressed, and that exclusion of Claude Barnes from the student election was in fact the basic reason for the protests. When school officials adamantly refused to discuss these issues with parents or community leaders, the committee declared, "the students were left to create situations that would force the officials to take notice. . . . It is a sad commentary that the only group in the community who would take the Dudley students seriously were the students at A&T University."

Moving on to A&T, the committee severely criticized both city and National Guard officials. Given the paucity of weapons found and the absence of any disturbance at the time of the sweep, the committee concluded that there was no justification for dropping tear gas from the air or forcibly destroying locks and doors. Indeed, such actions emphasized "the lawlessness and the disorder with which this operation was executed." In light of the abundant evidence of racial discrimination that it found in Greensboro, the committee questioned the accuracy of blaming Nelson Johnson and other "outside agitators" for the disruption. Instead, the committee was impressed with how consistently state, local, and school officials had acted to corroborate the charge that "the system" paid no attention to black problems in Greensboro.

IV

More than a decade later, an air of mystery and uncertainty still surrounds the tragedy at Dudley and A&T in the spring of 1969. No one is sure who killed Willie Grimes; nor is anyone certain who wounded the police or organized the gunfire from Scott Hall. Law enforcement officials who cited "confidential informants" as the basis for their charges at the time refuse to provide any additional information. Students and university officials have offered valuable testimony on the black perspective, but they, too, are unable to provide precise data. Nevertheless, it is still possible—and important—to venture some generalizations about the Dudley and A&T tragedy.

First, there is no way to escape the contradictions that run through the public police record—more contradictions than a reasonable person can accept as natural or incidental. Repeatedly, Chief Calhoun and others declared it would have been impossible for police to have killed Willie Grimes because no law enforcement official used a weapon of less than .32 caliber. It required an investigative reporter to disclose the fact that the police used both rifles and shotguns that could have fired the bullet which killed Grimes. Police insisted that the car carrying

Grimes to the hospital had fired upon the police cruiser following it; yet when the students' car was overtaken at the hospital there were no weapons inside it. For two days police circulated news reports about the arsenal of high-powered and semiautomatic weapons that had been captured during the National Guard sweep; all along, they knew that only three of the guns were operable. Finally, although Chief Calhoun asserted that there was heavy sniper fire when the National Guard began its sweep, most witnesses testified that the campus was quiet. The discrepancies seem neither small nor unimportant.

Second, a significant double standard—based upon race—appears to have characterized police and newspaper treatment of the disruptions. Although it would be difficult to imagine a more tragic event than the killing of an innocent student, Grimes's death received little attention in the media, certainly far less than did the stoning of cars containing white motorists or the destruction of white-owned property. In one editorial, the Greensboro *Daily News* detailed a litany of outrages, including "the sniping, the rock throwing, the bottle barrages, the assaults on delivery truck drivers and motorists." The editorial failed to mention either the death of Grimes or the shooting of another student. Nor did the white newspapers at any point question police or National Guard conduct. The same double standard carried over to sentencing procedures. One Dudley High School student was given an active sentence of twelve months on a charge of disorderly conduct and assault with a deadly weapon—his umbrella. The student claimed to be protecting female friends during fighting between police and Dudley students. Franklin Williams, a staff member of FCD, was sentenced to either six months in prison or a $500 fine for violating the curfew. Most others charged with the same violation were placed on probation after payment of court costs. Finally, Eric Brown—an admitted Black Panther—received a sentence of two to six years for ransacking a grocery store and stealing three cartons of cigarettes during the cafeteria workers' strike.

Third, in all of this, police, National Guard, and local officials overreacted. The hard-line stand of school representatives, the indiscriminate use of tear gas after students had been dismissed from Dudley on May 21, and the wanton exercise of force by National Guardsmen in breaking down doors in the A&T dorms—all suggest the absence of a sense of balance. As he listened to National Guard plans for the sweep, one city official recalled becoming "very much concerned about what I was hearing."

They were going to be shooting into these windows and all this
stuff . . . and I told a friend that if somebody didn't do something we were going to get about 150 people killed over
there. . . . I'll never forget going down to Scott dormitory the
next day . . . and seeing that place all shot to hell. . . .

By contrast, President Lewis Dowdy, who over and over again had
demonstrated his ability to deal effectively with student protest, was
never called upon to play any part in the crisis.[8]

Fourth, the overreaction of authorities was rooted in a state of near-
paranoia that swept state and local officials. In part, that hysteria reflected national events. In a year when blacks entered the state legislative building in Sacramento carrying guns (it was legal to do so), and
students took over buildings on campuses as diverse as Antioch, Duke,
and the University of North Carolina at Chapel Hill, public officials
were given to seeing conspiracies. President Richard Nixon condemned
"minority tyrants," and Attorney General John Mitchell called for a
crackdown on extremist demagogues. It sometimes seemed that the
entire country was under attack from young people who rejected the
rules and values of middle-class white America.

But the near-paranoia was also a response to local circumstances.
Never before had white political and economic leaders faced such a
profound threat. The challenge consisted not of weapons, but of an
approach to power that questioned the very ground rules by which city
leaders functioned and remained in control. By organizing poor people,
public-housing tenants, cafeteria workers, and high school students to
reject the definition of their proper "place" handed down by white
authorities, Nelson Johnson and his associates were undercutting the
very foundations of white power. No longer would blacks defer; no
longer would they allow someone else to set the agenda or determine
the scope of possible compromise. In effect, Johnson was asking blacks
to create their own base of power and solidarity, to shape their own
political program, and to do so independently of what whites thought. If
blacks created their own ground rules, they would cease to be vulnerable to white attempts to divide and conquer them through traditional
white rules.

In this sense, the new black insurgents were rejecting the heart of
North Carolina's progressive mystique. Black Power assaulted the assumption that whites should control the political agenda available to
blacks. By wearing bib overalls, "Afros," or dashikis, black young people

were launching a cultural attack on the right of whites to dictate black standards of dress. Whenever GAPP representatives arrived late to a meeting with white officials, or mobilized tenants to reject out-of-hand official rationales for urban redevelopment, they were defying white concern about manners and "civility." Thus, in almost every respect— their language, their cultural goals, their involvement with the poor, and their determination to build a revolutionary politics—the new insurgents posed a radical threat to the status quo. Indeed, they were striking at the very base of white control—the power to define what is real and unreal, permissible and impermissible.

Neither Greensboro's white leaders, nor those in the nation at large, proved able to deal with this political and cultural challenge on its own terms. The issues of self-definition, self-determination, and autonomy were too large, or perhaps too threatening. Instead, white leaders perceived a conspiracy—violent in nature—to commit illegal acts, to overthrow the government, to kill and maim white people. By defining the challenge in such a manner, it became easier to avoid confronting the underlying questions and yet to feel comfortable with a response to black insurgents of total rejection and hostility.

This insistence on finding a violent conspiracy, however, caused white leaders to ignore legitimate grievances and to overlook important distinctions within the black movement. In 1968 the Black Liberation Front had been dedicated to armed insurrection. But there were few vestiges of the BLF still in existence by 1969. Eric Brown and the Black Panther party had relatively little support at A&T. Furthermore, Nelson Johnson and his co-workers rejected Panther rhetoric and methods of organization. They sought to build a coalition around issues such as housing and to develop a sense of political efficacy both on campus and in the ghetto. To embrace the Panthers would automatically have sheared off large parts of that coalition. Johnson was too shrewd to engage in such self-destructive behavior. He and his associates did ally themselves with the Foundation for Community Development, and they did seek to radicalize youngsters in high school. But they were not reckless. As one member of the group later said: "The notion was to put as much pressure on as we could, but not to be insane. Let's not delude ourselves. The police, FBI included, would be very happy to pull out their pieces and blow your brains out. . . . It was always our orientation to put pressure on people but not get innocent people into a position where they could possibly get hurt."

Although such statements are self-serving, the evidence suggests that

Nelson Johnson and his associates were more committed to building the community than destroying it for the sake of armed revolution. On the basic issues, black ministers, lawyers, and bankers supported the young activists, particularly on questions involving the Dudley High School elections and the excessive use of force by the police. Once city officials became tied to a belief in a monolithic conspiracy, however, they overlooked the multiple constituences among black students and imputed a set of motives to every act of protest that made it impossible to address the substantive questions at the root of the protests. Since every expression of dissent was seen as part of a subversive plot, there was no possibility—or need—to distinguish legitimate demands from violent insurrection.

The result was the irrational use of force in 1969. Despite evidence to the contrary, city officials disregarded the existence of divisions among the student protesters. It was as if they needed to see a conspiracy in order to justify their own instinct to strike out and destroy the enemy. Once Nelson Johnson and his allies had shown their contempt for the progressive mystique, they had moved beyond the pale. Thereafter, white leaders seized any evidence of radicalism to create a picture of black insurgency that would warrant all-out retaliation. Hence the Viet Cong imagery. State Attorney General Robert Morgan insisted that the Black Panthers were so clever that one could not "distinguish between the militants with guns and the merely innocent." The implication: the Panthers melted into the population just as the Viet Cong did among the Vietnamese. When the Greensboro *Daily News* denounced black protesters for engaging in "guerrilla warfare," it was in a very real sense explaining why the use of any degree of force, however awesome, could be justified in response.

In this context, the violence of 1969 can be seen as a ritual acting out of the need to destroy an enemy who challenged one's most dearly held values, even if the exact nature of the challenge or the reasons for the reaction were never fully articulated in a conscious manner. "It was almost like watching something unfold that, once you started, it's out of everybody's control," former Mayor Jack Elam recalled. Moreover, since the enemy refused to play according to the rules of the progressive mystique, there was no need to worry about the harshness of one's response. In 1963, white leaders had chosen compromise rather than repression because making some concessions seemed the only way of preserving the city's progressive reputation. Now the rules had changed, both among the protesters and among the city's leaders. Repression had become a legitimate way of saying "never." Significantly, Captain William Jackson, who earlier had proven so adept at dealing with civil rights protest, played no role in formulating police policy. Instead, he was "pushed back" and "eased away" by superiors who wished to adopt a tough stance without encountering any opposition.

Perhaps above all, the tragedy of 1969 confirmed how powerless black people in Greensboro were—despite the efforts of Johnson and others—when white authorities chose to resist change. As soon as the disturbances began at Dudley, the white superintendent of schools sent a white associate to take over. When the action moved to A&T, local officials disregarded university leaders in shaping their response. The hard reality, the *Carolina Peacemaker* editorialized, was "that when the chips are down, most so-called black power rests in the hands of whites." Whether on the school board, the city council, or other city agencies, black perceptions and priorities were either discounted or interpreted only through white eyes. Nothing could do more to give credibility to the charges of Nelson Johnson. The troubles at Dudley, Dr. George Simkins told the North Carolina Civil Rights Committee, were just one more manifestation of an ongoing racial double standard. Not only was Dudley allowed to operate illegally as an all-black school in disregard of the Supreme Court, but whenever trouble occurred there, white people came in and began "cracking black heads." Would the same thing have happened, he asked, at a white high school or university?

V

Appropriately, the use of massive force at A&T occurred the same month that the Greensboro school board resolved to defy HEW. In both instances authorities chose to resist rather than concede on issues of civil rights. In both instances also, whites insisted on dictating the terms under which relationships with blacks could occur. Significantly, the school board's brief against HEW concluded that forcing white parents to send children to previously all-black schools "would be disastrous to the public school system of the community." In terms reminiscent of the Pearsall Plan debate, white support for the public schools became the primary point of reference, with blacks left out. The same rigidity characterized discussion of student protest at A&T and Dudley. In putting down student disorders, Guilford County prosecutor Douglas Albright declared, "the police haven't been brutal enough." Polarization around both issues could hardly have been greater.

In retrospect, at least part of that polarization appears to have been the work of agents of the state. Throughout the late 1960's, George Dorsett continually inflamed Ku Klux Klan members with his calls for violent repression of blacks. Typical of Dorsett's demagoguery was a statement to a Raleigh rally that "the white man of America will be pushed only so far. We are only backing up to the attack. We don't believe in violence, and we won't have it if we have to kill every nigger in America." Dorsett helped to trigger the violence that occurred around the housing issue in Greensboro during 1967. Yet throughout this period, he served as an FBI informer.

Most of the rumors of violent plots among black insurgents in Greensboro may also be traceable to an FBI agent provocateur. During the early part of 1969, a visitor who identified himself as a Black Panther came to Greensboro and joined the large group of black protesters who regularly congregated at Nelson Johnson's home. Mr. X, Johnson recalled, "put people in awe. He was big, bearded, very dark complexioned, [wore a] dashiki, and looked like what people thought Black Panthers should look like." After boasting of his exploits, the newly arrived Panther tried to incite his comrades to blow up buildings, ambush policemen, and start a violent revolution. Johnson and his friends became suspicious of the new arrival both because of his rhetoric and his effort to introduce drugs into the group. When Mr. X began to travel around the country with no visible means of support, their suspicions intensified. Yet FBI intelligence reports cited conversations led by Mr. X as examples of violence being plotted by black insurgents. Significantly, these conversations provided a chief point of reference for Chief Calhoun's narrative before the McClellan committee. Thus, the evidence of a black conspiracy to foment violent revolution may have had as its source a man distrusted by black protesters and suspected of being an FBI informer paid to provoke blacks to engage in illegal activity.[9]*

The ironies of such a situation abound. The leader of violent right-wing forces was a paid agent of the government. In all likelihood, the primary supporter of black revolutionary violence occupied the same position. If the bullets which wounded police at A&T came from National Guard rifles, as some officials speculated, nearly all the violence associated with the Greensboro tragedy, including the sweep of the dormitories, would be traceable to government actions. In Greensboro,

*For a full review of the evidence on this matter, see note 9.

as elsewhere in the nation, government counterintelligence operations seemed most effective in creating a specter of violence which then could be used to justify massive counterviolence by other government agencies.

Whatever the validity of such speculation, by the summer of 1969 racial hostility in Greensboro had reached an unprecedented level. Older blacks felt systematically excluded from the economic and political mainstream of the community. Denied access to decent housing, prevented by the election system from achieving representation on the city council, and ignored by the board of education, most felt alienated and powerless. Younger blacks, less optimistic in the first place about securing justice through "the system," also became increasingly radicalized when they could not secure action in the areas of housing, poverty, and education. Although the two generations sometimes disagreed over tactics and approach, they recognized how much they shared a common enemy, even when they were most at odds.

On the other side, white political and educational leaders displayed a remarkable insensitivity to black grievances and interests. Nothing reflected this more than the refusal to seek black representation either in the councils of government or in the process of making decisions about the black community. As long as public policy could be conducted on terms acceptable to the white leadership, peace held sway. But young black insurgents would not permit that to continue. When they questioned those terms, insisted on defining their own agenda, and assaulted the fundamental values underlying the existing structure of power, the response was massively negative. Although Nelson Johnson did not speak for all black adults in Greensboro, or even for many young people, there were few who would have disagreed with his open letter to the black community in June of 1969:

In our efforts to promote changes, unimaginable obstacles have been placed in our way. Whenever we took action, only those things that could be made to appear bad were reported. . . . We have been made to seem stupid, hateful, and violent [but] it has never been a case of outsider versus insider; instead it has been right versus wrong.

The new protest led by Johnson had not been able to achieve victory. But it had provoked white leaders into a response of harsh repression. If nothing else, the new insurgency had clarified the issues and created a new agenda for decision.

CHAPTER EIGHT
The End or the Beginning

When I first got to Greensboro I heard the white power structure condemning the four sit-in demonstrators as if they were subversives . . . Five years later I heard the Mayor of the city brag about the fact that we were the home of the nation's first sit-in, as if we had invented the electric lightbulb. By that time it was a resource, but in 1966 it was a painful memory.

Hal Sieber, Greensboro Chamber of Commerce

The Chamber of Commerce wanted to be on top of what was going on in the community, . . . using people to get information . . . . We were concerned about how the system did things in the community. They tried to get around us.

A young black activist

We do have freedom of choice in Greensboro. We have the choice to make the next few weeks and months the most productive and educationally rewarding in the history of our community, or we have the other choice, to drag our heels, to put up unnecessary obstacles, . . . to blame inanimate school buses for our unwillingness to make the school transition work.

Joan Bluethenthal, a parent volunteer

Just as insurgents must continually devise new strategies to undermine the status quo, those who hold power must constantly invent new methods of containment. In 1969 Greensboro's white authorities had met the challenge of black radicalism with repressive force. But military confrontation offered no permanent solution to the city's racial crisis. As awareness seeped in of how destructive further civil strife would be, established leaders of both races started to explore ways to prevent additional polarization. Business interests in particular groped for a program of conciliation. Their search was informed by the tactical judgment that, as one prominent white put it, "Nelson Johnson did not want peace . . . and would have been bitterly disappointed if the community had met all his demands." Acting on this assessment, Greensboro's white leaders sought an accommodation with the black middle class, hoping in the process to accomplish two objectives at once: to refurbish the city's progressive image and to drive a wedge between black radicals and reformers. If middle-class leaders of both races could move forward on a new agenda of cooperation, Greensboro might yet recover from her momentary lapse into reaction and redeem her reputation.

Three issues distinguished the history of Greensboro's race relations during the years after May 1969. First was the question of whether the white community would support efforts to build new structures of inter-racial cooperation. The tragedy of Dudley had clearly awakened some whites from their complacency, but would a program of concessions to blacks win broader backing? Second, could black unity be maintained in the face of white conciliation attempts? In the past the black bour-geoisie had supported the radical organizing activities of GAPP despite a profound antipathy toward black nationalism and socialism. Con-versely, Johnson and his allies had helped established black leaders to win concessions through traditional channels, despite their contempt for "the system." Could this solidarity continue if whites appealed to one group against the other? Finally, how would school desegregation inter-act with the other two issues? For more than twenty years, school integration had ranked high on the agenda of black protest. Now, at precisely the moment when substantive action was forthcoming, other black concerns competed for first priority. How would desegregation fit into the white strategy of conciliation? And what effect would it have on black attempts to maintain solidarity?

As each of these themes evolved from 1969 to 1972, the story of Greensboro began to come full circle. The old issues of the progressive mystique, white paternalism, and differing styles of black insurgency still dominated the larger drama, but the play was now being acted out on a new stage with slightly different characters. How these old issues were resolved in a new setting would say much about what had and had not altered in Greensboro's long struggle to come to grips with the question of black civil rights, and what the future might hold for those seeking a transformation of the existing social and economic structure.

I

Just one day after violence erupted at Dudley High School on May 21, 1969, a committee of the Greensboro Chamber of Commerce con-vened hearings on the confrontation. Within a week the committee proposed that Dudley High School students decide for themselves whether they wished Claude Barnes excluded from the ballot. The

Chamber of Commerce report was important, not because it transformed the immediate situation, but because it was the first time that a powerful white organization had clearly sided with black insurgents. At that moment little happened as a result of the hearings. But they represented a significant move by at least part of Greensboro's white elite to move away from polarization and toward a framework for building a new interracial alliance.[1]

Chamber of Commerce involvement in racial issues reflected in large part the work of one man—Hal Sieber. Reared in western North Carolina and a graduate of the University in Chapel Hill, Sieber became public relations director of the Greensboro chamber in 1966. Over the following three years he thoroughly redirected the chamber's activities, emphasizing social progress as the primary prerequisite for community development. Under Sieber's prodding, the chamber created the Community Unity Division to reach hitherto uninvolved citizens, sponsored neighborhood "cell" meetings to discuss racial questions, recruited hundreds of black members, and became a pivotal force supporting school desegregation. Although some believed that the chamber would have pursued these paths regardless of Sieber's presence, most agreed that Sieber was the "indispensable core" of the chamber's community-action program.

Sieber's interest in discrimination was an outgrowth of his childhood and adolescent experiences. As a first-generation German-American living in North Carolina's mountains, Sieber saw very few blacks; but very early he developed a sensitivity to prejudice. While in elementary school during World War II, Sieber was awarded a DAR citizenship medal. Yet on the day of the prize ceremony, the principal of the school told Sieber that the DAR had rescinded the award because of his German background. Shortly thereafter, a poem by Sieber about the evils of racial discrimination appeared in a local newspaper. By the time he arrived at UNC in the late 1940's, he found it natural to join the coterie of students who gathered each weekend on the steps of Frank Porter Graham's house to hear the gospel of racial tolerance preached by UNC's distinguished president.

Even though the next fifteen years brought varied occupations, the Graham legacy remained a continuing presence in Sieber's life. In 1950, at the urging of the UNC president, Sieber attended a New York Ethical Culture Society conference, where for the first time he had close contact with blacks. The experience altered his life permanently. Subsequently, Sieber wrote two volumes of poetry, one of which was nominated for a National Book Award. He also worked in Washington for Senator John Kennedy and Senator Ernest Gruening, and directed a congressional study of the incarceration in a mental institution of poet Ezra Pound. Later, Sieber returned to Chapel Hill, where for six years he served as public relations director for the North Carolina Heart Association. It was from that position that Sieber moved to Greensboro in June of 1966.

Chamber executives hired Sieber at a sensitive point in the organization's history. Local chamber officials talked constantly about Greensboro being a "modern, progressive, and dynamic" community, yet civil rights battles had already tarnished the city's image. Despite continuing announcements of business expansion, chamber leaders saw a need for new blood and new direction. Sieber's job was to "put some sparkle" into the chamber, to polish its image as an "innovative" organization, and to develop new programs—all at a minimal cost. Race was never mentioned as an overt issue during the interview process. Indeed, the chamber was still a classic booster organization, concerned with industrial development and convention solicitation. But underneath the traditional rhetoric was a budding awareness of "social issues."

Within weeks after Sieber's appointment, he began to reshape chamber priorities, albeit indirectly and with a subtle touch. Though Sieber claimed not to have race on his mind, he operated in such a manner that the issue could not long remain off the chamber's agenda. Sieber genuinely believed that Greensboro was "the most progressive city in the state," but that "didn't mean it didn't have a damn long way to go." Thus, whenever the public relations director wrote a speech for a chamber official he emphasized how much still remained to be done. Words by themselves, Sieber believed, exerted little impact on people's actions. But they could establish standards and expectations that then could lead to substantive action. "When you have a chance to write the speeches as well as to manage the way that things get into the press," Sieber noted, "you start seeing some results." Unabashedly, Sieber insinuated new symbols and concepts into the public realm—symbols that soon carried a political message. For example, after creating the cartoon character "Nat Greene" to represent the the city's namesake, Sieber had the cartoon figure alternately appear with a black or a white skin.

Sieber built his approach around having people discover for themselves how central race was to their lives. The public relations director initiated conversations throughout the community, supposedly to discover the major problems in the city. As different issues surfaced, it quickly became clear that most of them were related to race. Sieber applied the same techniques to small group meetings. There, he would repeat back to community representatives, with uncanny skill, the essence of what they had just described as pressing problems, in the process underlining the "race-relatedness" of the issue. Throughout, Sieber appeared to be totally neutral, simply a facilitator of dialogue. In addition, he earned praise for his powers of recall, reassuring people that they were receiving a fair hearing. By the end of the meeting, participants shared a sense of having arrived at a new insight about the importance of race in their community.

The "cell" group became Sieber's organizing signature, serving as both a means of extending the Chamber of Commerce into the community and bringing the community into the chamber. The discussion groups began under the label "Curbstone Conferences," and initially involved only chamber members who came to a local cafeteria each week to have coffee and to discuss issues such as downtown development, zoning changes, or education. Within a few months, however, Sieber had labeled the meetings "discussion cell" groups, consciously playing on the term's public association with communism. "The Chamber . . . normally starts off by talking about how it supports free enterprise and the American way of life," Sieber noted; "[the cell group put the chamber] publicly on record as supporting free enterprise in the marketplace of ideas, and not just in goods and services."

In the natural course of things, the cell groups focused frequently on "race-related" questions. As they did, more and more blacks became involved. By late 1969 the groups were meeting in the black community as well as the white community, in people's homes as well as in public places. The "cells" had become the principal instrument of broadening the chamber's outlook and extending its outreach.

The cell groups provided the centerpiece of Sieber's plan to involve the chamber in "total community development." Sieber chose the phrase in a calculated effort to attract chamber conservatives to the campaign for social change in race relations. From the beginning, some chamber members protested his activities, but no one, he believed, would object to "total community development." But after writing the slogan into the speeches of chamber officers until it became a cliché, he dropped the word "development," making the phrase "total community" instead, with all that the new slogan signified for blacks as well as whites. Through such devices, Sieber reversed the traditional posture of the chamber. Instead of being identified with the theme, "What's good for business is good for the community," the Greensboro chamber accepted the slogan, "What's good for the community is good for business."

The theme of "total community" provided the vehicle through which Sieber injected non-chamber issues onto the chamber's official agenda. "If you are involved in a total community approach," Sieber noted:

you are sooner or later going to be involved with people who have a lot of bottled up reactions to . . . the established ways of doing things . . . and you are going to be exposed to the very intense feelings that have developed over a period of time among the white poor, the black poor, the Indian poor . . . and if you are exposed to those things you are going to be exposed in human terms rather than statistical or paternalistic terms and you are probably going to be more responsive than you might be if you had never opened up that Pandora's box.

By tying the Chamber of Commerce to such a community approach, he made issues such as housing, political representation, and school desegregation legitimate chamber concerns.

The "total community" theme coincided with a soaring increase in black membership in the chamber. In the initial issue of *Greensboro Business* that Sieber edited, he featured an article on a black A&T professor. Shortly thereafter, Lewis Dowdy became the first black member of the chamber's board of directors. By the spring of 1968 three additional blacks had been named to the chamber's board. When Allen Wannamaker was elected president of the chamber for 1968, he asked Sieber what issues he should emphasize in his conference with the press. "Minority recruitment," the two agreed. That year more than two hundred additional blacks joined the chamber.

Nevertheless, the chamber experienced difficulty in gaining credibility with many blacks. Lawyers, doctors, and university officials were ready to join, once they sensed a welcome environment. But others viewed both Sieber and the chamber with suspicion. Dr. George Simkins, for example, kept a careful distance from the chamber, anxious to preserve his independence and leverage even after the chamber presented him with an award for his leadership. Sensitive to this suspicion, Sieber moved to win over blacks he perceived as most influential. Thus, he early recruited David Morehead of the Hayes-Taylor YMCA; Otis Hairston and Cecil Bishop, two prominent activist ministers; and John Marshall Stevenson, editor of the *Carolina Peacemaker*. Still, many other black community leaders—less prestigious and more radical in white terms—shunned what they perceived to be a devious effort being made by the white establishment to co-opt them.

In response to such opposition, Sieber encouraged the chamber to form the Community Unity Division (CUD). Established after the death of Martin Luther King, Jr., the CUD represented the institutional embodiment of Sieber's outreach strategy. Although an official committee of the chamber, the CUD was to consist primarily of "average" community people who were encouraged to maintain their independence. The King assassination highlighted how little real communication existed between whites and blacks and how widespread was the disaffection of the black community from existing white leadership. The CUD represented an explicit attempt to overcome that disaffection and expose white chamber leaders to black community sentiments.

The CUD proved its worth during the tragedy at Dudley and A&T. At a time when other community organizations were unable to mediate, the CUD heard testimony from all sides and offered specific recommendations. In addition to proposing a referendum in which Dudley students could decide if they wanted new elections, the CUD also recommended reinstatement of suspended students, a review of the high school constitution, and measures to establish more meaningful communication between students and administrators. "We heard no evidence from any source," the CUD declared, "that Claude Barnes was a person of other than good character and citizenship." Given Barnes's past record, the chamber committee called "debatable" the school's decision to exclude him from the election. Thus, the CUD had acted decisively on an issue of extreme volatility. Even leaders of GAPP grudgingly praised the CUD report. A school spokesman, by contrast, declared that education officials would treat the document as they would any other report from an organization such as HEW or the NAACP.

The CUD hearings represented a public "coming out" of the Sieber strategy. Prior to that time, most of his organizing activities had been hidden from outside view. Although the analogy of undercover intelligence is not exact, there was a *sub rosa* quality to the chamber's shifting political orientation. Intentionally, Sieber disguised his approaches to black community leaders with the language of traditional chamber concerns for business and membership. Neither Sieber nor the chamber had actively opposed the position of city leaders on an open-housing ordinance or school desegregation, preferring to work behind the scenes to change people's assumptions and perceptions. Nor were they involved in decisions over the use of force against black protesters. Now, however, the potential impact of the chamber's activities upon traditional patterns of race relations became dramatically visible. Not only was a chamber committee intervening; it was siding with the "radicals."

The most decisive aspect of the CUD action in this respect was the support given it by chamber executives. The CUD, almost by definition, consisted of people sympathetic to the black community. By standards of white power, therefore, what mattered was how the chamber's executive committee reacted. Most of its members agreed with the Greensboro *Daily News*, which mockingly praised the CUD for its "pure heart" but declared that "no concessions . . . ought to be made to gratify unruly and disruptive tactics." Chamber President Al Lineberry, however, had listened carefully to the testimony on the school crisis as an ex officio member of the CUD. (Lineberry was also on the school board.) If a mistake had been made, he believed, the only answer was to acknowledge it. In the end, Lineberry decided that school officials had committed a tragic error at Dudley. "After Al took such a strong stand," Otis Hairston recalled, "a lot of executive committee members changed their minds," even if only out of personal loyalty. Caught in a difficult position, the chamber president had followed his conscience, knowing that his position would alienate the chamber's business constituency. But in doing so, the chamber won an incalculable increase of respect from blacks, who saw for the first time a prestigious white organization willing to risk controversy on an issue of social justice.

With the CUD victory behind him, Sieber and his allies moved overtly to attack institutional racism. Testifying before the North Carolina Advisory Committee on Civil Rights, Sieber declared that all the problems at Dudley were "related to a community's inflexibility during a time for change." For too long, he said, Greensboro had been victimized by "cultural taboos and institutionalized responses" that had failed to deal with underlying issues of racial oppression and cultural miscommunication. The white ghetto, Sieber declared, was just as tragically separated from the "total community" as the black ghetto. Hence, both had to learn about the other, not with the goal of "making Milquetoasts out of militants" or "Amy Vanderbilts out of bigots," but with the intention of confronting directly the legacies of centuries of racism. To implement such a goal, the chamber began, in the summer of 1969, to sponsor sensitivity-training institutes and human-relations workshops where fifty or more people—half black and half white, half male and half female—would explore each other's perceptions of race and become better able to work with others to overcome discrimination.

Through all of this, Sieber inevitably became a figure of controversy himself. In the beginning, he had moved behind the scenes, almost invisible as he worked to alter chamber policies. "Hal had a way of getting across varying viewpoints and getting other people to champion a cause," one of his friends recalled. "I felt like I was watching a maestro." As Sieber's politics became more visible, however, dissention increased. White conservatives attacked him as a subversive trying to destroy the chamber as a business institution. Some white liberals, in turn, criticized the chamber for behaving as though it had invented civil rights. A few white radicals ended up on both sides. "When I first met you about three years ago," one activist white minister wrote, "I thought of you as a smooth-talking con-man trying to divert the community's attention from the real issues of community change . . . . I now realize that you were in the forefront of community change."

Black perceptions of Sieber were equally mixed. Many welcomed his commitment to social justice. "I don't think anybody will ever know," Lewis Dowdy said, "how many things were prevented from occurring because of [Hal] getting us together." Others admired his manipulative skills, seeing them as necessary assets in the struggle of social change. "He was able to move people without people realizing that he was moving them," Cecil Bishop noted. "When they did realize it, there wasn't much they could do about it." Above all, Sieber's black friends valued his role as an intermediary between the white and black communities. "[He] was somebody who would get somebody else to hear us," one man noted. Another added, "If you had nobody on the other side to talk to us, it could have been hell."

On the other hand, the same qualities generated suspicion. "Sieber was a snake in the grass," one young black declared. "He used people in the community to get information . . . . In some quarters black people thought he was the greatest thing that ever existed because he was doing favors, but he was out to destroy us." From the perspective of some black radicals, Sieber represented the ultimate example of paternalism, using flattery or the offer of jobs and political help to win allies. "He wormed his way around to everybody," Nelson Johnson commented, appearing to take the side of insurgents, but only for the purpose of controlling them. Sieber "tried too hard" to be genuine, skeptics said, and seemed to feel that "whenever or wherever a meeting went on in the black community, he was supposed to be there." A few viewed this as simply a psychic need to identify with blacks. But to some it suggested a determination to infiltrate the black movement and destroy it through a strategy of divide and conquer.

Whatever the verdict on Sieber personally, there could be little question that by 1970 the Chamber of Commerce had become a central presence in Greensboro's racial situation. Through its emphasis on "total community," the creation of cell groups, the recruitment of more than three hundred black members, and the activities of the CUD, the chamber had moved from being just a booster of big business to serving also as an advocate of racial reconciliation. Chamber leaders had recognized, Al Lineberry noted, that "as long as you've got that tall dry grass growing there is always a danger of fire; and when you break the ground and turn the grass under, the fire dangers are much less. So the Chamber was breaking new ground." With the aid of men like Lineberry and Allen Wannamaker, Sieber had persuaded chamber leaders, for the moment at least, that change in the racial status quo would serve Greensboro's best interests. Chamber of Commerce identification with that proposition, in turn, provided important legitimacy for those supporting a shift in the racial status quo. "For the first time," one businessman observed, "a lot of people changed a part of their mind and said . . . maybe it is socially acceptable to allow some integration." Clearly, Sieber had brought the Chamber of Commerce a long distance in four years. Whether for the purposes of subtle social control or radical social change, the organization was destined to play a pivotal role in Greensboro's future racial politics.

II

The second major ingredient in those politics consisted of the agenda set forth by the black community. If the Dudley tragedy of 1969 spurred new efforts by the white elite to seek racial reconciliation, it also forged new bonds of unity between young radicals and older reformers in the black community. In the past the two groups had often been split by dissimilarities of style and philosophy. Traditional protest leaders operated through existing channels of power. Despite their anger at specific injustices, most accepted the ground rules of the prevailing economic and political system and sought reform rather than revolution. The younger insurgents, by contrast, rejected "the system" and attempted to create both new ground rules and new values. Issues such as black separatism and revolutionary denunciation of capitalism symbolized continuing divisions in the black community. With white use of violence at A&T, however, these differences were set aside, dwarfed by the dimensions of the common enemy. The question now was whether old and young, reformer and radical, could create a program of demands that reflected areas of agreement and at the same time avoid issues that dramatized their profound differences over how to deal with the white "establishment."

One of the strongest voices supporting black unity was the *Carolina Peacemaker*, begun in 1967 by John Marshall Stevenson, a drama professor at A&T. Among the few faculty members who openly sympathized with student activists, Stevenson had first come to A&T during the 1950's. After alienating university officials by his strong commitment to racial protest (he wished to donate faculty funds to the NAACP Legal Defense Fund rather than for a bust of President Bluford), Stevenson was forced to leave. But in 1961 Lewis Dowdy urged him to return, and from that point forward, Stevenson became a charismatic figure in the community, not only stimulating students with his dramatic tours de force but also providing crucial support for those who questioned the racial politics of the city and campus.

Like Sieber, Stevenson was driven by an almost religious sense of mission. His uncle was the oldest practicing black physician in the state of Arkansas; his mother had been one of the first black nurses in the public health service. Although orphaned at an early age, Stevenson felt compelled to repay all that his family had given him by devoting his own energies to the advancement of the race. To the young drama teacher, Martin Luther King, Jr., represented the quintessence of service to black America, a man who could speak both to the generation that had gone before and the one that would come after. Stevenson hoped to emulate his hero and carry on that struggle to unite generations. Appropriately, the *Peacemaker's* name referred to a combination of force and love—Wild Bill Hickok's Colt .45 and Jesus' Sermon on the Mount.

The *Peacemaker* espoused two primary goals: achievement of an integrated society and development of a strong power base within the black community itself. Only when the second goal was accomplished, Stevenson believed, could the first become a possibility. Blacks required a position of strength from which to negotiate with the white community. To that end Stevenson urged blacks to stand together and to build powerful community institutions. Why was it, he asked, that with electricians being trained at A&T, the college hired white repairmen to fix its television sets? Why did stores serving ghetto customers not have black managers and staffs? The *Peacemaker*, Stevenson believed, could galvanize people to act on these issues. Significantly, the editor reserved his harshest barbs for the black bourgeoisie, particularly those intellectuals who believed that "with a new car and a mortgage, they had arrived." It was time, he argued, for blacks to "be purged of the do-nothing attitude which causes them to play footsie with uptown intellectuals passing as born-again liberals."

With the *Peacemaker* sounding the charge, black protest organizations concentrated on winning economic and political gains. The time had come, the *Peacemaker* announced, "to bring smoke to the pocketbooks of business and industry until they push their time clocks forward and bring American and Greensboro into the twentieth century." Black activists focused on supermarket chains that took dollars out of the black community but refused to employ black managers. After the King assassination, a negotiating committee succeeded in getting the A&P to hire a black manager. Within two months, Kroger and Colonial stores had followed suit. At the same time, Stevenson pointed out that even states like Mississippi had elected blacks to their state legislatures, while North Carolina—supposedly the most progressive state in the South—had done nothing. Local blacks, Stevenson said, should stop being "duped" and start supporting their own candidates. By the spring and fall of 1968, that effort started to bear fruit, with the election of Henry Frye to the state legislature and Elreta Alexander to a district judgeship.

The campaign for political recognition achieved substantial success, however, only after the tragedy at Dudley and A&T. Prior to that time white leaders had for the most part turned a deaf ear to black protests about the absence of political representation. Now, the combination of black insistence and white desires to avoid further polarization produced results. Some white leaders claimed that such concessions "were waiting in the wings anyway," but even these observers acknowledged that "the riots . . . speeded things up." Whites were not "willing to tolerate these moves being made," Mayor Jack Elam said. "They had not been aware before how important these seemingly token things were to the people in the black community. Now that they knew that it constituted a direct threat to their own well being, they accepted it."

The first breakthrough came in May when Jimmy Barber was elected as the first black city councilman since 1963. Then came what seemed to be a deluge of appointments. In July of 1969 a black was appointed assistant to the City Manager—an office long sought by Greensboro Negroes in acknowledgment of their 26-per-cent share of the city's population. For the first time also, blacks were named to the Alcoholic Beverages Commission, the Guilford County Draft Board, and the Housing Commission. When white members of the Economic Opportunities Council in Guilford County attempted to name a white Northerner to head the antipoverty agency, black protests led to the selection of Charles Davis, a black from Greensboro who long had been active in the Negro protest movement. Perhaps most important, the city council named Vance Chavis to a council seat left vacant by death, thereby giving blacks two of the seven seats on the council. Significantly, through most of these ventures, young black activists such as Nelson Johnson worked alongside older and more traditional leaders in pressing for change. The united effort appered to be producing dividends. In an editorial entitled, "Is the Pendulum Swinging Towards Justice?" Stevenson noted that black citizens "were being afforded opportunities to serve the total community . . . in capacities which never before have been open to them."

Even the school administration showed signs of flexibility, at least in the area of administrative appointments and policies toward student dissent. Just two months after the Dudley disruptions, Fred Cundiff became the first black to hold the position of assistant superintendent of schools. A man who believed that students should not be punished for thinking critically, Cundiff was placed in charge of the "freedom of choice" pupil-assignment plan. His influence soon was felt in Dudley High School. For the first time students there were given the right to eat their lunches outside of school; Claude Barnes was a finalist in the election for senior class president; and a new student group committed to black unity was approved, with Barnes as senior adviser. Another sign of change came when Dr. George Evans resigned from the school board in March of 1970; his replacement was Walter Johnson, a black lawyer who had participated in the original A&T sit-ins and had been the first black to be graduated from Duke Law School. Johnson represented a new breed of activist leadership, his selection perhaps a sign that change would even invade the school board, the city's last bastion against change.

Throughout these battles, division in the black community over competing racial and political ideologies lurked just beneath the surface. Usually the differences were contained as each side worked to maximize cooperation; but on occasion they threatened to explode into public conflict, destroying the solidarity that had come at such a high price. In almost every case the underlying issue was how much to work with whites, or trust "the system." In one instance, for example, GAPP initiated a rent strike against John Taylor, the owner of several apartment complexes in the black community. To young activists Taylor typified the white slumlord, notwithstanding his "liberal" political views. Yet many older blacks remembered that Taylor had risked his career to desegregate the Holiday Inns he owned, and that he had always supported integrated housing. Taylor's friends pointed out that he was correcting problems brought to his attention by tenants and had displayed good faith in negotiations. From their point of view this kind of tactic showed how easy it was to carry Black Power too far.

A similar conflict emerged around differing approaches to community organization. GAPP had always been separate from OEO, the two organizations having opposing methods of operation. GAPP believed in living in a community and organizing residents around issues like welfare and housing that directly impinged on their lives. OEO, by contrast, worked through official agencies on programs such as redevelopment and job training. In 1969, however, Tom Bailey was hired to direct community development for OEO, and he brought with him an orientation much more similar to that of GAPP. In the spring of 1970 more "established" blacks accused GAPP and Bailey of trying to brainwash innocent youngsters, turn them into revolutionaries, and incite them to illegal activities. The Bailey faction, in turn, perceived the attack as an effort sponsored by downtown leaders to defuse political insurgency and ensure that antipoverty activities would remain antiseptic and impotent.

The OEO conflict dramatized how volatile was the issue of trusting "the system," especially the Chamber of Commerce. Black radicals were convinced that chamber officials were trying to eliminate Bailey and Johnson from any influence with anti-poverty organizations. Indeed, rumors circulated that the chamber had proposed funding an OEO faction to fight the "Black Panthers." Hal Sieber, of course, personified the threat with his successful attempts to woo established black leaders to his "total community" alliance. When the *Carolina Peacemaker* announced its intention to "lock arms with the developing [white] power structure," Johnson and his followers erupted in anger, accusing Stevenson and others of allowing themselves to be duped by an insidious conspiracy to co-opt blacks into the white capitalist system.

More often than not, however, the competing black factions found ways to submerge their differences and form an effective coalition for common objectives. In many cases individuals from the two camps were close friends. They liked and admired each other. More important, each recognized what the other side had to contribute because, despite different methods of proceeding, each gained more from cooperation than from allowing differences to dominate. Thus, a banker from a savings and loan company was a close ally of GAPP in the antipoverty fight. Through pursuing a strategy that was "a combination of negotiations and some element of confrontation," both sides benefited. When GAPP activists widened the parameters of protest through their aggressive organizing, they helped confer greater legitimacy on the demands of traditional black leaders, who now appeared to be "moderate." Ministers and NAACP leaders could now ask city officials, "who do you want to deal with, . . . us or these radicals?" Cecil Bishop noted that "those of us who were establishment types knew that we needed the troops." The young radicals, in turn, understood how much support from older black leaders meant for their ability to work in the community day to day. "Most of us would be in jail today were it not for [traditional leaders]," Tom Bailey noted. "Those men and women . . . were able to make the jump and understood very clearly that it was the entire black community versus the established order . . . . Otherwise, we would not have survived."

The extent to which solidarity prevailed, despite continuing tension, became apparent during the spring and summer of 1970, when radicals and reformers alike rallied behind a series of strikes by city cafeteria workers, housing tenants, sanitation men, and blind workers in a skillcraft factory. In each case, GAPP provided initial leadership for the organizing campaigns, but almost immediately black ministers, the NAACP, and black business leaders joined the cause—raising money, supplying food, and mobilizing community support. Housing kicked off the new protests. In November 1969 hundreds of black residents testified before a city council hearing about substandard conditions, rentgouging and the refusal of landlords to provide plumbing facilities or repair inadequate heat and lighting. Among the demands were strict code enforcements, the creation of a rent-control system, and a requirement that housing be in good repair before being rented. By January all these issues came to a head in a strike against the AAA Realty Company. Constant agitation, as well as support from some of the largest black churches in Greensboro, finally resulted in a settlement that addressed tenant grievances.

Soon thereafter attention shifted to the city's school cafeteria workers. Again, GAPP members organized the workers to strike, but the entire community rallied in support. At the end of May more than two hundred and fifty people marched from St. Stephens Church to the school administration building in support of the workers; the strikers' case, in turn, was argued before the school board by three of the most prominent black leaders in the city, with Walter Johnson leading a fight within the board for recognition of the workers' grievances.* The degree of support, Tom Bailey noted, reflected the fact that these issues, "didn't come out of the sky. They were very real. They were community problems that people could see and feel, and it was for that reason that these [community groups came] together, sat down, and tried to organize." The black community provided similar support for the sanitation workers' strike and the blind workers' strike; although neither of these walkouts resulted in victory, there could be little question that the older generation willingly supported the objectives sought by more militant and younger activists.

Nothing dramatized this underlying unity more vividly than the black community's response to the jailing of Nelson Johnson and Robert Evans for their role in the Dudley disruptions. Both men had been given sentences longer than the legal maximum for a misdemeanor. After repeated appeals, the sentences were reduced by two months. Writing from jail in the summer of 1970, Johnson exhorted his fellow blacks not to allow white authorities to divide them by making Johnson a scapegoat for the Dudley tragedy or a figure of contention. Instead, the young activist pleaded, blacks should display solidarity across class and political lines and demonstrate their refusal to be manipulated. In an impressive display of unity, black bankers, preachers, lawyers, and protest leaders rallied to Johnson's side, lambasting "the system" for trying to blame him for the city's tragic errors. Only hypocrites, Cecil Bishop told a mass rally, could accuse Johnson of irresponsibility and at the same time ignore the murder of Willie Grimes. If city leaders had any intelligence, "Ole Nosey," the *Peacemaker's* gossip columnist, concluded, they would recognize that Johnson was the most important positive force keeping violence out of Greensboro.

With such episodes in mind, John Marshall Stevenson had reason to feel somewhat optimistic about the two goals he had articulated in 1967

---

*Otis Hairston called Johnson and asked him to come to St. Stephens to hear the workers' complaints. At the time the school board's attitude was hostile to the workers. After attending the meeting, Johnson sent a certified letter to all his colleagues detailing why he supported the workers' demands and urging a fair hearing on the issues. If nothing were done, Johnson said, he would make his letter public. At that point the school board adopted a more sympathetic stance.

when the *Peacemaker* began publication. Despite divisions over philosophy and style, black unity appeared to be a high priority. When Howard Fuller moved Malcolm X Liberation University—an alternative college committed to Black Power and culture—from Durham to Greensboro, virtually the entire roster of established black leaders turned out to welcome the new facility. He had chosen Greensboro, Fuller said, because of the support the black community gave to students, cafeteria workers, and sanitation men. A new sense of reconciliation also existed between student activists and university administrators. Stokely Carmichael came to A&T in May and criticized those who carried guns and tried to incite violence. By December, the Student Organization for Black Unity (SOBU) was holding a "save black schools dinner" at A&T, with principal speeches by Lewis Dowdy, state representative Henry Frye, and Nelson Johnson.

The evidence also suggested that Stevenson's goals of adequate political representation might be closer. After Vance Chavis was appointed to fill a city council vacancy in 1969, Greensboro's black community had two representatives on the seven-man board—representation approximately proportionate to the black percentage of the city's population. In May of 1970 the police department finally named a black as commander of the police community relations division—a long-time demand of black activists—and Cecil Bishop was named head of the Housing Authority. When Otis Hairston was added to the school board in March of 1971, black representation on that body also came to two out of seven seats. Even Governor Scott appeared somewhat responsive to the changes. One month after Nelson Johnson and Robert Evans were jailed, he granted them an executive pardon, citing the recommendations of Greensboro leaders "interested in making progress."

Thus, by 1971, Greensboro's blacks had achieved a degree of political strength unprecedented in their history. Through both unity and skill, black leaders successfully won concessions from city leaders intent on rebuilding Greensboro's image of progressivism in race relations. The key question that remained was whether black leaders could retain their unity and political representation without foundering on the ideological shoals of black separatism and contempt for "the system."

On that issue, the signs were mixed. During the city cafeteria workers' strike, Thomas Bailey had been forced to leave his OEO position because of charges that he helped organize workers in violation of rules governing federal employees. Lewis Brandon, a teacher in a public school and a GAPP member, was also pressured into resigning because of his support of the strike. Both episodes confirmed black radicals in their conviction that "the system" was committed to destroying any serious challenge to its power. On the other side, black reformers reacted angrily when GAPP leaders barred Hal Sieber and another white official from a meeting of black tenants. From the point of view of GAPP, Sieber's presence represented one more attempt by "Whitey" to control the decision-making process of black people. But to blacks who had come to trust Sieber as a powerful ally in a joint struggle, such actions smacked dangerously of racial separatism for its own sake. During the sanitation workers' strike, the whole issue surfaced again. Black workers accused a white organizer of betraying them, while the organizer claimed that GAPP activists insisted on working only with blacks. By 1970, little if any contact existed between young white radicals and young blacks. As one white activist recalled of his visits to Malcolm X University, "it would take fifteen or twenty minutes to get in the door . . . and when you came in you [had to be] escorted."

Given the specific issues of 1969 and 1970, it had been possible to contain these tensions. The community stood as one in support of workers victimized by an unfair wage system and leaders unjustly imprisoned by white authorities. Yet it was by no means clear that such unity could be sustained. As the new home of Malcolm X University and the headquarters of the Students Organized for Black Unity, Greensboro had become by 1971 the center of Black Power in the South. Moreover, organizations such as GAPP were increasingly critical of both white involvement in black activities and blacks who accepted the ground rules of capitalism.

In that context, the ability of black leaders to retain a united front would depend on the issues of the 1970's. No question was likely to generate more internal conflict among blacks than school desegregation, particularly the elimination of black-run schools and the imposition of a white majority in all educational facilities. Yet by 1971, that was precisely the issue at stake in Greensboro. Nearly twenty years after the *Brown* decision, substantive school integration was finally on the horizon. The results would say much about Greensboro's progressive mystique and the solidarity of the black protest movement.

III

In 1971 Greensboro was one of only five North Carolina school systems still not in compliance with federal civil rights guidelines.* Twelve

---

*There were 152 school districts in all. Greensboro, the local paper noted, was the largest city still maintaining a "freedom of choice" policy.

all-black schools still existed in the city, and the board of education had no intention of altering that pattern. After an HEW examiner issued a final ruling against Greensboro in August 1969, the school board voted to continue the appeals process, this time through the courts. As a result federal funds were deferred and the amount of money coming annually from Washington declined from $1.5 million to $423,000. Programs to sensitize teachers about the different cultural backgrounds of their students were among those closed down.

Judical action, meanwhile, continued to undercut Greensboro's legal position. In the aftermath of the *New Kent County* case, district courts ordered local communities in North Carolina and elsewhere to adopt HEW-suggested methods to achieve desegregation. When High Point, a neighboring community, refused to do so, Judge Edward Stanley in Greensboro decried the school board's "lack of fortitude."

You have been more sensitive to local clamor than to your responsibilities. It is not a matter of what you or I think should be done. It's the law and people must understand that.

In December 1969 the Fourth District Court ordered High Point to desegregate all its schools with a seventy/thirty white/black ratio in each school.

George Simkins and ten other black parents then filed suit, on February 24, 1970, demanding the immediate desegregation of Greensboro's schools. The plaintiffs charged the board of education with intentionally perpetuating a racially discriminatory school system and providing unequal educational facilities and opportunities for black students solely on the basis of their race. School board attorneys responded that freedom of choice had already led to desegregation of local schools. Although admitting that forty-two of the city's forty-seven schools were "racially identifiable," the board insisted that it had already accomplished "as rapidly as practicable, the complete elimination of any and all discrimination." When Judge Stanley suggested that the school board seek HEW assistance in working out a more acceptable plan, its attorney responded that he had no desire to put thirty thousand pins on a map of Greensboro solely to achieve rigid ratios of black and white in every school. Seeking the advice of HEW, he declared, was like asking for help from the NAACP. In the absence of any prospect for compromise, Judge Stanley suspended action on the Simkins case in October 1970 pending the Supreme Court's decision in *Swann v. Mecklenburg*.

On April 30, 1971, Judge Stanley rejected, once and for all, Greensboro's contention that "freedom of choice" constituted a legal means of pursuing desegregation. In light of the *Swann* decision upholding busing as a means to integrate schools, Stanley ordered the Greensboro school board to produce a plan providing for complete desegregation by June 18, with implementation to occur the following school year. Everyone recognized that large-scale busing and a universal ratio of black to white in each school would be necessary components of any acceptable plan. On the day of the decision, twenty-seven schools in Greensboro were more than 95 per cent white or black. Although more than ten thousand students were bused daily, only one hundred and fifteen were transported from the black section of the community to predominantly white schools. For more than a decade, the school board had argued that such a situation amounted to elimination of a dual school system. Now, the city had less than five months to compensate for the failures of past policies. As the city moved to confront the crisis, two questions dominated the scene. Would a school board that had said "No!" for so long respond affirmatively to the desegregation challenge? And would the white and black communities of Greensboro be able to accept what amounted to a transformation of the city's school system?[2]

IV

The answer to the first question revealed how quickly a strategic elite could reverse its field and effectively implement a policy that for so long had been resisted. Almost immediately, it became clear that the time for nay-saying was past. Just as the city's economic and political leaders had responded with concessions in the aftermath of the Dudley crisis, school officials now chose to comply without hesitation and to implement complete school desegregation.

The process was aided by the rise to leadership of a new generation of school board officials. During the preceding two years, three of the men most closely identified with "freedom of choice" had died. A different position by any of the three—Superintendent Philip Weaver, School Board Chairman Richard Hunter, or School Board Attorney Robert Moseley—might have altered school board policy earlier. Now, all were gone. At the same time, three new men joined the board, including Walter Johnson, a widely respected black attorney, and Otis Hairston, the author of black desegregation demands in the early 1960's. The third newcomer was Carson Bain, a former mayor and a tough, result-oriented businessman.

Presiding over the reconstituted school board was Al Lineberry, a former president of the Chamber of Commerce and owner of one of the city's largest funeral homes. Elected to the chairmanship the same week as the *Swann* decision was handed down, Lineberry was the white leader most capable of forging a creative, compassionate alliance with community groups interested in desegregation. "The first thing to know about Lineberry," Lewis Dowdy noted, "is that he is a Christian." Deeply committed to acting on his faith twenty-four hours a day, Lineberry saw his task of leadership and reconciliation as a religious mission. Lineberry defended the school board's actions during the late 1960's, believing that its members, including himself, had acted in pursuit of the best educational policies. But Lineberry's own views had been altered during the CUD hearings on the Dudley crisis. That involvement, Hal Sieber later noted, was probably the "single most sensitizing experience" that Lineberry could have had in preparation for being school board chairman.

When Lineberry took the chair for the first time shortly after Judge Stanley's decision, he charted a firm course. "We're going to comply," he told the board. "We're not going to fight the court, we're going to satisfy the court." From that point forward, complete cooperation—not resistance—marked the school board's posture toward desegregation. The Greensboro school board submitted its desegregation plan to Judge Stanley on May 26. The NAACP presented its proposal on June 2. The two plans were similar in outline, except that under the school board proposal five schools would have remained all-white and three would have remained predominantly black. The NAACP, by contrast, insisted that all schools , should have the same racial proportions. Judge Stanley—with the school board's acquiescence—supported the NAACP, and the issue was decided. In a little less than two months, the school board had accomplished, on paper at least, what for almost twenty years it had said would be educationally impossible.*

School board action meant little, however, without community acquiescence. To that end, white-led citizen groups had begun to mobilize citizen support for desegregation even before the case was decided in court. For more than three years the Chamber of Commerce's Community Unity Division had been building a framework in which white

---

*The similarity of plans submitted by the NAACP and school board reflected the new alliance being created by middle-class leaders across racial lines. Dr. Simkins invited Walter Johnson to his home at a time when Julius Chambers, the NAACP attorney, was visiting. After getting a thorough briefing from Chambers on what the plaintiffs wanted, Johnson went back to the school board. The result of such "backdooring" was a school board proposal remarkably parallel to that of the NAACP.

and black citizens could confront and resolve their problems. In addition, a small group of Greensboro women decided in the winter of 1969–70 to study the issue of social change in education for their "Great Decisions Club." The activities of both groups created a structure within which popular support for desegregation could be rallied once the decision was handed down.

The three-person "Great Decisions" team was headed by Joan Bluethenthal, a Philadelphia native who had moved to Greensboro in 1950 and had become involved in a variety of activities including public housing, day care, and the Council of Jewish Women. Impatient at the superficiality of many "great decisions" discussions, Bluethenthal and her compatriots set out to examine the unmet needs of the school system. Not surprisingly, the group concluded that human relations represented the number one problem of the schools. Everybody talked about the issue, but no one was prepared to do anything about it. "In spite of the fact that the *Brown* decision . . . was over fifteen years old," Bluethenthal later wrote, "we had no plans." If only money were available, Doris Hutchinson, director of school staff development, told the group, teachers, parents, and students could be brought together to look down the road and make those plans.

When Bluethenthal and her friends delivered their findings to the Great Decisions Club in January, 1971, they had completed their assignment. But at almost the same time Bluethenthal attended a conference at A&T entitled "Getting To Know You." There, Dr. Dorothy Williams of Shaw University presented a poem on the dilemmas of racism. The poem read:

Prejudice is cancerous to mind,
It eats and eats at soul 'til blind;
Blind and weak the soul is pained,
All is lost—nothing is gained;
The prejudiced soul must now take heed,
Or it is doomed to hell with all deliberate speed.
Prejudice, what is it?

The conference, together with Bluethenthal's own instinct for action, convinced her that more than study was needed. "The time was ripe," she later wrote. "Responsible, caring people wanted to do something and we just happened upon a course of action—positive action— and . . . offered anyone who wanted it a chance to participate."

Bluethenthal and Doris Hutchinson of the school system worked out a four-stage human-relations program, beginning with a series of week-end retreats for students, parents, teachers, and administrators in the spring of 1971. Each retreat sought to find ways to avoid racism in the schools and promote justice and communication between blacks and whites. To implement the plan, Bluethenthal raised $25,000—half from United Community Services, and half from the Chamber of Commerce. The first retreat was already scheduled when the Supreme Court handed down its *Swann* ruling.

The so-called "Chinqua-Penn" retreats became the training ground for hundreds of Greensboro residents who subsequently worked on be-half of the transition to integration. Held in an old mansion surrounded by grassy slopes, each of the three retreats involved two hundred people. Those attending represented a cross-section of the community: black and white students, parents, teachers, and administrators. With the assistance of psychologists, the participants learned to interact closely with someone of the other race, often for the first time in their lives. Those attending spoke candidly about their fears, the stereotypes they harbored, and the specific problems the community faced in preparing for desegregation. Parents learned that principals were human, and administrators heard, for perhaps the first time in depth, a student and parent perspective on education. "Most of us," Bluethenthal recalled, "experienced a oneness as we struggled with feelings and challenges which we all shared and of which we were all a part. We left knowing we had to do something." If nothing else, the retreats created cadres of individuals who, through their experience together, found a common commitment to make desegregation work.

Like Lineberry, Bluethenthal occupied a position of maximum re-sponsibility at a critical time. Many talented women, a friend wrote her, spent their lives searching for an identity and purpose without ever finding it. "[That is why] I envy you three girls," the friend continued. "You're where the world is at. As I weed my vegetable garden, I am well aware that this is temporarily what I need, but . . . it's just a pacifier when the world is on fire. It's really exciting to see someone in the right place at the right time . . . it's almost as if you had been preparing for this moment." In fact Bluethenthal had been "preparing" for nearly a year, and as the spring turned into summer, she, as much as anyone, shaped the nature of citizen response to desegregation.

In the meantime, the Chamber of Commerce pursued its own pro-gram. Hal Sieber had admired the efforts of the three women, especially their ability to communicate with the conservative community. In his own work he sought a similar base of operations. "I felt the day of reckoning would come," he commented, "and when it did come there [would be] a need for a coalition of community leaders to say that we in Greensboro are going to comply with the law . . . that we support the public schools, and that we believe in improved human relations." In order to establish such a coalition, Sieber recognized the need to avoid debate on issues such as busing. Rather, he emphasized the importance of committing people to obey the law of the land, however the court might interpret it. Through such a device, individuals of different persuasions could maintain their own points of view even as they joined in an alliance dedicated to upholding the law. During the winter of 1970–71 the CUD established a subcommittee to build the alliance that Sieber envisioned. Significantly, the new organization was to be called "Concerned Citizens for Schools," (CSS), a name consciously chosen to preempt the "concerned citizens" label that White Citizens Councils had so often used in the past to oppose desegregation.

In the months prior to the *Swann* decision, the CCS operated as an extension of the Community Unity Division. While the staff compiled a mailing list of 1700 influential community leaders to be mobilized when a court decision was handed down, informal discussions continued with the aim of building a broad base of support for the public schools, regardless of which way the court decided. While some staff people planned publicity, others discussed such issues as how to control rumors. Most of the chamber's energy went into a continuation of the human-relations workshops and cell groups that had been an integral part of the CUD program since 1968. Meeting on a weekly basis, the cell groups involved anywhere from five to 150 people discussing a broad range of community problems. The human-relations workshops, on the other hand, were one-time events designed to bring together representatives from all segments of the community to focus specifically upon race relations. Like the Chinqua-Penn retreats, the human-relations workshops were intense experiences, "You're taking a close look at yourself, and other people were criticizing [you]," one participant recalled, "and that's the part most people can't accept . . . you feel like you're being exposed." Yet those who joined such sessions inevitably gained a deeper understanding of the racial dynamics at work in themselves and the community. From 1968 through 1971, more than 2400 Greensboro citizens took part in these chamber-sponsored workshops.

At the end of May, the CCS went public. Inviting a representative segment of the community, the Chamber of Commerce convened the first official meeting of the CCS "to foster community cooperation with Greensboro's school system in order to assure quality and equality education as designed and required by law." Although no final judicial decision had been handed down, the CCS emphasized that "[our] organization is concerned about one thing—to make sure that all of us do our best to make a necessary school assignment transition as educationally helpful, productive, and dignified as possible." By the end of June, the CCS had elected Cecil Bishop, a black, and Robert Mayer, a white, as co-chairmen. By July more than one thousand members were enrolled.

The Bluethenthal group, in the meantime, had persuaded the board of education to establish its own Human Relations Advisory Committee. Chaired by Bluethenthal, the Lay-Professional Advisory Committee (LPAC) was divided equally between blacks and whites, and drew upon many of the people who had emerged as leaders during the Chinqa-Penn retreats. Like the CCS, the LPAC attempted to mobilize all the forces it could. "We weren't fighting [others]," Bluethenthal noted; "we're just saying, if it's going to happen anyway, [let's do it right]." The major difference between the two groups was the the CCS dealt primarily with the larger community, while the LPAC concentrated on solving problems inside the schools.

During the early part of the summer, the coalition created task forces to deal with crises that would arise when desegregation began. One group worked on publicity, another on setting up a rumor-control center where parents could call to verify or report news of trouble. Desegregation supporters identified parent and student leaders who could develop a positive atmosphere in the new schools. The LPAC focused especially on student council representatives and PTA officers from the old schools who might provide a leadership core in the new schools until elections could be held. Another task force, called the Problem Solving Group, brought together students from different geographical and cultural backgrounds to discuss fears and concerns.

Paralleling these efforts, school administrators moved to facilitate the transition. Under pressure from Carson Bain, Otis Hairston, and Walter Johnson, the Superintendent appointed blacks to a series of high-level positions. Mel Swann, a black named to be assistant superintendent of schools for student affairs, became a pivotal figure, working as coordinator with the LPAC, establishing a liaison with each school in the community, and communicating directly with parent and student groups.

Under Swann's leadership, new assistant principals were named for each high school to work primarily with student affairs. Each high school appointed a black head coach in at least one major sport. Schools also introduced new courses on black history and culture. In addition, new black principals were named, and the school board took care not to demote or dismiss principals or assistant principals affected by the transition.

At the same time school administrators implemented their own four-stage human-relations program devised in conjunction with the Bluethenthal group. An outside expert conducted an eight-day workshop for principals on the importance of providing for the individual needs of the students. Later in the summer the supervisory staff met to develop strategies for dealing with interpersonal problems. School board officials, meanwhile, did their part to overcome the communications barriers that had existed in the past. Al Lineberry spoke to 111 meetings and was constantly available for consultation. "Whoever calls," he told his wife, "they've got a problem and somebody needs to listen to them."

The primary burden for communicating with the outside community, however, rested with the CCS. The CSS set out to combat the greatest obstacles facing desegregation—ignorance and fear—and to make known as much of the unknown as possible. To cope with parent fears about busing, the CCS published statistics on how safe school buses were. For those concerned that children might be unruly on the buses, the chamber advertised the presence of adult bus monitors. The new chamber president, W. A. Pittman, and Sieber met with more than one hundred community and church groups. Perhaps most important, the CCS mounted an intensive advertising campaign designed to create a positive community attitude toward the transition. "It Can Work," was the message delivered by thousands of bumper stickers and billboards. Community-service television programs, radio talk shows, and frequent newspaper stories provided an ongoing forum for CCS representatives to drive home the theme that Greensboro could make desegregation a positive experience. A six-page brochure depicted the back of a school bus, with black and white faces in the window, headlining the slogan, "Maybe We'll All Learn Something." Brimming with information, the pamphlet answered every conceivable question that parents might ask: how PTA's would be reorganized, what the white/black ratio would be in different schools, how teachers were being prepared for the transition, where parents might call for information, and how long the longest bus ride was (forty-five minutes). As the summer wore on, there was hardly a person in the entire Greensboro area who did not see or hear each day the CCS message that desegregation could work for the benefit of everyone.*

None of this, of course, occurred without significant opposition. Whites who were angered at the prospect of "forced busing" organized two groups, one called Positive Leadership for Education Action (PLEA), the other Americans Concerned about Today (ACT). Each campaigned for a constitutional amendment that would prohibit compulsory school assignments for teachers and students, and recruited support for alternatives to the existing school system such as "Christian Academies." At times, as many as two hundred people attended meetings of PLEA. Resistance also appeared among some people who attended CCS meetings. Why should whites be made to feel guilty about race? one woman asked Joan Bluethenthal. Blacks already had their "quota of jobs assured under federal legislation."

But the greatest opposition came from within the black community. As early as April, a group of blacks mobilized to oppose "mass forced integration, particularly busing." With integration, these parents believed, black children would be made to feel inferior. Black culture and leadership would be de-emphasized, and Negro pupils would lose the positive sense of identity associated with schools such as Dudley and Lincoln. Some blacks perceived the integration order as "a calculated plan to keep our people down" through the destruction of black pride and institutions. At an early meeting of one black PTA group, a majority voted to oppose the integration plan. "The 1954 decision," Nelson Johnson told the audience, "was based on aspirations for quality education. Integration was only a tactic. Today black pride has led to cohesiveness; therefore the whites want to integrate in order to break this down and control our schools." In the view of Johnson and some other black activists, attending school with whites ensured neither quality nor equal education. Rather, integration was being substituted as a panacea to divert attention from real issues like jobs and housing. Ironically, many adopted the position taken earlier by foes of the *Brown* decision.

*The coalitions supporting school desegregation were also successful in getting the Guilford County Commissioners to add $154,000 to the school operating budget for emergency assistance in helping with desegregation. "Our children are going to schools in the belief that their parents have left no stone unturned in making preparations for the most momentous school event in many decades," Joan Bluethenthal told the commissioners. She asked whether the commissioners wanted the responsibility in the decade hence for not having done all they could to make the transition successful. The money helped to pay for teachers and principals to come back to school early and attend preparatory meetings designed to sensitize them to the problems they would be facing in the fall.

Racism, they said, could not be legislated out of existence. According to this point of view, freedom of choice represented the only viable alternative.

Through the weeks and months after the court decision, debate over the issue raged inside the black community. Many black parents insisted that some schools should retain a black majority, both for purposes of cultural identity and because it seemed advisable to keep control over at least some institutions. White parents would not want their children to be a minority in other schools, these black parents argued; both races legitimately feared that their independence would be compromised in a school dominated by the other.

Yet the plantiffs in the Greensboro court case all had been black. It was they who had insisted on a 70/30 ratio in *every* school within the system. Speaking for those who had long struggled against segregation, John Marshall Stevenson asked editorially: "are we doomed to re-live our past?" Eloquently, Stevenson asked his readers to remember Edward Edmonds and other black teachers who had been fired from their jobs for fighting on behalf of integration. He recalled the common laborers who had stood guard over homes assaulted by white opponents of desegregation. It was true, he acknowledged, that white leadership had shown a massive capacity for duplicity and exploitation; it was also important that GAPP and SOBU and Malcolm X University should continue to free the minds and bodies of blacks. But, he concluded, "time has run out on freedom of choice. What a sad commentary for black citizens who now stand on the brink of true freedom for the first time to be willing to run back into the dark forest of segregation, of second-class citizenship."

As the internal struggle continued, the pro-integration point of view gradually gained the upper hand, at least publicly. Most black leaders had been identified with the fight for school desegregation too long to now abandon it. Cecil Bishop was co-chairman of the CCS. Otis Hairston served on the school board. Julius Douglas and Dr. George Simkins both had devoted their lives to the cause of integration. Even though some established blacks wished privately that a few schools could retain a black identity, they were unable to say so because of the precedent of their own past actions. In addition, the school board's selection of blacks for prominent administrative positions provided important ammunition for those supporting desegregation. "The sun do move," Ole Nosey declared in his gossip column after the rash of black appointments. Instead of being "dragged screaming into the twenty-first century, the school board [is] walking into the new day with pride and dignity."

As a result, black community leaders eventually came down on the side of busing. To have done otherwise would have precipitated a devastating internecine war. Not only had blacks initiated the desegregation suit; prominent members of the community had been involved at every level of the effort. In effect, they were taking the calculated risk that "if we go along with [whites] we'll get where we ought to be—eventually." Younger blacks such as Nelson Johnson and Tom Bailey justifiably perceived the school board plan as a threat to their hopes for Black Power and community development. But compromise on this issue— unlike others—could not be reached because the underlying principles were too basic. Once it became clear that Black Power advocates could not carry their fight without creating permanent divisions within the community, the younger leaders played down their hostility to the desegregation plan. "Our base was really not that strong to survive without [the older leaders]," Tom Bailey recalled, "and it became more and more apparent to us that that was the case." Particularly devastating was support for desegregation by men such as Hairston. "It was hard to criticize Otis," Walter Johnson noted, "because [he] was out in front of all the others. He was taking risks when it wasn't [fashionable], . . . Everything they were talking about doing, he'd already done." By midsummer even those who still led the black opposition had adopted a flexible position. Cecil Rouson, a black activist who was a member of PLEA, announced that even though his supporters opposed forced pupil assignment, they supported obedience to the law. Intentionally or unintentionally, white leaders had finally found an issue on which they could defeat Nelson Johnson and his allies, even while creating divisions of class and ideology in the black community.

As August began, supporters of desegregation mounted their final mobilization drive. "The sand bags are all in place," one supporter wrote Mel Swann. "Everyone seems outwardly relaxed [even if] inwardly braced for whatever." In order to prepare for "whatever," the CCS and LPAC coordinated a blitzkrieg of activity. The LPAC and the school board sponsored a four-day period of parent hearings where individuals could receive answers to their questions. More than 1500 people attended one meeting. The CCS, meanwhile, intensified its cell discussions, with more than one hundred meetings held in local neighborhoods. Such discussions not only brought people of different backgrounds together; they also created a new reserve of leaders who, as a result of their experiences, developed an investment in making desegregation work. Parents could remain indifferent as long as their own children were not involved, but once the issue struck home, many began to work actively for the cause.

In its most ambitious effort, the school desegregation coalition declared August 15 "Public School Sunday." Ministers emphasized the importance of "beginning to learn how to live with each other in an open community," urging Greensboro's citizens to be gentle and kind, honest and open, and prepared to answer for past mistakes. The next Sunday, words gave way to action. Knowing that fear of the bus ride represented the greatest concern of parents, desegregation supporters sponsored a mass visitation of parents and students to the schools. Along with the pupil assignment letters sent to parents, the school board issued invitations for an open house to be held on Sunday, August 22. Parents rode on the buses their children would take. They were met by teachers, students, and administrators who conducted guided tours of the new schools. In each place, core members of the new PTA's served refreshments as teachers answered parents' questions. More than 30,000 parents visited Greensboro's schools on Open House Day, with 1000 greeted at Dudley High School alone during one forty-five-minute period. Each parent was handed a copy of the CCS brochure, "Maybe We Will All Learn Something," as well as school bus schedules and a sheet giving parents advice on how to prepare their children for the transition.

Not to be outdone, student leaders demonstrated the extraordinary measures they had taken to prepare for the new school year. From the very beginning, student representatives had actively participated in the Chinqua-Penn retreats and the meetings of CCS and LPAC. Recognizing the importance of athletic contests and student government, the young leaders worked to ensure fair racial representation in those areas. School athletes and their fathers met with coaching staffs and were urged to go out for sports again. Student representatives wrote regulations assuring that at least two cheerleaders in each school would be black, and that a biracial committee would make the selection. In addition, plans were made for biracial School Action Councils to act as student governments until new constitutions could be written and new elections held. Typical of the preparations were the three orientation sessions planned for Dudley. At the first, former Dudley students were to gather and express their feelings. At the second, new students would meet to air any problems they anticipated. Finally, all would meet together and share a discussion of the major problems perceived by each group. The attitude of students was perhaps best expressed by Maurice Hundley, a black student leader from Page High School. "Students will make the change if parents stand behind them," he noted. "If parents open up, that will be three-fourths of the problem."

By the time "Public School Sunday" occurred, practically every contingency had been dealt with. Each day for more than a week the local newspapers had presented lengthy descriptions of each school, featuring pictures of libraries, cafeterias, and recreation facilities. School personnel, together with numerous volunteers, had moved more than 12,000 pieces of furniture and 70,000 library books into their new facilities. More than a thousand adults had been recruited to serve as bus monitors, with a guarantee that each trip to and from school would be accompanied by adults and met at the school gate by a parent volunteer. Sixty more adults had been trained to handle the telephones at the rumor control center. So thorough was the preparation that CCS officials invited members of PLEA and ACT to bring their case to the final meeting of the CCS so that each side might have the opportunity to air its point of view. By the time the meeting occurred, Cecil Rouson, a black executive committee member of PLEA, criticized plans to boycott city schools. It was time, he told the meeting, for the opposition to "open their eyes and learn from the positive attitude and constructive spirit which characterizes Greensboro here on the eve of the school opening."

When the day for desegregation of Greensboro's schools finally arrived, the battle had already been won. Two buses did get lost, and a few children ended up going to the wrong school. But most observers agreed that it would have been difficult to imagine a smoother transition. Three months earlier there had been twenty-seven schools in the city that were nearly all white or all black and only five that could reasonably be called integrated. Now the entire system had been transformed. Within days a new world of busing, integrated PTA's, and biracial student governments had become routine. A local journalist who served as a "bus father" concluded that "the slogan 'it will work' can be changed to 'it is working.' . . . The people of Greensboro have every reason to be proud of themselves and even more of their children." Although all the underlying problems of race and discrimination remained, Greensboro had reached a milestone. "I feel so proud to say that I'm from Greensboro," Dr. George Simkins declared.

Within a few months, experts were citing Greensboro as proof that blacks and whites could work together to make desegregation work. In a survey of forty-three school districts in the South, the NAACP Legal Defense Fund and four other organizations concluded that Greensboro's desegregation process was "probably superior to that of almost any other city in the South." The Chamber of Commerce was especially singled out for its role in "stepping into the leadership vacuum which is often filled by vocal opponents of desegregation." Two years later, beset by a desegregation crisis in its own city, the Boston *Globe* called Greensboro "a model" for others to emulate. "Desegregation in Greensboro was not an accident," the paper said. "It was a case of community leaders setting a goal and capitalizing on community pride, respect for law, and recognition that children should have the same educational opportunity."

Thus, seventeen years after leading the nation in declaring it would comply with the *Brown* decision, Greensboro was once again in the headlines as an example of racial progress. As observers from other communities took note of the city's desegregation procedures, local leaders boasted of their "feeling of pride that Greensboro was different from other cities, that it was a city interested in improving human relations." Yet, if it was important to ask how Greensboro had accomplished so smoothly the transition to integration, it was also important to ponder why the process had taken so long. As Joan Bluethenthal told a meeting in August 1971:

We are the ones who always believed in E-Quality education, we always wanted to live by the law of the land. . . . We always wanted to, but what did we do about it?

V

In looking back at Greensboro's history after 1969, the one theme that stands out above all others is the speed, efficiency, and skill with which white leaders implemented a radical change in policy. Clearly, the use of force at Dudley and A&T had gone too far. Not only did it provoke an angry response from blacks that could not be tolerated on a long-term basis; it also shattered Greensboro's reputation for racial enlightenment. "We had been through 1969," one observer remarked. "Were we going to do it all over again? The answer [was] no. We're going to do what's good for business. Which is the reason we settled in 1963. It's a question of economics." Yet if a progressive image was to be retrieved and made creditable, a new tack was necessary.

Much of the groundwork for the new strategy was laid through the subtle organizing skills of Hal Sieber. But once his purpose became visible, figures in the white business and political community aligned themselves on Sieber's side, even if reluctantly. Through an effort notable for its sheer intensity, new forums for interracial communication were established, long-standing black grievances were addressed, and a framework was created for middle-class cooperation across racial lines. The desegregation drive of 1971 simply culminated the campaign, crystallizing strategic developments that had been evolving over the preceding two years. Almost overnight, the city accomplished what for ten, fifteen and twenty years white leaders had described as impossible to attain.

In the face of this effort, black activists displayed a remarkable degree of unity in working toward common objectives. Nelson Johnson and GAPP participated in NAACP voter registration drives, worked for the election of blacks to city offices, and cooperated with the leadership agenda set forth by black ministers and businessmen. More traditional leaders, in turn, provided substantial support for most of the radical organizing activities championed by the "young turks." Because of their unity, blacks achieved more victories in the years after 1969 than ever before. In addition, the black community pulsated with political energy as different groups debated how to defeat slumlords, whether to work within "the system," and when to resort to strikes or boycotts. Yet this solidarity and dynamism could continue only by avoiding issues that evoked deep-seated conflicts over black separatism and political radicalism.

When school desegregation became the primary focus of attention, it was inevitable that unity would break down. For most young radicals, going to school with whites had never occupied the same symbolic or substantive importance that the older generation had attached to the issue. School desegregation represented a priority of another era. From a radical point of view, the issues were class and race oppression, creation of distinctively "black" values, and the development of independent community institutions. Older black leaders, however, had sacrificed too much for desegregation to dismiss it now as secondary. For most of them, integration still exemplified what the struggle was all about. They believed in it, they had bled for it, and they would not move to new priorities—not, at least, until that victory had been won. For such individuals, giving up the goal that had driven them for so long would be tantamount to rejecting a segment of their lives. Clearly, such a step was impossible. Both for reasons of ideological conviction and psychic integrity, they needed to see the battle through—even if the price was a break with the younger generation of more radical activists.

There are two ways of viewing these developments. From one perspective, Greensboro had achieved a new maturity of race relations. For the first time in their history, white city leaders had operated straightforwardly in an interracial coalition to bring about significant change in the racial status quo. More than at any time in the past, the alliance had been based upon a recognition that the contribution of each side was indispensable for success. With skill, imagination, and, above all, dedication, black and white leaders had worked together to move Greensboro in the direction of racial progress, in the process burying traditional modes of paternalism and white supremacy.

From another perspective, however, the older forms of control had simply taken on a new appearance. Through black political appointments and capitulations on issues like school desegregation, white leaders had successfully "coopted" members of the black middle class, giving them an investment in the prevailing system of political and economic authority. Yet had power really changed hands? Were blacks any more in control of their own fate? Was not the primary achievement of the post-1969 period the polishing of Greensboro's progressive image and the isolation of her young black radicals? In short, did not the victories of the post-1969 years simply reflect paternalism raised to a new level of shrewdness and sophistication?

In the end, such questions may have no definitive answers. But they remain the crucial issues of Greensboro in the 1970's—and 1980's—joining the history of those years to the history of all the generations that have gone before.

CHAPTER NINE
Struggle and Ambiguity

It seems to me that this community in a real sense is realizing its
potential for leadership in the South.
> *Susie B. Jones, former Dean of Admissions at Bennett College*

To me the single most important thing that came out of the
1960's is how the superstructure was able to absorb a revolutionary thrust for a long period of time [without ever really
changing].

> *Nelson Johnson*

"Some things have changed a lot, some things haven't changed at all,"
a black lawyer observed. "[At] Shiloh Baptist Church . . . the baton was
passed from J. T. Hairston to Otis Hairston. But the philosophy didn't
change. 'Let's push in all areas as much as we can for the benefit of
those we serve.' In the civil rights area George Christopher Simkins,
Sr., made it possible for George Christopher Simkins, Jr., to do what he
did. The father passed on to the son a perspective of how things ought
to go and allowed him to become active in the community. . . . Now,
another generation of folk are being given an opportunity to be heard
[and] you have different voices. But there is a continuity among some of
the voices that reaches back fifty years."

I

Continuity: the theme is an anchor in the shifting currents of Greensboro's racial history. From the church to the school to the NAACP, a
thread of protest links one generation to another. Vance Chavis refused
to ride Jim Crow buses or to attend Jim Crow movie theaters; his
students addressed envelopes for voter registration and became leaders of
the sit-in movement; and in 1969 Chavis himself became black Greensboro's spokesman on the city council. Otis Hairston grew up in his
father's Shiloh Church, organized student civil rights protests at Shaw
University, and returned to Greensboro to spearhead the civil rights
battle as chairman of the Greensboro Citizens Association. The
NAACP Youth group, founded in 1943 by Randolph Blackwell, produced a roster of leaders destined to transform Greensboro's history—

Ezell Blair, Jr., Bill Thomas, Tony Stanley, and Walter Johnson. If the strength of black protest in Greensboro seems remarkable, it is because the roots of that protest go back so far.

Continuity exists also in the attitudes that have prevailed in the white community. Committed to political moderation as the best means of guaranteeing continued economic growth, Greensboro's white leaders have consistently boasted of their support for reasonableness and tolerance in race relations. No single family or corporation set this policy; nor has there ever been a power elite enforcing it, at least not in the classic sense of a few people meeting regularly to make decisions. Rather, the heads of the city's large industrial and commercial enterprises have shared a series of assumptions on how to regulate conflict and preserve harmony.

These assumptions constitute the progressive mystique that has dominated North Carolina from the early twentieth century to this day. Every social system, Erich Fromm has observed, generates values and modes of behavior that help existing structures perpetuate themselves. The progressive mystique fulfilled that function for North Carolina's economic and political leaders. Openness to new ideas conveyed a sense of enlightenment and tolerance. Insistence on consensus ensured that any political programs that generated too much conflict would never be acted upon. And paternalism smoothed over the rough edges with those—blacks and labor, especially—who might otherwise become a source of conflict. Good manners surrounded all these values with an aura of civility, reinforcing the notion that this was a genteel way of life. Woe be to anyone who dared to challenge these ground rules or question the virtue of those who subscribed to them!

In racial politics, the progressive mystique operated in both positive and negative ways. Because of a concern with paternalism and civility, white supremacy in Greensboro and most of North Carolina never exhibited the viciousness associated with it in Mississippi or Alabama. As one black woman observed approvingly, "[the worst things] just never happened here . . . you can be disappointed with the progress, but there is something here that is fundamental. [Greensboro] never goes overboard." As a result of this absence of racist terror, blacks in Greensboro had the psychological space to protest. Without the politics of moderation, it is unlikely that Greensboro would have been the birthplace of the student civil rights movement.

Yet the progressive mystique also served as a masterful weapon of social control. By promoting the appearance of enlightenment and tolerance, the mystique obstructed efforts to mobilize sustained protest. The enemy was elusive and flexible, not immediate and brutal. In effect, North Carolina's image of progressivism acted as camouflage, obscuring the extent to which underlying social and economic realities remained reactionary. Although the world of Frank Porter Graham appeared contradictory to the world of labor and racial oppression, in fact the relationship was complementary. Graham's liberalism kept observers from probing North Carolina's conservative core, serving ultimately to protect that conservatism against attack either from insiders or outsiders. After all, North Carolina was progressive. It did not treat people brutally, as did other states. Therefore, people concerned with oppression should concentrate on the worst offenders and let North Carolina take care of itself.

The use of the progressive mystique to forestall substantive change reached a pinnacle, of course, with enactment of the Pearsall Plan. Never before had the rhetoric of moderation been used so effectively to implement a politics of reaction. Significantly, the results were the same as they had been historically in trade unionism. Just as North Carolina was last in the proportion of workers organized for collective bargaining, the state also ranked near the last in desegregating its schools, largely because outside officials were convinced that the state was "moderate" and "progressive" and should be left alone.

It was within this over-all framework of continuity that the struggle for black civil rights in Greensboro was waged. If one of the characteristics of the progressive mystique was its promise that progress would be forthcoming if only blacks showed patience, one of the characteristics of black protest was its persistence in developing new tactics to test that commitment. The civil rights movement in Greensboro was like a series of waves on an incoming tide. Each time a civil rights protest took place, pledges of improvement caused the wave of protest to recede in the expectation that the promises would be acted upon. When they were not, a new wave developed, carrying insurgency to yet another level. Incredibly, at each stage blacks continued to believe that concessions would be implemented, leading to substantive breakthroughs. Yet, each time, those who held power performed only the minimal acts necessary to forestall protest, thereby inevitably calling forth still another wave of insurgency. From the politics of deference during the 1930's and 1940's to the protests and petitions of the post-*Brown* years to the direct-action sit-ins of 1960, each stage of black assertion developed new techniques designed to overcome the obstacles placed in the path of racial justice by white leaders. With the massive demonstrations in 1963, these waves of protest reached a new crest, frontally challenging the effort of white political and economic leaders to use voluntarism and civility as defenses against change.

Even as late as 1963, however, black protesters accepted the framework established by the progressive mystique. Although demonstrators broke the rules in order to call attention to their grievances, they retained faith in the system itself and believed that appropriate reforms would make a reality of the democratic dream. Petitions, protests, even massive sit-ins—all operated on the premises that the existing ground rules were consistent with the achievement of equality.

It was only after 1963 that blacks began to question those ground rules. The most visible and dramatic symbols of discrimination were gone, making demonstrations difficult if not impossible. At the same time white economic and political leaders proved adamant in opposing any substantive progress on issues of institutional racism. Black radicals who came to political consciousness in the years after the sit-ins felt that there was no longer any reason to have faith in "the system." Whites had engaged in a series of cosmetic concessions that altered the appearance of race relations, but they had left completely intact the structure and foundation of racism. Only by attacking the structure itself could the struggle of black independence be won.

It was for that reason that black radicals in the late 1960's began to assault the very premises of the progressive mystique. No longer would they permit whites to establish the framework for interaction between the races, nor would they accept white definitions of what was appropriate or not appropriate to discuss. Instead, they sought to build a coalition of poor people, college students, workers, and professionals to establish an independent black base from which to attack the white structure of power. By rejecting civility, consensus, and paternalism, Black Power advocates attempted to strike at the heart of the white progressive hegemony.

Yet in doing so they also placed themselves beyond the protection of the progressive mystique. Paternalism had certain advantages. If blacks accepted its constraints, they received protection. Once they rejected those constraints, on the other hand, they placed themselves at risk—beyond the pale. Clearly, the protests of Black Power advocates no longer fell within white definitions of acceptable dissent. Since black radicals had rebelled against the white-controlled system of civilized discourse, there was no need for white authorities to obey traditional restraints in their response. The repression at Dudley and A&T was the result, setting the stage for one last attempt to restore progressivism.

In the aftermath of the violence at A&T, white leaders recognized that new initiatives were necessary if the community was not to lose forever its reputation for tolerance and enlightenment. "The business community," one white woman recalled, "realized the city was either going to have to integrate or it was going to destroy itself. It was purely a survival necessity." Pulling back from the brink, white political and educational leaders reached out to their middle-class colleagues in the black community. The effort to retrieve "progress" from the rubble at A&T would test Greensboro's capacity for change as never before.

Clearly, the black community was divided over how to respond. Blacks had their own agenda, which they effectively presented to city leaders. But beyond the issue of black appointments to city agencies and political offices, there existed larger questions of division over class, racial ideology, and political conviction. "There were sharp differences," Nelson Johnson noted, "over the extent that we would go to represent the masses of people." To Johnson and his allies, the reconciliation attempt by white leaders was one more slippery effort to co-opt black protest and destroy the movement for independent black power. Leaders such as Otis Hairston and Cecil Bishop, on the other hand, perceived the white conciliation attempt as a venture worth exploring. Ultimately, the conflict boiled down to a simple question: was it worth the chance of being burned again to see whether the white community was serious this time?

Desegregation of the public schools crystallized these divisions within the black community. To Nelson Johnson, the school issue was a diversion, deflecting attention from more basic concerns. "The essence of the struggle," he said, "was against real things; jobs, housing and education [were] simply reflected in the schools. [But] the whole integration thing . . . replaced the real issues [by making it seem] that the solution to our problem was proximity to somebody else physically." From Johnson's point of view, the concessions were designed to "destroy the unity that was capable of making demands, and replacing it [by naming] individuals to certain official positions." Reformers, by contrast, saw school desegregation as one step in a series of advances necessary for the realization of equality. Members of the black middle class, in particular, were willing to sacrifice unity with radical young activists for the possibility that integration would create a better life for their children as well as provide a foundation for securing the age-old promise of full participation in the American Dream.

II

How one judges the results of the risk depends in large part upon one's perspective. With the help of black leaders, Greensboro accomplished the transition to desegregation better than any other city in the South. In that enterprise Walter Johnson and Otis Hairston were crucial. Benjamin Mays, the president of Morehouse College in Atlanta, had told Johnson in 1970 that the key to successful integration was placing enough blacks in policy-making positions to ensure an adequate black voice in the process of arriving at decisions. Johnson learned the lesson. "One black in any structure can't do anything," he said. "But get him some company, and you'd be surprised what he can do." Together with white allies such as Carson Bain and Al Lineberry, Johnson and Hairston were able to persuade the school board to name blacks to crucial positions both in the central administration and in the individual schools themselves. In 1974, Johnson himself became chairman of the school board, dramatizing the change that had taken place.

Despite significant problems, Greensboro's desgregation process proved both stable and effective. Predictably, there was some racial strife, with blacks concerned about inadequate representation on student governments, cheerleading squads, and committees, and whites concerned about the possibility of violence. But most of these episodes were handled effectively by a fully biracial staff. Over a period of seven years the school population declined by 5000 students and the ratio of white to black shifted from 68/32 to 55/45. Much of the decline could be traced to a declining birth rate, out-migration to new suburbs in the county, and the shifting age-structure of the population; but between 25 and 30 per cent of the downturn represented a move by whites to private schools. Four schools had a black majority by 1978, with whites in one school comprising only 22 per cent of the student body.

In handling this issue, Greensboro opted for stability of school assignments over wholesale redistricting. Faced with the prospect of redrawing attendance zones so that every school would have the same racial proportions, most parents—black and white—emphasized their commitment to the schools their children were then attending. In many instances, parents had invested hundreds of hours to make the new school pairings work for their children; now these parents were unwilling to go through the process all over again. There seemed a consensus among school board members and parents alike that the existing school assignments—allowing a 20 per cent variation from the city-wide ratios in any school—provided the best opportunity to preserve the benefits of both desegregation and stability.

But if school desegregation worked relatively well, there were also reasons to question the advances made after 1971, especially their depth and direction. Integration entailed losses as well as gains; all along some blacks recognized the profound gap that would be left through losing institutions that had meant so much to black community life. Whatever its shortcomings as a hierarchical, sometimes authoritarian school, Dudley High School symbolized the pride, standards, and strength of black Greensboro's striving and achievement. Now, along with the retirement of Nell Coley, Vance Chavis, John Tarpley, and other dedicated teachers, the school also lost its black identity, the élan that accompanied its teams and clubs representing black Greensboro in local and state competition. Walter Johnson recalled that he had had opportunities at Dudley and A&T that never would have been available in a white setting. A black school provided a familiar environment. There an individual could aspire to be class president, stretch his horizons, and develop a core of strength from which to engage the white world outside. What would happen to racial pride, some blacks wondered, when integration eliminated black institutions? By the mid-1970's not only schools, but also voluntary groups like the YWCA had lost their "black" outposts and identity. One did not have to believe that integration was a white supremacist conspiracy to recognize the importance of this loss of a home base for future black generations.

Just as disturbing was the resignation—under pressure—of Hal Sieber from the Chamber of Commerce. Although Sieber's leave-taking had many causes, including complicated personal reasons, many believed that his politics had gone too far for white leaders who resented the pressure Sieber brought to bear for continued change in racial matters. "Hal went to the well so many times to get the chamber to change things," one observer noted, "that by 1973 he had probably dropped his bucket . . . once too often." To some blacks in particular, Sieber's leaving suggested that the Chamber of Commerce no longer wanted substantive racial change. At the time of his resignation, Sieber was pressing for investigation of police brutality in Greensboro—one of the sorest points in Greensboro's black community. He also challenged the chamber's right to hold committee meetings at segregated locations such as the Country Club. Similarly, he insisted on a continuation of encounter groups—now without outside funding—so that the gains in racial understanding achieved during the desegregation crisis could carry into new issues of racial conflict. From the point of view of friends, it was Sieber's advocacy politics that prompted the pressure for his resignation—not "personal" considerations. "Too many people were afraid," Eula Hudgens observed. "They hadn't gotten sensitivity training [themselves] and they had started up lies about it to escape being involved." According to this perspective, Sieber was the heart of the chamber's community-action program; without him, it would collapse; hence, his resignation signified that the chamber no longer cared about racial progress. Even Sieber's radical critics saw politics involved in his leaving. Sieber "worked himself out of a job," Nelson Johnson said; "after the real edge is off of this [kind of thing], those kinds of guys are not generally liked. So he got fired."

Whatever one believed about the reasons for Sieber's departure, there could be little question that his resignation signified a retreat from activism by one of the leading white institutions of the community. For good reasons or bad, as long as Sieber remained there was likely to be agitation on racial issues. But chamber leaders now decided that the time had come to restore stability. As Joan Bluethenthal noted, "more conservative people come on board at some point, and they are usually the people who see you through." But if encounter groups and sensitivity sessions were ended, how would the community combat the resurgence of racial stereotypes? If racial inequality still existed (and no one really believed that it had been eliminated), how could progress occur without agitation? In short, did not the abandonment of special programs geared to end racial discrimination automatically mean a pullback from substantive breakthroughs?

Perhaps the greatest loss of the post-1971 period was the demise of an active civil rights movement. By almost anyone's standards, the years after 1972 represented a nadir of civil rights protest. In many respects, the absence of a dynamic movement simply reflected the latest swing in the pendulum of protest. Yet the response of Greensboro's white leaders also played a crucial role in the decline of activism. By focusing on school integration and dividing black activists along class and political lines, white leaders had destroyed the unity so helpful to the effectiveness of black protest in 1969, 1970, and 1971. During the ensuing years the divisions between black radicals and black reformers became even deeper. Black radicals turned inward, seeking an intellectual and cultural strategy that would explain the past as well as inform future activities. Traditional black leaders, in turn, became more and more suspicious of anything resembling the radicalism of the late 1960's. When one former student sought a job teaching black studies at one of Greens-boro's universities, he was told that the school would never hire anyone who had been a student there from 1967 to 1971.

The demise of a united black movement completed the retreat from activism generally. If it was true that white leaders responded only to black pressure, then the absence of united black protest inevitably assisted in bolstering the status quo. Thus, an integral relationship existed be-tween the Chamber of Commerce's withdrawal from activism on race, divisions within the black community, and the lack of a strong black protest movement. In part, the pattern could be explained simply as exhaustion from the frenzied intensity of the late 1960's; but it also suggested larger forces of social control present in the country as a whole.

III

In all these developments, Greensboro represented a microcosm of what was taking place in America generally. The stages of black insurgency that evolved in Greensboro paralleled the stages of black insurgency in the country at large. From the politics of deference and petition in the 1930's and 1940's to the politics of assertion and protest in the late 1950's, Greensboro's black community mirrored trends prevailing among blacks elsewhere. The sit-ins inaugurated a wave of direct ac-tion, expressing in a creative new language the determination of black Americans everywhere to be free. Similarly, the confrontation and po-larization of the mid-1960's reflected shifts on the national scene as well. In some ways Greensboro simply exemplified national trends; in others, it helped to create them, particularly with the sit-ins and the evolution of Black Power ideology. But in either case, the city's history suggests the extent to which these stages reflected a shared history of black struggle, and grew out of circumstances that were more than local in nature.

Significantly, the system of white control against which blacks re-belled in Greensboro also represented a larger national phenomenon. Greensboro's progressive mystique paralleled in many ways the style of moderate liberalism prevalent in the country's national politics. There, too, the focus was upon stability, with change in race relations occur-ring only when concessions offered a means of restoring peace and retaining an effective image in the world. While free expression of ideas has usually been tolerated nationally, action on those ideas, particularly in the area of race, has taken place only under forceful pressure—almost never voluntarily. In the nation, as well as in Greensboro, civility and the manners of reasonable discourse have been used as a primary means of channeling dissent, not through forbidding the articulation of radical ideas, but through controlling the framework in which they can be considered and discussed.

The history of the national civil rights movement exemplifies the extent to which similar constraints on change have operated. The 1963 March on Washington, for example, was initially conceived as a massive act of civil disobedience with demonstrators sitting in at the Capitol until a Civil Rights Act was passed. In the face of that threat to the structures of national power, white political leaders and their more moderate black allies adopted a compromise that would make the march "respectable" and civilized. Instead of sitting in for days or weeks, the marchers would come for one day, leaving by sunset. They would wear coats and ties, demonstrate their commitment to established middle-class mores, and restrain their attack on existing political structures. Thus, John Lewis of the Student Non-Violent Coordinating Committee was prevented from blasting the national Democratic and Republican parties as equally responsible for America's racial shame. Instead of moving to the Capitol to sit in, demonstration leaders went to the White House for tea.

For good political reasons, Martin Luther King, Jr., and his allies accepted this compromise, hoping to build additional political support in the established parties for a civil rights bill. The only way to hold together a biracial coalition of white liberals, labor unions, Northern urban politicians, and blacks was to accept the framework of the dominant culture. Civility was the minimum common denominator for that compromise— playing by the rules of the game, not breaching propriety, acting in a reasonable and dignified manner. Yet civility was also the instrument through which the dominant culture regulated social and political discourse and, therefore, in the largest sense, retained control of the political agenda. The underlying issue, then, was how much, and whether, one could trust the good faith of those who said that they would secure change as long as it was done on *their* terms.

In that sense, the ultimate theme that ties the story of Greensboro to the story of America is the capacity of reform—within the existing system—to correct past errors. Historically, most black protestors have believed that white America, once shown the error of its ways, will support remedial change; that the system is inherently good; that inadequacies can be corrected; and that racism is a function of individual mistakes or historical circumstance, not an inherent element of the social structure. Over and over again, in Greensboro as well as nationally, blacks have wanted to rely on the good faith of white leaders, and to believe that protest will lead to the creation of a just society.

The experience of the 1960's, in Greensboro and in the nation at large, called into question that faith. Despite massive gains in combating overt discrimination, institutional racism remained. Nor did there appear to be a desire on the part of white leaders to attack problems of housing, income distribution, welfare, employment, or political recognition. When the Mississippi Freedom Democratic Party (MFDP) arrived in Atlantic City in 1964 with overwhelming evidence to justify its demands for representation at the Democratic National Convention, white political leaders responded with a token concession of two delegates to be chosen by white convention leaders rather than by the blacks themselves. The incident crystallized the underlying issue of whether equality was possible as long as leaders of the dominant political system dictated the rules of the game and dealt the cards. Black supporters of the MFDP had fulfilled to perfection all the procedures they were told to follow for their petition to be successful. They had believed in "the system" and had proven beyond doubt the justice of their protest. And then they were betrayed—by precisely those who had enlisted their good faith in the first place.

Black Power represented the answer of one segment of civil rights protesters to this issue of white cultural hegemony. On the basis of white failure to follow through on promises, blacks started to attack the entire basis of belief in the existing political system. Black Power was revolutionary precisely to the extent that it rejected traditional white definitions of success, achievement, political dialogue, and social manners. The white response, in Greensboro as in the rest of America, was resistance, repression, and, subsequently, an effort to separate black reformers from radicals. The use of FBI agents provocateurs to destroy the Black Power movement in Greensboro simply illuminates the extent to which national and local processes were related. Similar activities were taking place throughout the country in a massive counterintelligence effort to undermine black radicalism. And in the nation at large, as well as in Greensboro, repression was rooted in the conviction that Black Power advocates had put themselves beyond the limits of traditional political dissent by questioning the basic ground rules. They therefore no longer merited protection. Because they had proclaimed themselves enemies of "the system," they would be treated as such, with no holds barred in the war to destroy them.

IV

The conciliation efforts of the post-1969 years represented the latest attempt to persuade blacks that white promises could be trusted. On the basis of history, there seemed little reason to think that this time the results would be any different from the past. Yet most black leaders took the leap of faith once again. Unable or unwilling to support revolution, they cast their lot with those who believed that change could occur one step at a time and bring a better life for some, even if not a transformation of social and economic circumstances for all.

From the point of view of people like Nelson Johnson, the compromise simply reflected paternalism in a new form—middle-class co-optation sanctioned and agreed to by middle-class blacks. "I have developed more respect for the sophistication of the ruling class," Johnson noted ten years later, "of how they're able to bend over a period of years while people struggling against them tend to think in shorter spurts of time, so they can [make concessions] as long as they're laying the groundwork to send things back the other way." But for reformers the changes were tangible enough to sustain hope in a better future. "Some of our young kids," Walter Johnson comments, "have never experienced another way. . . . They [have] relationships with one another that weren't possible when I was their age. That's a healthy sign. . . . If we can continue a society where young people can learn from one another without letting too much institutional racism stifle one group, . . . it will be a better place in the year 2000."

No one knows who is right. But the story of Greensboro does offer these certainties. First, it makes clear that white Americans will respond to the issue of race only when forced to. As the Southern historian Anne F. Scott has noted: "Blacks simply had to come to the boiling point and become just as threatening to white peace of mind as they did. . . . Nothing less would have shaken the status quo. All the Hal Siebers and Al Lineberrys were made possible, as it were, by black assertiveness."

Second, the progressive mystique has been a decisive instrument for white leaders to maintain their dominance, even in the course of making changes. Despite efforts to blame prejudice on "poor whites" or "rednecks," control all along has been in the hands of white leaders. Although a classic "power elite" may not have existed in Greensboro, the swiftness and effectiveness with which change finally occurred in 1970 and 1971 illustrates the ability of political and economic leaders to act decisively when it is in their interest to do so. The same kind of decisiveness could have occurred earlier. In the 1950's Luther Hodges could have led a movement for compliance rather than resistance. Greensboro's educational and economic leaders could have desegregated many schools rather than one in 1957, and they could have moved quickly to increase the numbers of children attending integrated institutions. Pressure from above could have led to rapid desegregation of public facilities. The evidence suggests that in all of these areas change was not forthcoming, not because of protest from below, but because of resistance from above among those who held power. A central vehicle for the effectiveness of this resistance was the progressive mystique, with its insistence on consensus, voluntarism, and the preservation of civility. Far from being a contradiction to North Carolina's conservatism, the progressive mystique ultimately served as its cornerstone.

Finally, there is the certainty that the struggle will continue. For black reformers and their white allies, it will be in the context of ambiguity, always involving the risk of betrayal and disillusionment but driven forward by the passionate conviction that a change in one life today will bring a change in others tomorrow, with the rewards of protest measured in tangible change. For radicals, struggle must mean a continuing battle for transformation—politically, culturally, economically. With the acuteness of prophets, radicals see the sham of moderation and the sophistication of those who guard power under the guise of sharing it. But theirs is a struggle also crippled by the very alienation of their premises. For how can converts be made or constituencies be developed when one's potential recruits believe in "the system," when the "enemy" is elusive, controls schools, politics, and the media, and above all, has the capacity to quell revolt through "reform?"

Are civility and civil rights compatible? Will they ever be? The answer, it would seem, is no—at least not as long as those who take part in traditional political discourse do not begin from the same place and do not share the same resources. Civility within a context of oppression simply provides a veneer for more oppression. Only within a context of freedom can it be a vehicle for self-realization and fulfillment. Where equity prevails and people control their own lives, where they have equal access to power and deal from a position of autonomy, communication across race and class lines can be free of manipulation. But where one group dominates another, the ground rules of discourse will always serve as an instrument of control.

The final lesson of Greensboro, therefore, is that the struggle will go on, even if in ambiguity and uncertainty. And although the results remain in doubt, we should at least understand who has carried the fight forward, and how we have come to be where we are.

Epilogue for the
Paperback Edition

On November 3, 1979, Greensboro became the site once again of confrontation and violence. The Communist Worker's Party (CWP)—a small Maoist sect which included among its members Nelson Johnson and at least one other Greensboro activist of the 1960's—had organized a "Death to the Klan" rally. The demonstration represented an effort to provide dramatic focus to an ongoing attempt to build a biracial, class-based struggle against the textile magnates and bankers whom CWP members saw as the primary enemies of social and economic justice. Frustrated by their failure to make rapid strides in mobilizing workers, CWP members hoped that a highly publicized march against the Klan might provide a vehicle to attract new recruits. Consequently, they challenged Klan members to appear at the rally and answer to "the people's" judgment. Instead, Klan and Nazi supporters delivered their own judgment. Arriving with a virtual arsenal of weapons, KKK and Nazi party members—after a brief scuffle—opened fire on CWP followers. Eighty-eight seconds later, five CWP demonstrators lay dead.

At the time, Greensboro's white leaders insisted that the violence had nothing to do with Greensboro itself. Race relations in the city were good, they said. This was simply a case of an enlightened community being victimized by two extremist groups seeking to use the city for their own purposes.

Nine months later, six Klan and Nazi party members were put on trial, charged with first degree murder and a series of lesser crimes, including inciting to riot. Prosecutors relied heavily on videotapes of the slayings which showed, among other things, one defendant pumping bullets into a demonstrator already on the ground. Defense attorneys pleaded self-defense, citing the inflammatory rhetoric of the CWP's "Death to the Klan" invitation, the use of clubs by CWP members against Klan vehicles and return shots from some CWP members after the Klan opened fire.

After a three-month trial an all-white jury returned a verdict of innocent on all counts.* Repeating their theme of a year earlier, city leaders stressed that the acquittal had nothing to do with race relations in Greensboro. "Fate just dealt us this blow," Greensboro Mayor Jim Melvin declared. "It has no relation to our form of government or to social attitudes in Greensboro."

In an immediate sense, there is some truth to these arguments. Most of the Klan members came from an area over an hour away from Greensboro. Most CWP members, in turn, had no local base. Very few blacks in Greensboro, either before the "Death to the Klan" rally or after the killings, wanted anything to do with the CWP campaign. Indeed, virtually every civil rights leader in Greensboro, of whatever age or background, rejected the rhetoric and tactics of CWP organizers.

Yet, on a deeper level, the slayings of November 1979 and the acquittal of November 1980 are part of Greensboro's—and America's—continuing history of race relations. Whatever its errors of ideology, style, and politics, the CWP sought to address issues of class and race, which were a direct legacy of Greensboro's past. The problems of poor housing, ghetto poverty, and manipulation of racial divisions to forestall worker unity all reflected the institutional and structural racism that the civil rights movement of the 1960's was unable to alter, either in Greensboro itself or in America generally. As the Greensboro Human Relations Commission pointed out, even if most CWP members did not come *from* Greensboro, they came *to* Greensboro because the issues of class and race were present there with such clarity.

Continuity with the past was evident also in the dialogue that transpired between white and black leaders in the wake of the slayings and trial. "I don't see how anyone can say the verdicts aren't related to racial attitudes in Greensboro," NAACP chief George Simkins said. "The verdict is tantamount to giving the Klan and the Nazis a license to kill. . . . This shows that Greensboro despite all its protestations, is still

---

*Most journalists covering the trial were shocked at the acquittal. As a Greensboro *Daily News* reporter wrote, the prosecution case "seemed compelling." Most observers attribute the verdict to the makeup of the jury (its foreman was a strongly anti-Communist refugee from Cuba) and the fact that the victims were self-avowed revolutionaries.

a racist town." But Simkins's observations were anathema to Mayor Jim Melvin, who in words reminiscent of those used by his predecessor fifteen years earlier, insisted that Simkins should talk privately with city leaders about racial grievances rather than engage in public protest. "Now is the time for us all to work hard at pulling together," Melvin said. "There may be some efforts to divide our community, but the positive spirit of Greensboro must prevail." Significantly, the demands put forward by Greensboro's black leaders in 1980—a ward system of political representation, passage of city ordinances against discrimination in housing and employment, and enforcement powers for the Human Relations Commission—were virtually identical to those advanced a decade and a half before.*

Most important for the long run, past and present were joined by the rhetoric of the progressive mystique. Greensboro's historic reputation for enlightenment, the news director of a local television station declared, was well intact. Justice had been served, and Greensboro had good reason to be proud. Other editorial writers in the state insisted that extremists were the only problem. With the same ease that Luther Hodges had equated the Ku Klux Klan and the NAACP in the 1950's, commentators now treated the hate-filled words of the CWP as equally deserving of contempt as the bullets of the KKK. The November 3 episode, one paper editorialized, was simply "a confrontation between radical groups, a two-sided gun-toting exercise in which nobody was without blame." Since both groups were extremist, neither merited any consideration. The argument even went so far as to dismiss those protesting the verdict as mindless supporters of the left giving aid and comfort to the CWP—hence beyond the pale. Through such reasoning, only the consensus of the politics of moderation had any standing. Those questioning that consensus were, perforce, an alien presence.

Perhaps the most fitting commentary came from Henry Frye, state senator from Greensboro, one of the first blacks elected to office in the midst of the changes of the 1960's, and a man who often in the past had made the leap of faith to trust whites and believe in gradual reform. "I really don't know what to think," he said after the trial. "I just didn't believe there would be a jury verdict of not guilty on all counts for all

---

*Another reminder of the past was the role of informers in the Klan/CWP confrontation. A federal agent was present at Klan-Nazi meetings prior to the march, and another police informer also was involved. What information these men had prior to the slayings and what role they themselves played, is not known because prosecutors and defense attorneys found it in their mutual interest not to call the informers as witnesses.

six people. . . . A lot of people said they were going to turn them loose and I [said], 'no way.' . . . I'm wrong. There is a way . . . . It just makes me wonder about everything. It makes me want to re-evaluate, re-evaluate my approach [to the whole society]."

If nothing else, events surrounding the Klan slayings and trial demonstrate how profound the gap between black and white remains in our society, how different are the definitions of reality, and how powerful is the legacy of the past. Our abiding national dilemma continues. So too does the struggle to overcome it.

Notes

For reasons of economy and space, these notes have been abridged for the paperback edition of *Civilities and Civil Rights*. What follows are summaries of the most important sources used in each chapter. More complete documentation can be found in the hardback edition of *Civilities and Civil Rights*.

Introduction

1. Perhaps the best studies of the civil rights revolution have come from participants and journalists. *See*, e.g., Debbie Lewis, *And We Are Not Saved* (New York, 1970); Cleveland Sellers, *River of No Return* (New York, 1975); Anne Moody, *Coming of Age in Mississippi* (New York, 1968); James Forman, *The Making of a Black Revolutionary* (New York, 1975); and Pat Watters and Reese Cleghorn, *Climbing Jacob's Ladder: The Arrival of Negroes in Southern Politics* (New York, 1967). One of the best histories of civil rights organizations is August Meier and Elliott Rudwick, *CORE: A Study in the Civil Rights Movement, 1942–1968* (New York, 1973). Other books on the civil rights movement include Louis Lomax, *The Negro Revolt* (New York, 1962); David Lewis, *King: A Critical Biography* (New York, 1970); and Howard Zinn, *SNCC: The New Abolitionists* (Boston, 1964), to name just a few. Carl Brauer, *John F. Kennedy and the Second Reconstruction* (New York, 1977), is one of those who argues the importance of presidential initiatives. Among public-opinion surveys of racial attitudes are the following: Samuel Lubell, *White and Black: Test of a Nation* (New York, 1964); and Richard Lemon, *The Troubled Americans* (New York, 1970); and Angus Campbell, *White Attitudes Toward Black People* (Ann Arbor, 1971).

Books on the South, and on southern personalities, include the following: V. O. Key, *Southern Politics* (New York, 1950); William C. Harvard (ed.), *The Changing Politics of the South* (Baton Rouge, 1972); Jack Bass and Walter

DeVries, *The Transformation of Southern Politics* (New York, 1976); Numan P. Bartley and Hugh D. Graham, *Southern Politics and the Second Reconstruction* (Baltimore, 1975); Morton Sosna, *In Search of the Silent South* (New York, 1977); Melvin Tumin et al., *Desegregation: Resistance and Readiness* (Princeton, 1958); and George B. Tindall, *The Emergence of the New South, 1913–1945* (Baton Rouge, 1957). Numerous oral history sources also contributed to the introduction, including interviews with: Joseph Flora; Warren Ashby; D. Edward Hudgins; Tart Bell; and William Snider.

2. The value of civility is referred to repeatedly by white political and economic leaders in North Carolina. The title of this book derives from an editorial, "Of Civil Rights and Civilities," that appeared in the Greensboro *Daily News*, March 2, 1960. It describes the conflict between the two alternative values. The paper declared its support for civilities, though not necessarily opposing civil rights. As the reader will note, the conflict between the two values accurately describes an on-going struggle that took place within Greensboro and the nation itself over our national priorities.

Chapter One

1. Secondary sources providing background for this chapter included Samuel M. Kipp III, Urban Growth and Social Change in the South, 1870–1920: Greensboro, North Carolina, As a Case Study, unpub. Ph.D. dissertation, Princeton University, 1974; Samuel M. Kipp III, "Urbanization, Employment, and Race Relations in Greensboro, North Carolina, 1870–1910," M.S. in author's possession; Samuel M. Kipp III, "Old Notables and Newcomers: The Economic and Political Elite of Greensboro, North Carolina: 1880–1920," *Journal of Southern History*, XLIII (Aug. 1977), 373–94; Frenise A. Logan, *The Negro in North Carolina, 1876–94* (Chapel Hill, 1964); Ethel Arnett, *Greensboro, North Carolina* (Chapel Hill, 1955); Melvin Tumin et al. *Desegregation: Resistance and Readiness* (Princeton, 1958): and Lawrence C. Goodwyn, *Democratic Promise* (New York, 1977).

Manuscript sources include the YWCA papers, Greensboro YWCA: J. D. Tarpley Papers, in the possession of J. D. Tarpley, Greensboro; Eleanor Roosevelt Papers, Franklin D. Roosevelt Library, Hyde Park, New York; Board of Election Papers, Guilford County Courthouse, Greensboro; Benjamin L. Smith Papers, William L. Perkins Library, Duke University; American Friends Service Committee Papers, Philadelphia; American Friends Service Committee Papers, High Point, North Carolina.

Oral history sources for the chapter include D. Edward Hudgins; John Foster; William Snider; Warren Ashby; Susie B. Jones; Joseph Flora; Louise Smith; Vance Chavis; Randolph Blackwell; George Simkins; Ezell Blair, Sr.; Otis Hairston; Nell Coley; J. D. Tarpley; A. Knighton (Tony) Stanley; William Thomas; David Morehead; Hobart Jarrett; Willa Player; Ella Baker; John Marshall Stevenson; Lewis Dowdy; Ezell Blair, Jr.; John Taylor; Betsy Taylor; Richard

Bardolph; George Evans; Kay Troxler; Helen Douglas; Margaret Falkener; Sara Mendenhall Brown; and Robert Ford. In subsequent years Ezell Blair, Jr. changed his name to Jibreel Khazan. John Marshall Stevenson changed his name to John Marshall Kilimanjaro. In the text and in these notes, I will refer to the names they used at the time.

2. From the point of view of many middle-class blacks, Randolph Blackwell recalled, "Brodie was kind of shady, questionable." He and his candidacy helped to challenge the notion that only a certain group of blacks should participate in the political process. Ironically, the presence of more than one black in the race proved troublesome to some liberal whites who could not decide which black they were supposed to vote for. "If they could just get together and run one," a white observed, "they would have a so much better chance at having that one elected. [One of the candidates] may not have had anyone behind him, I don't know. But the white community couldn't tell."

Chapter Two

1. Secondary sources providing background for this chapter include Benjamin Muse, *Ten Years of Prelude* (New York, 1964); Albert Blaustein and Clyde Ferguson, *Desegregation and the Law* (New York, 1962); Richard Klugler, *Simple Justice* (New York, 1975); William Bagwell, *Desegregation in the Carolinas* (Columbia, S.C., 1972); Melvin Tumin et al., *Desegregation: Resistance and Readiness* (Princeton, 1958); Luther H. Hodges, *Businessman in the Statehouse* (Chapel Hill, 1962); Jack Bass and Walter DeVries, *The Transformation of Southern Politics* (New York, 1977); William Havard (ed.), *The Changing Politics of the South* (Baton Rouge, 1972); V. O. Key, *Southern Politics* (New York, 1970); and Samuel Lubell, *The Future of American Politics* (New York, 1951). Day-to-day events are described in the Greensboro *Daily News*, the Greensboro *Record*, the Raleigh *News & Observer*, and the Carolina *Times*. I am indebted to the Greensboro *Daily News* and Greensboro *Record* for making available to me their clipping files.

Manuscript sources for the chapter include the American Friends Service Committee Papers in Philadelphia and High Point; the Luther Hodges Papers, North Carolina Department of Archives and History, Raleigh; the Benjamin L. Smith Papers at Duke University; Greensboro School Board Minutes, Greensboro; and the YWCA Papers, Greensboro.

Oral history sources for the chapter include interviews with Vance Chavis; Ezell Blair, Jr.; Edward Edmonds; John Foster; George Simkins; Otis Hairston; Benjamin Smith, Jr.; D. Edward Hudgins; Sara Mendenhall Brown; Mrs. Raymond Smith; Louise Smith; Tart Bell; Mrs. Charles Bowles; Joseph Flora; John Marshall Stevenson; Cleo McCoy; Jack Elam; Walter Johnson, Jr.; Willa Player; Susie B. Jónes; George Roach; Kay Troxler; John Taylor; and Robert Ford.

2. Irving Carlyle subsequently wrote D. Edward Hudgins that had more

people joined the immediate cry for compliance, North Carolina might have avoided its subsequent policy of resistance. Despite the stereotype of massive intransigence, the initial reaction of the white South to the *Brown* decision seems to have been one of resignation rather than rebellion. Only James Byrnes in South Carolina, Herman Talmadge in Georgia, and Hugh White in Mississippi indulged in the rhetoric of outraged resistance. More representative were comments that showed regret at the *Brown* decision, but called for a calm process aimed at working out arrangements acceptable to the Court. Thus Governor Francis Cherry of Arkansas declared: "Arkansas will obey the law. It always has." And "Big" Jim Folsom stated: "when the Supreme Court speaks, that's the law." Only when the President of the United States and others in positions of leadership invited resistance by their own refusal to give active support to the *Brown* decision did the posture of massive obstruction to change become widespread in the white South.

3. Hodges's earlier statement on closing the schools denounced the possibility as "a last ditch and double-edged weapon"; yet four months later he raised the possibility himself. In fact, Hodges was already reaching out for right-wing support. In a letter to Hodges on July 19, 1955, Eugene Hood, a leader of North Carolina's White Citizen's Council, praised the Governor for attacking the NAACP. Hood noted that his confidence in Hodges was based on conversations with Thomas Pearsall and Rep. Sam Worthington. Worthington, in particular, was noted for his segregationist views and had evidently assured Hood that Hodges was sympathetic to segregation. In his private correspondence, Hodges signaled his strategy. On November 7, 1955, he wrote Congressman William Tuck boasting that North Carolina was much farther advanced in its plans to fight integration than Virginia was. On December 1 the same year—five months before calling for a special session—Hodges wrote Eugene Hood that he anticipated the development of conditions that would lead to a special session.

4. Throughout the papers of Governor Hodges and Governor Terry Sanford there appear intelligence reports on surveillance of Ku Klux Klan meetings. Sanford aides commented that there had never been a Klan meeting in the state without intelligence agents or police present. Many of the intelligence memos indicate the presence of police informers within the ranks of the Klan. For obvious reasons, these informers are not identified by name. In addition, FBI documents suggest that leaders of the North Carlina Klan were paid federal informers. For all these reasons, it seems sensible not to exaggerate the power of the Klan. (See Chapter Seven for further details on FBI involvement.)

5. Many of Benjamin Smith's friends supported him privately, though few were willing to state their opinion in public. One of these, William Caffrey, a prominent attorney, wrote prophetically: "to put the future of the youth of this state in the balance, in an effort to circumvent the law of the land, is akin to Russian roulette . . . It seems a shame that what is cried for is a step forward,

but what we are offered is a step backward." Fifteen years later Caffrey would be the School Board attorney when Greensboro was ordered to integrate.

Chapter Three

1. Secondary sources for this chapter include Howell Raines, *My Soul Is Rested* (New York, 1978); Miles Wolff, *Lunch at the Five and Ten* (New York, 1970); Clayborne Carson, *In Struggle* (Cambridge, 1981); August Meier and Elliott Rudwick, *CORE: A Study in the Civil Rights Movement, 1942–1968* (New York, 1973); and Howard Zinn, *SNCC: The New Abolitionists* (Boston, 1964). Other material on the sit-down strike includes Wilma Dykeman and James Stokeley, "Sit Down Chilllin, Sit Down!" *The Progressive*, June 1960; Paul Ernest Wehr, The Sit Down Protest: A Study of a Passive Resistance Movement in North Carolina, (M.A. thesis, University of North Carolina, 1960); David Halberstam "The Kids Take Over," *Reporter*, June 22, 1961; and Michael Walzer, "A Cup of Coffee and a Seat," *Dissent*, Sept. 1960.

Manuscript sources include the American Friends Service Committee Papers in Philadelphia and High Point; the Benjamin L. Smith Papers at Duke University; the Luther Hodges Papers in Raleigh; the Terry Sanford Papers, North Carolina Department of Archives and History, Raleigh; the Edward L. Zane Papers, William L. Perkins Library, Duke University; and the YWCA Papers, Greensboro.

Oral history sources for this chapter include Otis Hairston; Ezell Blair, Sr.; Louise Smith; Kay Troxler; Mrs. Franklin Parker; Edward Edmonds; Benjamin Smith, Jr.; George Roach; W. P. House; George Simkins; Hobart Jarrett; Willa Player; Warren Ashby; John Marshall Stevenson; Ezell Blair, Jr.; Joseph McNeil; David Richmond; Vance Chavis; Franklin McCain; Eula Hudgens; Walter Johnson, Jr.; Lewis Dowdy; William Jackson; McNeill Smith; Edward L. Zane; David Morehead; Ike English; R. B. Lincke; George Evans; and Nell Coley.

2. Throughout the sit-ins, white observers, regardless of their political persuasion, were impressed by the demeanor of the black protestors. Benjamin Muse, representative of the Southern Regional Council, traveled to North Carolina shortly after the sit-ins. Jonathan Daniels, publisher of the Raleigh *News & Observer*, told Muse of one elderly segregationist woman who, after seeing well-mannered Negroes turned away from lunch counters, declared: "they have no business refusing nice, polite, young people." Even the manager of Woolworth's, Muse noted, remarked that he would rather serve well-behaved Negro students than the "white bums" who came to heckle blacks. The most classic example of this perception among whites appeared in an editorial of the Richmond *News Leader*, one of the leading segregationist newspapers in the South. Describing the sit-ins, the paper wrote: "Here were the college students, in coats, white shirts, ties, and one of them was reading Goethe and one was taking notes from a biology text. And here,. on the sidewalk outside, was a gang of white boys come to heckle, a ragtail rabble, slack-jawed, black-jacketed,

grinning fit to kill, and some of them, God save the mark, were waving the proud and honored flag of the southern states in the last war fought by gentle-men: Eheu! It gives one pause."

3. The edition of the *Daily News* which hailed the students' decision as "an act of maturity" marked the first time the paper gave page-one coverage to the student movement. There are two copies of the students' statement in the Zane papers. Both appear to have been typed on an IBM executive typewriter, with changes marked in Zane's handwriting. One is entitled "Suggested Release." In addition, the statement contains language characteristic of pronouncements by Zane on the issue.

4. As revealed by transcripts of telephone conversations between Hodges and Woolworth's executives, the Governor was outraged at Woolworth's for permit-ting the demonstrations to continue. One executive told Hodges that the com-pany was hopeful that local people would find a solution. Hodges responded: "that is just a will of the wisp." Hodges went on to say that "the government of North Carolina is offering you a law which you can use." The Governor made his point even more clear to another executive, indicating that in at least half a dozen cases local managers had said they would use the trespass law if author-ized to do so. "That is the only answer," Hodges suggested.

Chapter Four

1. For general background, see William C. Harvard (ed.), *The Changing Politics of the South* (Baton Rouge, 1972); and James R. Spence, *The Making of a Governor* (Winston-Salem, 1958). Day-to-day events are described in the Raleigh *News & Observer*, the Greensboro *Daily News*, the Greensboro *Record*, and the New York *Times*.

Manuscript sources include the Terry Sanford Papers, Raleigh; The Ameri-can Friends Services Committee Papers in Philadelphia and High Point; the YWCA Papers in Greensboro; The Greensboro Community Fellowship Papers, in possession of the author; Papers of the Education Committee of the Greens-boro Community Fellowship, in possession of the author; the David Schenck Papers, privately held by David Schenck, Jr.; and the raw files of the Greens-boro *Daily News*.

Oral history sources include interviews with Terry Sanford; Willa Player; Warren Ashby; Hobart Jarrett; Vance Chavis; Tart Bell; Otis Hairston; Kay Troxler; Louise Smith; Eula Hudgens; Charles Davis; Anna Simkins; Robert Ford; Betsy Taylor; John Marshall Stevenson; Warren Ashby; Cleo McCoy; McNeill Smith; and George Evans.

Chapter Five

1. Day-to-day events during this period are described in the Greensboro *Daily News*, the Greensboro *Record*, and *The Candle*, a newspaper of the student movement.

Manuscript sources include the David Schenck Papers; the Terry Sanford Papers in Raleigh; Greensboro Community Fellowship Papers; the Robert F. Kennedy Papers, John F. Kennedy Library, Boston; the YWCA Papers, Greensboro; and the raw files of the Greensboro *Daily News*.

Oral history sources include interviews with A. Knighton Stanley; William Thomas; Lewis Brandon; William Jackson; Joe Knox; Ezell Blair, Jr.; David Morehead; Cecil Bishop; Cleo McCoy; Willa Player; Lewis Dowdy; Vance Chavis; Ezell Blair, Sr.; George Breathett; Terry Sanford; McNeill Smith; Nell Coley; J. D. Tarpley; David Schenck, Jr.; George Evans; and Joseph Flora.

2. The tone of the local CORE chapter changed from deference to anger and assertion once it became clear that the city was not going to respond. On April 24, 1963, Lois Lucas and William Thomas wrote to the Mayor: "this letter is being written in the hope that you will grant an audience to members of the Greensboro Chapter of CORE on Thursday, May 2, 1963. We thank you in advance for the consideration we know that you will give to this request." After it became clear that such "proper form" would not bring results, CORE became more demanding. The same evolution can be seen in almost every phase of the civil rights movement. It reflects both the degree of optimism that continually re-emerged during the movement and the inevitable disillusionment that followed when whites revealed that they would not change their practices voluntarily.

3. Numerous black organizations sent letters and telegrams supporting the demonstrators. For example, Edgar Shephard of St. John's Lodge #12 wrote Mayor Schenck that the 183 members of his Masonic Order had voted unanimously to endorse equal rights. "The students, who have borne the burdens of this fight, are our pride and joy. They have conducted themselves in such a manner as to touch the hearts of all right thinking men and women. No longer are they as one crying in the wilderness; no longer can the cry be ignored . . . We again emphasize our support in the movement to banish segregation and its evil influences from all walks of life. . . ."

4. Significantly, the federal government rarely, if ever, intervened in North Carolina's racial situation until the end of 1967. This was due, in large part, to the close friendship—personal and political—of Governor Sanford and the Kennedy brothers. It also reflected the presence in the Kennedy cabinet of former Governor Luther Hodges. The Kennedys trusted Sanford to handle the racial conflict in North Carolina, concentrating their energies instead on states such as Georgia, Alabama, and Mississippi.

5. The split between Jesse Jackson and other movement strategists was never fully explicit. The division turned on style and personality as well as tactics. Stanley and Thomas believed in detailed planning and discipline, fearing that spontaneous activity could lead to violence. Jackson, by contrast, was bold and dramatic, and more likely to seize the spirit of the moment. After the June 2 march, Jackson distinguished his own actions from those of CORE. CORE may

have declared a truce, he said, "but CORE can't dictate to the community." In the end, the two approaches complemented each other, although, for a few days there was significant tension.

Chapter Six

1. For a day-to-day description of events, see the Greensboro *Daily News*, the Greensboro *Record*, and the *Carolina Peacemaker*, a black newspaper published by John Marshall Stevenson starting in 1967.

Manuscript sources include the David Schenck Papers; the Terry Sanford Papers in Raleigh; Greensboro Community Fellowship Papers; the Papers of the Education Committee of the Greensboro Community Fellowship; the American Friends Services Committee Papers in Philadelphia and High Point; the Greensboro Human Relations Commission Papers, City Hall, Greensboro; the Dan K. Moore Papers, North Carolina Department of Archives and History, Raleigh; the Joan Bluethenthal Papers, privately held, Greensboro; and the raw files of the Greensboro *Daily News*.

Oral history sources include interviews with Cecil Bishop; A. Knighton Stanely; William Thomas; Otis Hairston; Kay Troxler; George Evans; Robert Ford; Anna Simkins; Warren Ashby; Hal Sieber; Joseph Flora; Michael Weaver; John Taylor; Louise Smith; and Joan Bluethenthal.

2. Conrad was well intentioned, envisioning a world where "progress unheard of before can be gained [if only] you can put your shoulder to the wheel with the rest of us, to impress upon the state and the nation, that the Negro is responsible element. . . ." Basic to Conrad's position was the belief that the responsibility for change fell upon Negroes. "The minds of many people [in Greensboro] are beginning to develop hatred rather than friendliness," he wrote. "That hatred can only lead to civil strife and an explosion of the time bomb. I believe that leadership such as yours can be responsible and take a position that can do ultimate good for the Negro unheard of in our past history. *You* can create a new image." (Italics mine.)

3. On November 12, 1963, Thomas Lambeth reported to Terry Sanford that no Klan meeting had been held in North Carolina during the preceding three years without complete intelligence reports on the activity prior to its occurrence. When the KKK burned a cross on the lawn of the Governor's mansion in August 1964, informants provided the names of the perpetrators immediately. Klan activity appeared to increase significantly during the next few years when Dan K. Moore was governor. Moore named I. Beverly Lake, his opponent in the first primary and a staunch segregationist, to the Supreme Court of North Carolina shortly after taking office. In addition, Moore continued Hodges's practice of grouping the NAACP with the Ku Klux Klan as an extremist organization. Governor Moore claimed to have no authority to bar the Klan from the State Fair, or to revoke the State Charter given to it by North Carolina's Secretary of State. However sincere Moore's commitment to

law and order, his political orientation was clearly sympathetic to conservative forces.

4. The issue of black political representation carried into other areas as well. Black leaders were infuriated by what they saw as a systematic disregard for their contribution to the community. Greensboro's white newspapers, for example, failed to report A&T's football scores or to acknowledge the academic contribution of the university. At high schools which boasted about their black athletes, blacks were not included in the cheerleading squads or the homecoming courts. Even where football games were interracial, black referees were rarely, if ever, chosen. And when the city named a new community information officer for the police department, he was white. In addition, there was no black reporter on the staff of the Greensboro *Daily News* or Greensboro *Record*.

Chapter Seven

1. For a general discussion of the emergence of black power within the civil rights movement, see Clayborne Carson, *In Struggle* (Cambridge, 1981); Stokeley Carmichael and Charles Hamilton, *Black Power* (New York, 1968); and James Forman, *The Making of a Black Revolutionary* (New York, 1975). Description of day-to-day events in Greensboro can be found in the Greensboro *Daily News*, the Greensboro *Record*, and the *Carolina Peacemaker*.

Manuscript sources for this chapter include the Terry Sanford Papers, Raleigh; the Robert Scott Papers, North Carolina Department of Archives and History, Raleigh; the YWCA Papers, Greensboro; and over a thousand pages of FBI files on the Black Panthers in North Carolina, obtained by the Greensboro *Daily News* under the Freedom of Information Act, and made available to me by Jack Betts of the *Daily News*.

Oral history sources include interviews with Nelson Johnson; Thomas Bailey; Terry Sanford; Lewis Brandon; Otis Hairston; Hal Sieber; Jack Elam; William Jackson; Michael Weaver; Cecil Bishop; Nell Coley; Vance Chavis; John Marshall Stevenson; Walter Johnson, Jr.; Carolyn Mark; Cleo McCoy; Lewis Dowdy; and S. N. Ford.

2. In establishing the North Carolina Fund, Sanford correctly perceived poverty and a lack of educational opportunity as principal components of discrimination. The problem with the North Carolina Fund was that, like the Good Neighbor Council, success depended upon private funds and local support. Nevertheless, with Ford Foundation backing, the Fund became a significant force for social change during the late 1960's, giving rise to organizations such as the Foundation for Community Development. Howard Fuller was the community organizer for the FCD and his name quickly became synonymous in many people's eyes with the more radical thrust of the North Carolina Fund. Coming to North Carolina in 1964, Fuller initially had worked for integration and reform within the established system. But he too had become alienated when opponents attacked him as a subversive and attempted to destroy his

ability to work with poor people for changes within existing structures of power. Fuller was a powerful, charismatic leader whose presence was felt throughout the state during the late 1960's, although he did not specifically play a major role in Greensboro during these years.

3. At each moment of crisis from 1968–1971 older black leaders stood solidly with the younger activists; the two sides worked together in major organizing campaigns around housing, redevelopment, political representation, and adequate wages.

4. Cafeteria strikes were going on at approximately the same time on other campuses as well. In addition to being underpaid and exploited, the cafeteria workers for the most part were denied permanent status as university employees. It was customary to hire them under the category of "temporary workers," and then release them after they had worked for the duration provided for "temporary help," only to re-hire them again as "temporary" staff after a few days.

5. The actions of police during the Malcolm X memorial service and the cafeteria workers' strike created a degree of political solidarity among black students that had not existed before. Earlier, during the February 5 protests against the A&T administration and faculty, students had responded negatively toward an alleged Black Panther spokesman who had sought to inflame the situation. By mid-March, however, the actions of city authorities had moved the students toward a more radical posture, minimizing the divisions that continued to exist within the student body. Local police, meanwhile, were receiving intelligence reports from the FBI that suggested a conspiracy led by Black Panthers to foment violence. FBI documents and confidential interviews suggest that the primary source of these violent plots may have been an FBI informer and not a Black Panther at all. In addition, most supporters of GAPP rejected the advice of the alleged Black Panther. Nevertheless, police tended to generalize from the information they received and to believe that all the black insurgents were part of a Panther conspiracy.

6. Subsequently, S. N. Ford, head of the Intelligence Division of the Greensboro Police Department, declared that the police had no evidence of Howard Fuller or other FCD staffers bringing guns or ammunition into Greensboro.

7. Significantly, Calhoun took whole chunks of his testimony directly from FBI intelligence reports. Yet these reports contained substantial contradictions and in all likelihood reflected the work of FBI agents provocateurs. Drawing together the loose connections between Claude Barnes, Nelson Johnson, GAPP, and alleged Black Panthers, Calhoun arrived at a conspiracy theory, the core of which lacked substance. In a subsequent interview, police officer S. N. Ford claimed that there was no evidence that either Johnson or Barnes was a Black Panther.

8. The belief that National Guardsmen had over-reacted was not limited to one city official. Other city leaders, as well as two high police authorities, felt

that the National Guard's plan represented a disproportionate use of force and threatened massive injuries. None of these objections was raised at the time.

9. For published material on FBI involvement, see Winston-Salem *Journal*, Nov. 23, 26, 1977; and Greensboro *Daily News*, Dec. 21, 1975; Jan. 3, 12, Mar. 4, Apr. 2, 1976; Sept. 29, 1977. Senator Robert Morgan of the Senate Intelligence Committee first identified Dorsett as an FBI informant. Subsequently, the Director of the State Bureau of Investigation in North Carolina noted that he was told in the 1960's that Dorsett was being paid a salary "tantamount to what an agent might make." Dorsett was recognized as the most effective organizer of the Klan in the 1960's. According to intelligence reports in the papers of Governors Sanford, Moore, and Scott, Dorsett appeared at nearly every Klan meeting that took place in the state during these years. For unpublished information, particularly on the Black Panthers, see FBI memoranda dated Jan. 13, Feb. 7, 12, 17, 21, Mar. 25, 27, 28, Apr. 18, 22, 23, May 6, 9, 10, 12, 1969. The conclusion that Mr. X was probably an FBI-agent provocateur is based upon two bodies of evidence. First, oral testimony suggests that Mr. X acted in a provocative way, proposing illegal activities such as bombing, arson, ambush of police, and the use of drugs—any one of which would have made black insurgents liable to arrest. According to oral sources, Mr. X espoused these activities in a reckless fashion. He offered to teach other participants in the group how to detonate explosives and bragged of his previous exploits. Johnson and others became suspicious of Mr. X both because of these suggestions and because of their own insistence that no drugs or alcohol be permitted within the movement. Second, and perhaps more important, the written evidence corroborates and reinforces the oral testimony. According to FBI documents, Mr. X portrayed himself as a section chief of the Black Panther party sent to organize new chapters in North Carolina. According to these same documents, Mr. X introduced plans at a meeting of a college and high school students to expel white merchants from the black section of Greensboro and to ambush a police car. Mr. X also suggested bombing a white grocery market. Copies of these reports were sent to the Greensboro police department and obviously helped to create the attitudes that prevailed among police during the spring of 1969 toward black insurgents. Other FBI documents, however, raised questions about Mr. X's authenticity as a Black Panther party member. An April memorandum, for example, notes that Mr. X left Greensboro for New York by air in February 1969 and for a month traveled to Connecticut, California, and Cincinnati. The same memo notes that Mr. X was suspended by the national Black Panther party for calling himself a field marshal when in fact he had no rank within the party. A second memo on April 23 reports that Mr. X called Black Panther party national headquarters asking David Hilliard, a national officer, for an organizing charter. He was advised that he had no authority to organize a Black Panther party chapter. In addition, FBI informants from the Charlotte office of the FBI reported that Mr. X was in difficulty with Black

Panther party leadership; nor could any Charlotte informer positively identify Mr. X as a member of the true Black Panther party. In a fall 1969 speech in Chapel Hill, national Black Panther party organizer Bobby Lee declared: "we got some niggers . . . in Greensboro who are running around here propagating madness, propagating racism, calling themselves Panthers . . . they are out of order . . . . We say you are either part of the problem or you're part of the solution, and these niggers are part of the problem." On the basis on this oral and written testimony, there seems to be good reason to suspect: (a) that Mr. X never was a Black Panther and (b) that he was acting as an agent provocateur. Since he would be acting under "deep cover"—i.e., other informants would not know about his true identity, and only a few people at the top would be aware of his mission—the fact that Mr. X's activities continually appeared on other informants' reports is no surprise. Indeed, having his activities reported to local police would be a prerequisite for effective counterintelligence work. All the FBI documents on which this assessment is based are heavily edited, with whole sections blacked out with magic marker. However, there are two memos—March 27 and May 6, 1969—which allude to the possibility of Mr. X being an informer. The second memorandum indicates that no Charlotte informant could positively identify Mr. X as a member of the party. At that point, two-thirds of a page are blacked out completely. The implications of Mr. X acting as an agent provocateur are startling, to say the least. As Chief Calhoun's testimony before the Senate in July suggests, official perceptions of black activism in Greensboro during the spring of 1969 hinged completely on belief in a Black Panther party conspiracy; yet the primary evidence cited for that conspiracy consists of intelligence reports focusing on suggestions for violence and sabotage that emanated from Mr. X—a man continually disowned by national Black Panther headquarters.

Chapter Eight

1. For a day-to-day description of events, see the Greensboro *Daily News*, the Greensboro *Record*, and the *Carolina Peacemaker*.

Manuscript sources include the Greensboro Chamber of Commerce Papers, Greensboro; Hal Sieber Papers, privately held; the Joan Bluethenthal Papers, privately held; and the Robert Scott Papers, Raleigh.

Oral history sources include interviews with Hal Sieber; William Little; Michael Weaver; Lewis Dowdy; John Marshall Stevenson; Otis Hairston; Al Lineberry; Nelson Johnson; Eula Hudgens; Warren Ashby; John Taylor; Lewis Brandon; Linda Bragg; Thomas Bailey; Carolyn Mark; Cecil Bishop; Joan Bluethenthal; Walter Johnson, Jr.; George Evans; Vance Chavis; and Jim Clark, interviewed by Scott Ellsworth.

2. On the day of Judge Stanley's decision, one of Greensboro's four high schools was all black as were three of its six junior high schools and seven of its twenty-nine elementary schools. Two additional elementary schools were more

than 99 per cent black. On the other side, one high school was 97 per cent white, another 80 per cent white, six elementary schools were comprised solely of white students, and an additional seven schools contained more than 95 per cent white students. All in all, 85 per cent of all black students attended schools that were either exclusively or predominantly black, while 82 per cent of whites attended schools having more than 86 per cent white enrollment.

A Note on Sources

Civilities and Civil Rights is based on a mixture of primary sources, written and oral.* Although oral testimony is often invaluable, it sometimes contains errors of fact or judgment that can be avoided if historians devote equal attention to written sources. By the same token, scholars who rely on written sources alone—particularly in writing recent history—run the risk of losing indispensable perspectives available through oral sources. The written record too often represents the experience of only a small segment of the society—usually white, male, and upper class—and hence ignores the experience of the vast majority of people. In writing about the history of black people and white people in the recent past, therefore, it becomes essential to draw upon both kinds of historical evidence.

The type of oral history research used here differs from that associated with most oral history programs. For the most part those programs have been archival in nature, with the interviewees chosen because of their individual fame or distinction, and the transcripts of the interviews deposited in libraries for use of scholars in the future. Because of this orientation, the interviews are ordinarily autobiographical in nature and somewhat unstructured. Since no common theme or focus ties one interview to another, oral history archives often contain material dealing with a multiplicity of subjects.

Civilities and Civil Rights, by contrast, is based upon a problem-centered approach to oral history. The individuals interviewed were selected not because of their fame or "standing" in Greensboro, but because of their ability to add significant information to the specific story of the civil rights struggle in that Southern city. The questions asked, therefore, were also specific. The purpose of these questions was to explore those research issues that could not be

*For a listing of the secondary sources used, see the notes, especially note 1 of the Introduction.

answered through looking at the written record alone. Nevertheless, the written record offered a crucial underpinning for the oral research, providing as it did vital evidence of chronology and a list of some of the historical "actors."

One of the advantages of using both written and oral sources is that information provided through oral history casts new light on how written sources should be read. Conversely, information from written sources can provide context and facts that will give new meaning to otherwise imprecise oral history generalizations.

Two examples from *Civilities and Civil Rights* may illustrate this mutual reinforcement. The historian looking at black political history in Greensboro during the late 1940's would learn from the written record that a major increase in black voter registration took place in 1949, and that in the same year two black candidates ran for city council, one a construction engineer and the other a restaurant owner. At that point, the written record becomes silent, leaving the historian to speculate as to why there were two black candidates and what connection there might be with the increase in voter registration. Oral sources covering the same period note a major increase in political activity in the black community, and discuss specifically an attempt to galvanize a segment of the black community that previously had been inactive. By putting the oral and written sources together and asking additional questions, a story emerges that would otherwise have remained invisible. The voter registration campaign in 1949 was a direct product of efforts to involve working-class people in the political process and move away from the domination of black politics by the black bourgeoisie on the one hand and black political brokers who bargained votes for a price on the other. Blacks who wanted to enlarge the black political constituency understood that they had to run a candidate for office who represented the "street" people, as opposed to the black middle class. Oral testimony provides a way to uncover and to make comprehensible this fundamental shift in black politics. The political candidate described in the white press as a "restaurant owner" was in fact the owner of a pool hall and café whose clientele consisted primarily of those working-class people who were being urged to register and vote. Clearly, only a combination of oral and written sources could make possible an understanding of these important dynamics.

A similar interplay between oral and written sources takes place in trying to understand the possible role of agents provocateurs in the Black Power movement of the late 1960's in Greensboro. Oral sources suggested that an individual or individuals within the movement acted in a manner that seemed reckless; a particular individual urged bombings and attempted to involve local black insurgents in other illegal activities. By themselves, however, such oral sources offered only hints. Those hints, on the other hand, made it possible to read the FBI records on black militancy in Greensboro with a much sharper eye. As a result, information that might otherwise have been inexplicable suddenly took on a new significance. It would have been impossible to suggest the likelihood of infiltration and provocation on the basis of oral testimony alone; it would also have been difficult to make a case on the basis of the written record alone. The two together, however, provide a plausible basis for suggesting that much of the violence that occurred in Greensboro in the spring of 1969 may have been at the behest of infiltrators sent in by government authorities. *

A variety of written sources deals with the history of Greensboro's race relations during this period. The gubernatorial papers of Luther Hodges, Terry Sanford, Dan K. Moore, and Robert Scott—all in the North Carolina Archives in Raleigh—offer interesting perspectives from the state's political leaders on issues of school desegregation and racial conflict in Greensboro. The papers of Hodges and Sanford are particularly rich in background material, including reports from the State Bureau of Investigation on Ku Klux Klan activity and civil rights activity in the state. The Moore papers are also interesting for what they reveal about state policy toward the Klan from 1965 to 1969, and the Scott papers are helpful in allowing us to understand official policy toward student demonstrations and the Black Power movement.

The papers of the American Friends Service Committee in High Point, North Carolina, and Philadelphia, Pennsylvania, offer perhaps the most valuable written source on Greensboro during the 1950's and early 1960's. The AFSC had its Southeast regional headquarters in Greensboro and conducted major operations in the city in the areas of school desegregation and "merit employment." AFSC staff members visited nearly every major employer in the Greensboro area at least once, and frequently three or four times. At the conclusion of each of these interviews, the AFSC staffer wrote lengthy memoranda recounting the response of corporate employers. As a result, historians have a firsthand account of attitudes toward racial change among white employers in the Greensboro area. It is interesting to note that the AFSC papers represent an intriguing combination of written and oral testimony, since they are comprised of oral interviews that were written up in memorandum form shortly after they took place.

Official records also provide a useful point of reference for Greensboro's racial conflict during these years. The Greensboro school board has a full file of school board minutes, as well as exhibits of petitions by various individuals seeking school desegregation. Benjamin Smith's papers at Duke University also offer interesting testimony on the pro-integration attitudes of Greensboro's school superintendent during the early 1950's.

Much of the most interesting written material bearing on Greensboro comes from private papers that have been made available to me through the generosity of the individuals holding them. Edward R. Zane's papers contain a rich variety

---

*For a full discussion of the evidence on this issue, see Chapter 7 and especially note 9 of that chapter.

of material dealing directly with the sit-in movement, and the effort by a city council committee chaired by Zane to find a solution to the first sit-ins. Otis Hairston, minister of the Shiloh Baptist Church, generously made available to me his own clipping file on civil rights activities in Greensboro. Dr. John D. Tarpley, principal of Dudley High School for more than thirty years and former supervisor of Negro schools, kindly made available to me some of his personal papers dealing with the history of black education in Greensboro. Kay Troxler, a member of an interracial group of Greensboro women who worked for more effective school desegregation, shared with me the minutes and records of her education committee and Warren Ashby, one of the founders of the interracial Greensboro Community Fellowship, did likewise with the records of that body. The board of directors of the Greensboro YWCA gave me complete access to the voluminous records of that organization—records that tell a great deal not only about Greensboro's racial situation but also about the relationships be- tween a leading voluntary association and the "powers that be" in the city.

Vance Chavis shared with me a history that he helped write of the Greens- boro Men's Club, one of the oldest black private associations in Greensboro. I also benefited greatly from the help of Anna Simkins, who provided important documents that would have otherwise been difficult to obtain. William Little, then executive vice president of the Greensboro Chamber of Commerce, gener- ously gave me access to the chamber's records on this period. In addition, Jack Betts, William Snider, Ed Yoder, and Alfred Hamilton of the Greensboro *Daily News* and the Greensboro *Record* allowed me to have access to many newspaper files. Hal Sieber, formerly of the Greensboro Chamber of Commerce, also shared with me letters he had received, as well as some of his personal writings.

I am particularly grateful to David Schenck, Jr., son of the former mayor of Greensboro, who together with his family agreed to let me use the extensive collection of papers in their possession that dealt with the 1963 demonstrations, when David Schenck, Sr., was mayor. I am also grateful to Joan Bluethenthal for her willingness to let me peruse the wealth of material that she has collected over the years about the final desegregation fight in Greensboro between 1969 and 1972.

Much of the chronological basis for this book is derived from the Greensboro *Daily News* and the Greensboro *Record*, daily newspaper published throughout this period. It is important to note, however, that these white-dominated papers rarely contained a black perspective on racial events, with the exception of the work of individual reporters who on occasion successfully crossed the cultural and personal barriers separating blacks and whites in Greensboro. Most notable among these reporters has been Jo Spivey of the Greensboro *Record*. Through most of this period there is no running file of a black newspaper available, although the *Future Outlook* was published during the 1950's and various issues are present in other collections. That situation changed in 1967 when John Marshall Stevenson (now Kilimanjaro) began the *Carolina Peacemaker*. Ever since, a comprehensive written record has existed, with the *Peacemaker* offering a considerably different point of view on Greensboro's racial experience than that found in the Greensboro *Record* or the Greensboro *Daily News*.

The indispensable core of this book, of course, remains the oral sources I interviewed. Their names are listed here in alphabetical order, with the exception of twenty or so individuals whom I talked with in briefer conversations or in off-the-record interviews and whose names I am not reporting.

These individuals do not represent a cross section of Greensboro, since they were not chosen by random sample; nor do they represent all the neighborhoods, churches, or economic classes of the community. Each person, however, played a significant role in Greensboro's racial history. There were many others who performed equally significant roles whom I did not interview. In no way do I intend to suggest that this list of sources is inclusive, or that there are not other individuals who played just as important a part in Greensboro's racial history. Approximately half of these oral sources are black.

Each individual was interviewed at least once for a period of an hour or more, and frequently two or three times, with the average interview per respondent taking two and a half hours, and some requiring as much as eight hours. All of the interviews, the transcripts, and the written sources upon which *Civilities and Civil Rights* has been based will be deposited in the Oral History Collection of the Perkins Library at Duke University.

Oral Sources

Carolyn Allen
Warren Ashby
Thomas Bailey
Ella Baker
Richard Bardolph
Tart Bell
Cecil Bishop
Randolph Blackwell
Mr. and Mrs. Ezell Blair, Sr.
Ezell Blair, Jr.
    (now Jibreel Khazan)
Joan Bluethenthal
Mrs. Charles Bowles
Linda Bragg
Lewis Brandon
George Breathett
Sara Mendenhall Brown
Vance Chavis
Nell Coley
Charles Davis

Lewis Dowdy
Edward Edmonds
Jack Elam
Ike English
George Evans
Margaret Falkener
Waldo Falkener
Joseph Flora
Robert Ford
S. N. Ford
John Foster
Otis Hairston
W. A. House
Eula Hudgens
D. Edward Hudgins
William Jackson
Hobart Jarrett
Nelson Johnson
Walter Johnson
Susie B. Jones

Joe Knox
R.B. Linck
Al Lineberry
William Little
Cleo McCoy
Joseph McNeil
Carolyn Mark
David Morehead
Mrs. Franklin Parker
Willa Player
David Richmond
George Roach
Terry Sanford
David Schenck, Jr.
Hal Sieber
Anna Simkins
George Simkins

Ben Smith, Jr.
Louise Smith
McNeill Smith
Mrs. Raymond Smith
William Snider
A. Knighton Stanley
John Marshall Stevenson
   (now Kilimanjaro)
Carol Stoneburner
J. D. Tarpley
Betsy Taylor
John Taylor
William Thomas
Kay Troxler
Michael Weaver
Edwin Yoder
Edward R. Zane

Other Interviews

Randolph Blackwell (by Sara Evans)
Jim Clark (by Scott Ellsworth)
John Lewis (by Jack Bass)
Franklin McCain (by Howell Raines)
David Richmond (by Clayborne Carson)
KKK members (by Scott Ellsworth)

Index